The Jewish Experience

"Writing in a clear and jargon-free idiom, Steven L. Jacobs addresses a synthesis of beliefs and concepts that describe the parameters of the Jewish value system: God, Torah (teaching and commandments), people (chosen, covenant, choosing), land (holy and home), doctrine (beliefs, practices, ethics, morality), holy space and time, and contemporary matters. This is not a comprehensive discussion of Jewish history, culture, and religion but **a balanced and focused exploration of sacred and secular sources on what is meant by Jewishness**, molded by a mosaic of Jewish ideas from Torah to today and beyond."

Zev Garber
Professor Emeritus and Chair of Jewish Studies and Philosophy, Los Angeles Valley College
Past President of the National Association of Professors of Hebrew

"Steve Jacobs has written a readable and thorough survey of Judaism with his usual touch of a passion to see religions, in this case Judaism, as living communities faced with the challenge to meet the contemporary, post-Shoah world. This makes this book a unique contribution to the materials on Judaism and **a vital addition for any class or student to read**."

James F. Moore
Professor of Theology, Valparaiso University
Author of *Toward a Dialogical Community: A Post-Shoah Christian Theology*

CYCLES OF TIME CYCLES OF LIFE CYCLES OF THE HERE AND NOW CYCLES OF HISTORY CYCLES OF TEXTS CYCLES OF THOUGHT CYCLES OF BELIEF

The Jewish Experience

An Introduction to
Jewish History and Jewish Life

Steven Leonard Jacobs

Fortress Press / Minneapolis

Cover image: *Judaica*, 2005, by Max Blumberg. © 2009 Artists Rights Society (ARS), New York/ADAGP, Paris. Banque d'Images, ADAGP / Art Resource, N.Y.
Cover design: Paul Boehnke
Book design: Zan Ceeley, Trio Bookworks
Image on opposite page: Itinerary of the Israelites in the desert, 1867. French map from a chapter on Ancient and Modern Palestine. Bibliotheque de l'Alliance Israélite Universelle, Paris, France. Photo: Snark/Art Resource, N.Y.

Library of Congress Cataloging-in-Publication Data

Jacobs, Steven L., 1947–
The Jewish experience : an introduction to Jewish history and Jewish life / by Steven Leonard Jacobs.
    p. cm.
ISBN 978-0-8006-9663-4 (alk. paper)
1. Judaism. 2. Judaism—History. 3. Jews—History. I. Title.
BM562.J33 2010
296—dc22
                    2009040667

The paper used in this publication meets the minimum requirements of American National Standard for Information Sciences — Permanence of Paper for Printed Library Materials, ANSI Z329.48-1984.

Manufactured in the U.S.A.

14   13   12   11   10   1   2   3   4   5   6   7   8   9   10

"... a people who wandered into history

on a postage stamp of a land."

———

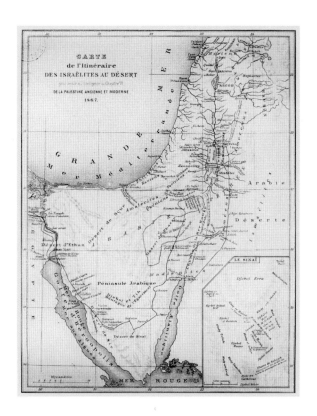

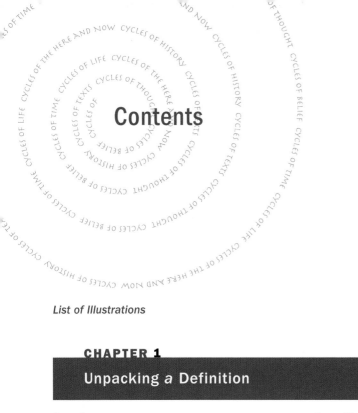

Contents

CHAPTER 3   51

Cycles of Texts: Building the Foundation

CHAPTER 4   83

Cycles of Thought: Judaic Philosophy

CHAPTER 5   107

Cycles of Belief: Judaic Theology

CHAPTER 6   123

Cycles of Time: The Judaic Calendar

CHAPTER 7 147

Cycles of Life: The Life-Cycle Journey

CHAPTER 8 169

Cycles of the Here and Now: The Twenty-First-Century Moment and Beyond

CHAPTER 9 183

Conclusion: The Future of Judaism and the Jewish People

List of Illustrations

CHAPTER 1

Unpacking
A DEFINITION

OVERVIEW

In this first chapter, we will introduce you, the reader, to the definition of Judaism, which frames this entire book, and make several observations regarding our definition. In addition, we will lay out the chapter-by-chapter "game plan" of the book you are about to read, and briefly introduce you to each. Have fun as you begin your journey of *The Jewish Experience*!

Introduction

Just as in the academic study of religion there is no one universally accepted definition of what we mean when we use the term *religion*, so too there is no one universally accepted understanding of what we mean by *Judaism*. Indeed, many years ago, in an introductory graduate level course in Jewish philosophy, on the first day of class, my professor announced, "There is no such thing as Judaism,

there are only Judaisms (and, by extension, there is no such thing as Christianity, there are only Christianities)!"[1] Shocked as we collectively were, over time, serious study of the Judaic experience continues to testify to the accuracy of his pronouncement.

Complicating this picture even more, there is equally no agreed-on understanding of who the totality of the Jewish people is, either historically or contemporarily. Biblically, the Israelites traced their status and lineage through their male parent, further subdivided into the three divisions within their society (high priestly families biologically connected to Aaron, Moses' older brother; others within the tribe of Levi; and, lastly, the remaining members of the Israelite community). Postbiblically, rabbinically, and talmudically, identity status was shifted to either one whose female parent was Jewish (a shift in collective identity from Israelite to Jew), or one who underwent the formal rite we know today as "conversion," though it did not even exist in the biblical period.[2] Thus, for approximately the first four thousand years of Israelite/Jewish existence, identity was male based; for the next two thousand years, it was and is female based. In 1983, the Reform or Liberal or Progressive religious denominational movement in the United States declared, through its rabbis at their annual convention, that the Jewish identity of children could now be determined through *either* male *or* female parent, *provided* the commitment was to raise that child within the orbit of the organized Jewish community, the child itself underwent significant Jewish rites of passage (brit milah [circumcision], naming, consecration, bar/bat mitzvah, and/or confirmation), *without* necessarily, however, undergoing any act formally recognized as conversion. This decision is still marked by rancorous debate and unresolved tension among the various Jewish denominational communities.[3] Today, then, the waters tend to be somewhat muddy as to who is or is not a Jew, depending on parental status or denominational affiliation includ-

---

BOX 1.1

Definitions of Religion

"Religion is (subjectively regarded) the recognition of all duties as divine commands."
Immanuel Kant (1724-1804)

"Religion is the sigh of the oppressed creature, the heart of a heartless world, just as it is the spirit of a spiritless situation. It is the opium of the people."
Karl Marx (1818-1883)

"[Religious ideas] are not precipitates of experience or end-results of thinking: they are illusions, fulfillments of the oldest, strongest and most urgent wishes of mankind."
Sigmund Freud (1856-1939)

". . . an absolute reality which transcends this world but manifests itself in this world, thereby sanctifying it and making it real."
Mircea Eliade (1907-1986)

"Religion, in the largest and most basic sense of the word, is ultimate concern. . . . [Religion] gives us the experience of the Holy, of something which is untouchable, awe-inspiring, an ultimate meaning, the source of ultimate courage."
Paul Tillich (1886-1985)

"[A] religion is: a system of symbols which acts to establish powerful, pervasive, and long-lasting moods and motivations in men by formulating conceptions of a general order of existence and clothing these conceptions with such a aura of factuality that the moods and motivations seem uniquely realistic."
Clifford Geertz (1926-2006)

"Religion is the audacious attempt to conceive of the entire universe as being humanly significant."
Peter Berger (b. 1929)

". . . a belief system that includes the idea of the existence of 'an eternal principle . . . that has created the world, that governs it, that controls its destinies or that intervenes in the natural course of its history.'"
Dorothy Nelkin (1933-2003)

ing conversionary practice—all this despite modern Israel's first prime minister, David Ben-Gurion's (1886–1973 C.E.), suggestion that "A Jew is anyone who considers himself such!"

The Operating Definition of *Judaism* in *The Jewish Experience*

Thus, attempting to define either *Judaism* or the *Jewish people* is a tricky enterprise at best. It is, however, a place to begin, as we explore a complex and complicated history, recognizing, even at the outset, that we simply cannot divorce the religion of Judaism from the people who continue to be its living embodiment. What follows, then, is this author's

working definition of Judaism, which will serve as the frame of reference around which this book is organized, and which we now unpack:

> **JUDAISM** *is the evolving cultural expressions of the people originally known as Hebrews or Israelites over the course of the generations, in response to their (and others') changing perceptions of themselves, their historical journeys, their stories and ideas, their celebrations, and their understandings of their relationship with their God.*

Sociologically Speaking . . .

First, sociologically, any group, however defined, expresses its collective identity through its behaviors

---

BOX 1.2

Definitions of Judaism

"Just as antisemitism drives the weak, the cowardly and the materialistic Jew into Christianity, so its pressure has strengthened my own Judaism powerfully within me."
Theodor Herzl (1860–1904),
the "Father" of modern political Zionism

"For the Jews the advantage of Hebrew over other languages is that it is the natural garment of Judaism."
Ahad Ha'am (Asher Zvi Hirsch Ginsberg, 1856–1927),
Hebrew essayist and pre-State Zionist thinker

"The Jew, by virtue of his origin, will always belong to Judaism, even if he or his ancestors have changed their faith . . . Judaism is an historical religion."
Moses Hess (1812–1875), secular Jewish
philosopher and one of the founders of socialism

"Unity of God, unity of the universe and unity of mankind are the spirit which moves Judaism."
Uri Zvi Greenberg (1896–1981),
Israeli poet and journalist

"Judaism is a nation and a creed at one and the same time."
Joseph Gedaliah Klausner (1874–1958),
scholar of Jewish religion, history, and modern Hebrew literature

"The division of Judaism into 'Orthodox', 'Conservative,' 'Reform,' etc. is artificial. For all Jews have one and the same Torah, given by the one and same G–d, though there are more observant Jews and less observant Jews. To tag on a label does not, of course, change the reality of Jewish essence."
Rabbi Menachem Mendel Schneerson (1902–1994),
Lubavitcher Hasidic Rabbi

"Where Jewish education is neglected, the whole content of Judaism is reduced to merely an awareness of antisemitism. Judaism ceases then to be a civilization, and becomes a complex."
Rabbi Mordecai Menahem Kaplan (1881–1983),
essayist, scholar, and founder of Reconstructionist Judaism

www.jewish-wisdom.com

Fig. 1.1 An American Jewish family celebrating a bar mitzvah Central to the coming-of-age celebration is the opportunity for the bar mitzvah to read a portion of the Torah scroll appropriate to the Sabbath. Photo: © SuperStock RF/SuperStock

(that is, its cultural *expressions* [note this emphasis on the plural]), bracketed by both its ideas and its stories or myths. Over time, those behaviors change, buffeted about by both internal and external threats to its survival and adapting itself to changing historical circumstances; new, different, and challenging reinterpretations of its own existence; and the like. Historical groups that have long survived—and the Jews certainly count themselves among them, following an historical trajectory close to six thousand years of continually identified existence—are those that continue to successfully negotiate and renegotiate both the internal and external understandings of what it means to be a member of the group.[4]

Second, *all* manner of group behavior constitutes the group's culture, from so-called high culture and ennobling behaviors (religion, the arts, literature) to "low culture" and disgracing behaviors (violations of moral and ethical norms in defiance of group ideals). And the Jews are no exception to the latter, to be sure, from those patriarchs of the Hebrew Bible who lied to protect themselves (e.g., Abraham informing Avimelech, the king of Gerar, that Sarah was his sister rather than his wife in *Bereshith*/Genesis 20) to those who deceived and manipulated those even within their same family (e.g., Jacob's deception of his father, Isaac, in his quest for the latter's blessing in *Bereshith*/Genesis 27 or his manipulation of his older brother, Esau, exchanging food for birthright in *Bereshith*/Genesis 25) to those who maintained themselves within the criminal elements of society, particularly in the nineteenth and twentieth centuries and some who do so even today (e.g., gangster Meyer "Little Man" Lansky [1902–1983 C.E.][5]). Thus, to tell the story of the "cultures of the Jews"—to use historian David

Fig. 1.2 Moses receiving the Ten Commandments at Mount Sinai According to the Jewish religious tradition, Moses received directly from God not only the *Aseret Ha-Dibrot* (Ten Commandments) but the whole of the Jewish interpretative tradition as well, *Torah sheb'al peh* (Oral Tradition). Photo: Scala/Art Resource, N.Y.

Biale's felicitous phrase[6]—is to attempt to tell the *whole* story of the Jews, without blinders, to include both the best and the worst in this migratory trek of several thousand years, especially through Europe, North and South America, and the Middle East.

The Importance of the Literary Tradition

Third, important in sustaining Jewish group survival have been both the stories that the Jews have told to themselves about themselves (those contained not only in the Torah/Hebrew Bible but in the Talmuds and other literatures as well) and those told to others about themselves and their relationship to Jews. Such stories (and myths) are powerful psychological tools, not only in times of stress and threat but in times of celebration as well. Added to these stories are the *ideas* that the founders of Judaism have crafted, that the Jewish people have embraced and that later generations have enlarged and reinterpreted in response to changing historical circumstances (e.g., the Sabbath, the so-called Ten Commandments, the interface between religion and ethics).

Significantly, at least for the last two thousand years, the Jews have valued literature and literacy, and the values reflected therein, in the production not only of their sacred Torah/Hebrew Bible but of their ancillary texts as well. Prior to this, it is our scholarly understanding that the stories, laws, poems, hymns, psalms, and the like were, at a minimum, at least a thousand years if not longer in their original Israelite formulations and tellings and retellings. Three thousand years at the very least from the original dreams to their contemporary manifestations; a long, if somewhat uneven, journey to be sure!

The Two Calendars of Jewish Life

Fourth, Israelite/Jewish identity as it behaviorally manifests itself is best perceived and understood when viewed through the dual prismatic lenses of two calendars, referred to in this book as "Cycles of Time" (chapter 6) and "Cycles of Life" (chapter 7). The former refers to those Jewish celebratory events marked annually—with the exception of the Sabbath, marked weekly. The latter refers to those celebrations that "mark the moments" of the life's journey common to all humanity—birth, growth, maturation, decay, and death—but which are uniquely expressed, in seemingly unique ways, by Jews. And, like the stories and the ideas, these celebrations, too, have changed over time—sometimes quite dramatically—not only in response to the "slings and arrows of outrageous misfortune,"

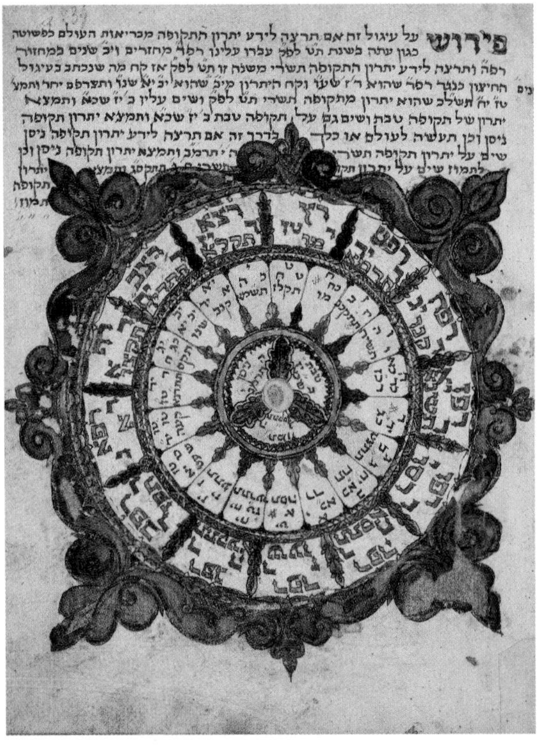

Fig. 1.3 Sefer Evronot (The Jewish calendar) Jehuda ben Schemuel Reutlingen Mehler, Germany, 1649. This page from the Sefer Evronot (Ibronot), a book on calculating the calendar, depicts wheels that the reader could cut out and rotate to compute dates and Jewish calendar cycles. Photo: Bildarchiv Preussischer Kulturbesitz/Art Resource, N.Y.

à la Shakespeare (e.g., Yom Hashoah/Day of the Holocaust, 27th of Nisan), but to positive moments as well (e.g., Yom Ha'atzmaut/Israel Independence Day, 5th of Iyar [May 14, 1948]; bat mitzvah, the coming of age of a young Jewish girl beginning at age twelve).

The Centrality of the God of Israel

Fifth, the interwoven story of the Jews and Judaism cannot fully be told without reference to the God of Israel already present in the first sentence of the Hebrew Bible (*Bereshith*/Genesis 1:1: "In the beginning of creating, God with [the use of] the heavens and the earth . . ."),[7] and even more fully present at Sinai with not only those Israelites already there but the generations yet to be born, entering into a covenantal relationship for all time (*Devarim*/Deuteronomy 29:14-15). This singular incorporeal creator God, vitally concerned with the affairs of humanity and, most particularly and especially Israelite humanity, remains a distinctive contribution of the Jewish people to the civilizing and humanizing of humanity, along with such concepts as the euphemistically labeled "Ten Commandments" and the Sabbath itself.

Judaism, Jewish People, and God

Thus, when all is said and done, the history or story of "Judaism" cannot be disconnected from either "the Jewish People" or "God" however each element of this tripartite entity is understood, both historically and contemporarily. Together they constitute a seamless garment, embroidered over countless generations by countless persons in countless locales. At the same time, this garment is always unfinished, as each generation of Jews continues to add its own distinctive features, changing that which was previously created to fit the moment and knowing only too well that the next generation of Jews will repeat this threefold tradition of preservation, adaptation, and innovation. Thus, throughout this book, the

Fig. 1.4 Prayers in the Western Wall Prayers have been placed in the Western Wall in Jerusalem, the remaining site of the Second Temple and traditional Judaism's holiest shrine. Photo courtesy Creative Commons, http://commons.wikimedia.org/wiki/File:A_prayer_to_God_in_the_Western_Wall_in_Jerusalem.jpg

concept of "cycles" best describes not only the journeys of the Jews ("cycles of history"), but the evolving nature of Jewish philosophical and theological ideas ("cycles of thought" and "cycles of belief"), the record of these ideas ("cycles of texts"), Jewish behaviors ("cycles of time" and "cycles of life"), and the Jewish present ("cycles of the here and now").

The Plan of This Book

Chapter 2, "Cycles of History: The Judaic Journey," tells the story of the Israelites prior to the inauguration of the monarchy under Samuel and Saul, from the migratory and settled periods of Judah and Israel to the destruction of the First and Second Temples (586 B.C.E. and 70 C.E.) to their two-thousand-year wandering primarily throughout the European continent and into the modern period, with the re-creation of the Third Jewish Commonwealth on May 14, 1948, and now the twenty-first century. It is a journey filled with peaks and valleys, successes and failures, creations and destructions, but eclipsed by the seeming indestructibility not only of the Jewish

People but of the Judaic religion as well.[8] It is also of necessity an all-too-brief history, globally attempting to tell a broad story while elaborating somewhat on many, many topics worthy of such elaborations, but not on all of them.

Chapter 3, "Cycles of Texts: Building the Foundation," addresses a singularly important fact of the Judaic journey: its emphasis on intellectual development and textual learning as the central building blocks of both communal and religiously defined development and identity. We may articulate its essential understanding of itself as a Judaic religious tradition as "biblically based but not biblically confined." Beginning with the Hebrew Bible—itself canonized in the year 90 C.E.

Fig. 1.5 Knesset sculpture celebrating Jewish history Opposite the main entrance of the Knesset, Israel's governing legislative body, is this chandelier made by Benno Elkan. It is 5 meters high and 4 meters broad and shows 29 reliefs of Jewish history. Photo courtesy Creative Commons: http://commons.wikimedia.org/wiki/File:Knesset_Benno_Elkan.jpeg

Fig. 1.6 The Aleppo Codex The Aleppo Codex is a medieval manuscript of the Hebrew Bible (Tanakh), associated with Rabbi Aaron Ben Asher. The Masoretic scholars wrote it in the early tenth century, probably in Tiberias, Israel. It is in book form and contains the vowel points and grammar points (nikkudot) that specify the pronunciation of the ancient Hebrew letters to preserve the chanting tradition. It is perhaps the most historically important Hebrew manuscript in existence. Photo courtesy of Creative Commons: http://commons.wikimedia.org/wiki/File:Aleppo_Codex_(Deut).jpg

legal tradition in both communities. Then it's on to the various Codes of Jewish Law (e.g., *Shulchan Aruch*, "Set" or "Prepared Table," originally published by Joseph Karo [1488–1575 C.E.] in the sixteenth century) and to the vast literature of communal and rabbinic questions and answers known as *Responsa*. Finally comes the kabalistic or mystical literatures of Judaism (e.g., the *Zohar* or "Book of Splendor," originally published by Moses de Leon [1250–1305 C.E.] in the thirteenth century). So vast is the literary enterprise of Judaism that no one person has ever mastered it all, leaving specialists to focus their quest for knowledge, in the main, on only one or more parts of this huge corpus. To provide you, the reader, with at the very least an introductory taste of each, brief representative selections are also included.

Fig. 1.7 The Center for Jewish History, New York The Center for Jewish History is located in New York City. It is home to five Jewish institutions dedicated to history, culture, and art: The American Jewish Historical Society, The American Sephardi Federation, The Leo Baeck Institute, Yeshiva University Museum, and The YIVO Institute for Jewish Research (www.cjh.org). Photo courtesy Creative Commons: http://commons.wikimedia.org/wiki/File:Center_for_Jewish_History_NYC.jpg

in the city of Yavneh under the Pharisaic Rabbi Yochanan ben Zakkai (who, it is believed, died shortly thereafter)—one moves quickly into the legal compendium known as the *Mishnah* ("Repetition" or "Second Teaching" after the Torah or Hebrew Bible) of Palestine redacted in the year 220 C.E. under the leadership of Rabbi Judah Ha-Nasi (135–220 C.E.) ("the Prince"; or recognized religiopolitical leader). From there one moves to the Talmuds of both Palestine (redacted in 350 C.E.) and Babylonia (redacted in 700 C.E.), themselves expanded commentaries and conversations regarding all the possible permutations of a developing

Chapter 4, "Cycles of Thought: Judaic Philosophy," and **chapter 5**, "Cycles of Belief: Judaic Theology," essentially follow a chronological approach, fully understanding that the *ideational*

content of Judaism always builds on the work of previous generations, with the following important caveat: This distinction between "philosophy" and "theology" is, from a Judaic vantage point, a false dichotomy. Those intellectual challenges, both internal and external, with which the authors of the Torah/Hebrew Bible and subsequent literatures wrestled, and also reflected in their own individual writings, can best be subsumed beneath the following overarching categories: (1) God and God's relationship both to humanity in general and Jewish humanity in particular, (2) Torah in both its ritual-ceremonial aspects and its moral-ethical aspects, and (3) Israel the people in its relationship to itself and to the larger, non-Israelite/non-Hebrew/non-Jewish communities. It is, therefore, only in the so-called modern period where we see the development of a "Jewish Philosophy" concerned with the very same issues addressed by the larger world of philosophers as distinct from so-called Jewish religious concerns (e.g., the nature and composition of the universe versus the election of Israel). As we reverse direction and go back into history, however, we see a true interweaving of all such ideas under this more general notion of "Jewish concerns." And, while the common myths that the development of

Fig. 1.8 Purim street scene, Jerusalem On a Jerusalem street, the festival of Purim is played out. This festival is associated with the celebration of the Book of Esther in the Torah/Hebrew Bible. Photo courtesy Creative Commons: http://commons.wikimedia.org/wiki/File:Jerusalem_Purim_street_scene.jpg

Jewish thought has been independent of the larger worlds outside the various ghetto walls, solid historical analyses continue to confirm and reconfirm cultural interaction at every step of the journey, sometimes public, sometimes private, sometimes well-known, sometimes little known.[9]

Chapter 6, "Cycles of Time: The Judaic Calendar," and **chapter 7**, "Cycles of Life: The Life-Cycle Journey," reflect, both separately and together, "life on the ground," as it were. For intellectual ideas, no matter how controversial or stimulating they may be, tend to attract only limited numbers both within any given group, and usually less so those outside the group. Thus, from an anthropological and ethnographic perspective, if one truly wants to learn who the Jews *are*, one needs to look most closely at what the Jews *do*, no matter how broad or narrow the diversity of such behaviors. Therefore, self-identifying Jews in the twenty-first century, as in every century prior, govern themselves as both individuals and as communities by not one but two calendars: one that marks holy days (or holidays), festivals, and fast days, and another that marks the moments of the journey of life itself, from birth to death. Yet such an examination of even these two calendars—unique to this people—are not without problems and difficulties, for there are and have been those Jews who see and understand themselves positively to be Jews but limit their active behaviors to certain aspects of Jewish life, and who, throughout this long journey, have never been "written out," as it were, of the community. For example, there are committed Zionist Jews who, while living abroad, stand fully with the State of Israel, defend it politically, participate in fundraising in support of its many and varied institutions, enrich themselves and their families with all manner of Israeli culture, and visit as often as possible, but who remain noticeably absent from religious life. There are other Jews who fully embrace the religious calendar in its totality but understand Zionism as a secular political enterprise divorced from the religion of Judaism, and who have never set foot in Israel and never intend

Fig. 1.9 Jewish town on the West Bank, Israel Communities such as these remain a contentious issue in Israeli politics as they are often located in predominantly Arab population centers. Photo courtesy Creative Commons: http://commons.wikimedia .org/wiki/File:YishuvEliShomron.jpg

to do so until the physical advent of the messiah. The vast majority of Jews, however, are of course to be found somewhere in the middle; and all Jews, no matter their individual or collective understanding, do tend to draw on the historical wellspring of religious Judaism for moments of birth, coming of age, marriage, and death.

Chapter 8, "Cycles of the Here and Now: The Twenty-first-Century Moment and Beyond," concretizes the classical French expression *Plus ça change, plus c'est meme chose* ("The more things change, the more they stay the same!") by reexamining three central issues of concern in modern Jewish life: survival of this minority people, antisemitism against this same people, and the latter's sixty-year redirected focus from western Europe and the Holocaust to the State of Israel and its neighbors. Though the specifics change every time the topics themselves are addressed (e.g., success-

ful integration and assimilation of America's Jews coupled with questionably dwindling numbers; less antisemitism in certain locales, increased antisemitism in others; periods of "cold peace" in the Middle East coupled with "hot wars"), the concerns of the Jews themselves do not. How these three crosscurrents continue to play themselves out reinforces not only the cyclical nature of the Judaic experience and Judaic journey but, equally, reminds the Jews themselves of the insight of the author of the Book of Ecclesiastes that, in truth, "there is nothing new under the sun" (1:9).

Chapter 9, "Conclusion: The Future of Judaism and the Jewish People?" is, in all truth and honesty, pure speculation. Futurology is far from an exact science, though some Jews and some Christians and some others have been reading the prophets of the Hebrew Bible as predictors of tomorrows for better than two thousand years. (Such unfortu-

Fig. 1.10 Man and child on Jerusalem street, 1898
This touching scene reveals part of life in nineteenth-century Jerusalem. Photo courtesy Creative Commons: http://commons.wikimedia.org/wiki/File:Jerusalem_quiet_street_with_donkey_1898.jpg

Fig. 1.11 Contemporary street party, 2009 This celebration in Jerusalem shows a party on Dorot Rishonim (literally, "First Generations," i.e., Founders) Street. Photo courtesy Creative Commons: http://commons.wikimedia.org/wiki/File:Jerusalem,_Dorot_Rishonim,_street_party_03.jpg

nates, however, find themselves constantly having to *revise* their own predictions of events by confessing to incorrectly reading those very texts that led to their assessments in the first place, and, even more unfortunately, attributing to Isaiah, Jeremiah, Ezekiel, and their associates events and happenings of which they, most assuredly, had no knowledge whatsoever.) Then too, such all-too-easy speculations possess the potential to be both right *and*

wrong, but if one is foolishly willing to extend one's own thinking beyond the period of one's own predictable lifespan, who knows? One could be wrong or one could be right, and only tomorrow's reader will know for sure, the author only a memory.

Enjoy the journey you are now about to undertake as you learn about one of the world's oldest surviving and thriving religious communities!

IN REVIEW

In this chapter, we have presented you, the reader, with the definition of Judaism that frames this entire text. In so doing, we have "unpacked" this definition by making a number of observations. We have also provided you with a brief summary description of each of the following chapters as you begin your own "Jewish experience." Welcome to my world!

KEY TERMS

Babylonian Talmud	Mishnah
bar/bat mitzvah	mitzvot
Brit Milah	Palestinian Talmud
Christianity	patriarchs
confirmation	rabbis
consecration	Reform Judaism
conversion	religion
covenant	*Responsa*
culture	Second Jewish Commonwealth
First Jewish Commonwealth	Second Temple
First Temple	Shabbat
Hebrew Bible	Ten Commandments
Hebrews	Third Jewish Commonwealth
Israelites	Torah
Jews	Yom Ha'atzmaut
Judaism	Yom Hashoah
Middle East	*Zohar*

Questions for Review, Study, and Discussion

1. Compare and contrast the various definitions of *religion* as presented in Box 1.1. Which do you like/dislike? Why? Try your hand at writing your own definition of religion. Does *Judaism* fit in with any of them? Does Christianity?

2. Compare and contrast the various definitions of *Judaism* as presented in Box 1.2 with that presented in this chapter. Which do you like/dislike? Why? Try your hand at writing your own definition of *Judaism*.

Suggested Readings

Biale, David. *Cultures of the Jewish: A New History.* New York: Schocken Books, 2002.

Konner, Melvin. *Unsettled: An Anthropology of the Jews.* New York: Penguin, 2004.

Seltzer, Robert. *Jewish People, Jewish Thought: The Jewish Experience in History.* New York: Prentice Hall, 2003.

CHAPTER 2

Cycles *of* HISTORY

The Judaic Journey

OVERVIEW

In this chapter, we broadly survey the history of the Jewish people, from antiquity to the present day. This survey helps to introduce the importance of "cycles" in the Jewish experience by highlighting the recurrence of episodes of community broken by episodes of dispersion. Thus, we may divide all of Jewish history into three periods: the prebiblical and biblical period (to 70 c.e.), the postbiblical or rabbinic period (to 1791); and the modern period (1791 to the present).

Introduction

In truth, the origins of the Israelites, Hebrews, Jewish people are shrouded in mystery—provided one departs from (or, possibly, incorporates) the story of their origins as presented in the Torah or Hebrew Bible. From minimalist historians who suggest that the biblical materials only hint at the truths of a much larger and ultimately far more complex story, and in so doing overlay the truths of history with religious-political-theological agendas, to scriptural-literalist readers in both the Jewish and Christian camps who regard the Torah/Hebrew Bible as a fully accurate description of the events it portrays, to all those who find themselves in between these two at times hostile camps, the origins of the people who presented their unique vision of a singular deity to the world remain the stuff of intrigue.

Historical Sources

Complicating the story is, in the main, the genuine lack of corollary historical materials from the various epochs portrayed in the text itself *and* the multiplicity of contemporary academic disciplines—from anthropology to archaeology, linguistics to literature, philosophy to political science, theater to theology—each of which has minutely examined the text from its own vantage point, oftentimes in opposition to other perspectives and, in so doing, expanded our knowledge of both text and context. Yet, in the end, the scholarly enterprise continues to present us with more questions than answers.

Ways of Reading the Hebrew Bible

At the outset, therefore, this author would suggest that there are, across the board, four "readers" of this Torah/Hebrew Bible: (1) the *Jewish* religious reader who tends more toward a literalist reading than even he or she may be aware, and who affirms the "truth" of the text; (2) the *Christian* religious reader who, like his or her Jewish counterpart, reads the text somewhat literally, but with an additional "bringing to the table" of that perspective of see-

---

BOX 2.1

Theophany at Sinai
(Exodus 19:16-25 New International Version)

On the morning of the third day there was thunder and lightning, with a thick cloud over the mountain, and a very loud trumpet blast. Everyone in the camp trembled. Then Moses led the people out of the camp to meet with God, and they stood at the foot of the mountain. Mount Sinai was covered with smoke, because the Lord descended on it in fire. The smoke billowed up from it like smoke from a furnace, the whole mountain trembled violently, and the sound of the trumpet grew louder and louder. Then Moses spoke and the voice of God answered him.

The Lord descended to the top of Mount Sinai and called Moses to the top of the mountain. So Moses went up and the Lord said to him, "Go down and warn the people so they do not force their way through to see the Lord and many of them perish. Even the priests, who approach the Lord, must consecrate themselves, or the Lord will break out against them."

Moses said to the Lord, "The people cannot come up Mount Sinai, because you yourself warned us, 'Put limits around the mountain and set it apart as holy.' "

The Lord replied, "Go down and bring Aaron up with you. But the priests and the people must not force their way through to come up to the Lord, or he will break out against them."

So Moses went down to the people and told them.

ing the Christ of the New Testament hidden in the "Old";[1] (3) the *academic* reader who, most assuredly, sees himself or herself as a nonliteral (or even at times antiliteral) reader of this same text, but whose self-perception is as one thoroughly committed to the ideal of scientific objectivity without the subjective investment of self; and (4) the *intelligent* reader outside the university, and, perhaps, even outside any religious community whatsoever, who finds himself or herself fascinated by these ancient writings about which we appear to know so much and yet, in truth, know so little. I leave it to you, the reader, to determine which of these four best describes your own orientation, and make no evaluative judgment about your choice. Each has its merits and demerits. Indeed, if we could gather representatives of the four around the conference table and listen attentively to their (ideally civil) conversations, we would not emerge from the encounter full of certainties and answers but full of uncertainties and questions. Which is as it should be when studying the past or present, for it is the questions which propel us forward; not the answers.

What follows, then, in relatively briefest outline and knowingly incomplete, is the story of the Israelites, Hebrews, Jews from their earliest beginnings to their present moment. (Readers who wish to go further are urged to consult "For Further Reading" at the conclusion of the book or the "Suggested Readings" at the end of this chapter for fuller presentations of the history of this people.)

Two Notes on Calendaring

Lunar versus Solar Calendars. The Hebrew or Jewish calendar is a *lunar-based* calendar, following the cycles of the moon, while our Western calendar is *solar based*, following the cycles of the sun. This same calendar is also framed by early postbiblical, rabbinic attempts to date the origins of creation based on the chronology of the ancient kings of Judah and Israel and, while today scientifically inaccurate, retains its hold because of the power

of the Judaic religious tradition. Thus, the year (Fall) 2009–(Summer) 2010 equates to the Judaic religious year 5770, the Jewish New Year of *Rosh Hashanah* always beginning in September–October.

Fig. 2.1 Beit Alpha Zodiac The Beit Alpha ruins are in the Beit She'an Valley in Israel. Discovered in 1929, this zodiac has been dated to the Byzantium era of the fifth–sixth centuries B.C.E. The zodiac was used as a decorative element in synagogues at this time. Each symbol has the corresponding Hebrew name beside it. In the center, the Sun God Helios is depicted in a chariot drawn by four horses. At each corner are the four seasons, with their Hebrew names—Nisan (Spring); Tamusz (Summer); Tishrei (Autumn); and Tevet (Winter). Photo: Art Resource, N.Y., Synagogue, Beth Alpha, Israel

B.C.E. and C.E. Though Jews the world over agree with everyone else on the Western (Gregorian) dating system presently used, the rationale of B.C. ("Before Christ") and A.D. (Latin *Anno Domini*, "in the year of our Lord") remains problematic. Thus, one finds not only among Jews, but in the literature as well, the alternative designations B.C.E. ("Before the Common Era," i.e., as everyone understands the date) and C.E. ("Common Era," i.e., same understanding).[2]

Beginnings
until the Monarchy

If one fancies oneself a devotee of the so-called great man (person) theory of history, largely attributed to the nineteenth-century Scottish essayist, satirist, and historian Thomas Carlyle (1795–1881), Israel's beginnings, at least according to the Torah or Hebrew Bible itself, can well be told in terms of its patriarchs Abraham, Isaac, Jacob, Joseph, and Moses. Collectively larger-than-life figures, their stories dominate the first two books of the Hebrew Bible or Torah, *Bereshith*/Genesis and *Shemot*/Exodus (more on these naming conventions and their content in chapter 3).

In doing so, however, one tells only a partial story, a series of *biohistories*—if we may invent such

a term—and misses a far larger picture as well as the insights of the various aforementioned academic disciplines. For the story of the Israelites or Hebrews or Jews is not only the story of individuals writ large, however large they were and are, but instead the story of an ancient people, a collectivity as it were, whose present-day descendants perceive themselves as lineal inheritors of that which has preceded them.

Migratory Tribes

Scholarly consensus suggests that the group's origins lay among the western Semitic migratory tribes of the region who traveled its highways and byways during the second millennium B.C.E., approximately 3,500 to 4,000 years ago. Organized along patriarchal and tribal lines, they were primar-

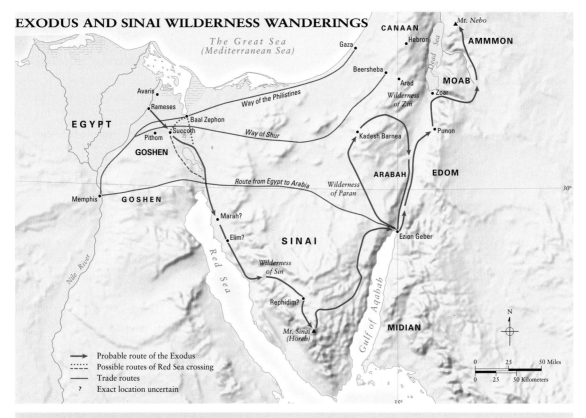

Map 2.1 Exodus and Sinai wilderness wanderings Map from *The People's Bible* © 2009 Fortress Press

ily shepherds whose own flocks, herds, and cattle dictated their journeys in their constant need and search for food. Some among them, how many we cannot say, hired themselves out as mercenaries, traveling not only with their portable wealth but with their families and tribes as well. At a time when the Egyptian empire dominated that part of the world, their journeys took them into and out of Egypt and into and out of their own lands as well.[3]

Egyptian Monarchy

With the gradual integration of the Asiatic tribes known to us as *Hyksos* (a term possibly meaning "foreigners"), their takeover of the Egyptian monarchy between 1655 B.C.E. and 1570 B.C.E., life continued as it had under the Egyptians. (The story of Joseph, who attained eminence at the highest levels of Egyptian government, may very well date from this period.) However, with the end of their period of hegemony and its reclamation by so-called native Egyptians, the tide turned against these migrants, ultimately resulting in their enslavement under pharaonic leadership. According to *Shemot*/Exodus 1:11, it was the slaves, not only Israelites, who built the store cities of Pithom and Ramses for the Pharaoh (now identified as Ramses II [1290–1224 B.C.E.]). And it was during his reign, a period of corruption and disintegration, that the Judaic archetypal redemptive experience known as *Y'tziat Mitzrayim*, the "going forth from Egypt"—the exodus—took place, an event of such magnitude that it will forever be enshrined as one of the two central themes of Judaic religious life (the other being the *theophany* at Sinai, the "giving of the Torah").

Though nowhere recorded by Egyptian or other non-Israelite chroniclers (or at least not yet unearthed by archaeologists), within two centuries, these same Israelites conquered much of their former home and resettled in the land of Canaan. In so doing, they turned from their previous preslavery nomadic ways of life to becoming agriculturalists, farmers, and craftspersons, constantly on guard against invaders.

Confederation of Tribes

Subsequent to the solitary leadership of the Egyptian court prince Moses, his designated nondynastic successor, Joshua, and Moses' priestly older brother, Aaron, leaders known as "judges" stepped forth to govern what, for all intents and purposes, was a confederation of tribes, none acquiring full supreme sovereignty over either the people or the land itself. It will then be at the end of this period of a series of transitional leaders, by the beginnings of the eleventh century B.C.E., that the Israelites will usher in their monarchy.

Fig. 2.2 Moses (c. 1250 B.C.E.) Michelangelo Buonarroti (1475–1564). This statue is located in the church of St. Peter in Chains (San Pietro in Vincoli), Rome. The "horns" appearing on Moses' head resulted from a mistranslation of Exodus 34: 29-35, which describes Moses having "shining" or "radiating" skin, not "horns" as was translated for Michelangelo. Photo courtesy Creative Commons: http://commons.wikimedia.org/wiki/File:Michelangelo-Moses-2.jpg

Kingdoms of Judah and Israel

Reign of Saul

According to the books of the Hebrew Bible, specifically 1 and 2 Samuel, we learn that the eleventh-century prophet *Shemu'el*/Samuel (whose own story is one of the most fascinating in the whole of the Hebrew Bible) is tasked with the communal responsibility to find a king for his nation after first communing with the God of Israel, whom he regards as Israel's *only* legitimate ruler. To his surprise, according to the text, the God of Israel accedes to this request, and the necessity for a strong military leader who can unite the tribes finds him anointing *Sha'ul*/Saul, the son of Kish, a member of the tribe of Benjamin, as Israel's first king (1 Samuel 9–11). Though strong in the ways of the military and nearly successful in fully routing the Philistines, and fully aware of the need for tribal unity in a confederation-style government, his failures at the helm ultimately result in his break with Samuel. A later battle with the Philistines at Gilboa and looming defeat force Saul to take the dramatic action of his own suicide by falling on his sword and avoiding the humiliation and ignominy that would come with capture.[4]

A close reading of Saul's story presents us with a personality seemingly suffering from a quasi-legitimate paranoia. After all, as Israel's first king, he is, potentially, the target of assassination, the norm in his world, with which he certainly was familiar. To assuage his own fears, his son-in-law, popular in his own right as a poet, singer, and lesser military hero, David, is brought in to work his therapeutic magic, but to no avail. Saul perceives David's growing popularity as reason for concern, and it is David himself who must flee the royal court as Saul becomes more and more convinced that his own death is part of David's agenda. With his suicide, however, the people *do* anoint David as Israel's second king, leaving us to wonder, perhaps, whether or not David himself does in fact have his own "royal agenda."

Reign of David

Reigning for almost forty years (1011–971 B.C.E.), David is successful in uniting the northern and southern tribes, and, most significantly, establishing Jerusalem, the former hilltop fortress city of the Jebusites, as his capital, and with it bringing the ark of the covenant, symbol of Israel's religious authority and divine favor, to rest there. All this during the military and political decline of the powerful nations of both Egypt and Mesopotamia. Said to be the author of many of the psalms contained within *Sefer Tehillim*/Book of Psalms (evidence of his poetic genius as well as his love for God), David is also successful in engaging in peace treaties with his neighbors, for example, Hamath and Tyre. Thus, even today, many religious Jews regard the period of David's monarchy as Israel's historic "golden age," made even more positive for those who affirm belief in a personal messiah that will trace his own lineage back to the royal Davidic household.

However, whatever plans David had for a dynastic chain of succession initially went awry with the death of his son Amnon (responsible for the rape of his sister Tamar) by his third-born son, Absalom, and Absalom's own death at the hands of David's general, Joab, during the course of a rebellious military campaign (2 Samuel 13–18). Adonijah, David's firstborn son and the legitimate claimant to the throne is passed over in favor of Solomon, David's *sixteenth* son and son of Bathsheba, to assume the throne. He, in turn, will rule the kingdom for more than thirty years (970–928 B.C.E.).

Here too, a close reading of the text certainly addresses David's initially adulterous relationship with Bathsheba but, on reflection, may also suggest not that she was seduced and ensnared by a powerful king, but rather that she was a women whose own agenda was ultimately to see one of her own sons sit on the throne of Israel. And the vagaries of history being what they are, she saw her dream realized.

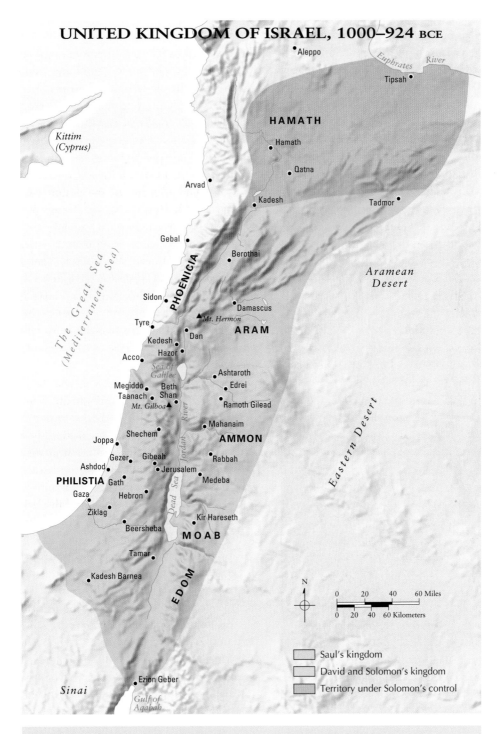

UNITED KINGDOM OF ISRAEL, 1000–924 BCE

Aleppo

Euphrates River

Tipsah

HAMATH

Hamath

Qatna

Arvad

Kadesh

Tadmor

Kittim (Cyprus)

Gebal

Berothai

Aramean Desert

PHOENICIA

Sidon

Damascus

Tyre

Mt. Hermon

Kedesh

Dan

ARAM

Acco

Hazor

The Great Sea (Mediterranean Sea)

Sea of Galilee

Ashtaroth

Megiddo

Beth Shan

Edrei

Taanach

Mt. Gilboa

Ramoth Gilead

Mahanaim

Shechem

AMMON

Joppa

Gezer

Gibeah

Rabbah

Ashdod

Jerusalem

PHILISTIA

Gath

Medeba

Gaza

Hebron

Eastern Desert

Ziklag

Kir Hareseth

Beersheba

MOAB

Tamar

Dead Sea

Jordan River

Kadesh Barnea

EDOM

N

0   20   40   60 Miles

0   20   40   60 Kilometers

Sinai

Ezion Geber

Gulf of Aqabah

☐ Saul's kingdom

☐ David and Solomon's kingdom

☐ Territory under Solomon's control

Map 2.2 United Kingdom of Israel, 1000–924 B.C.E. Map from *The People's Bible* © 2009 Fortress Press

Reign of Solomon

Be that as it may, *Shelomo*/Solomon becomes Israel's third king in a time of relative peace and is recognized far and wide for his wisdom, as evidenced by the parable of the two harlots both claiming motherhood of the same child (1 Kgs 3:16-28).[5] His genius, however, lay in his ability to enter into alliances with his neighbors as well as his success in realizing his father's dream of building in Jerusalem a temple to the glory of God. Both successes, however, come at a price, and cause us to realize a more nuanced portrait of him than the overwhelmingly positive one in the popular imagination.

Normal in nation-state relationships, these alliances resulted in ambassadorial entourages journeying to Jerusalem, together with their own idol-worshiping religious representatives, to take up residence, which the populace, in turn, viewed as acts of desecration of a holy city. Even more, the Temple would require vast corvée (unpaid labor) drawn from the Israelite population as well as vast sums of capital to purchase the required goods, purchases that could only have been gotten by extraordinarily heavy taxation, again a significant source of discontent. And while the Babylonian Talmud (more on this text in chapter 3) indicates that the Temple may in fact have been one of the wonders of the ancient world, it would take a long passage of time for it to be viewed as such in the minds of the ordinary citizenry.

Fig. 2.3 David (c. 1000 B.C.E.) Donatello (c. 1386–1466). Immortalized in 1 Samuel 17 for defeating Goliath, David ruled as Israel's second king and is depicted in this statue which resides in the National Museum of Bargello, Florence, Italy. Photo: Alinari/Art Resource, N.Y.

Downfall of the Two Kingdoms

Unfortunately for Israel, with Solomon's death, there was no designated successor, no great unifier able to maintain such, and the nation splits into the northern kingdom of Israel under Jereboam, with its capital at Shechem, and the southern kingdom of Judah under Rehoboam, with its capital at Jerusalem. For the next three-plus centuries, the thrones of both the North and the South will experience all the court intrigues associated with royalty, including murders and assassinations, some occupying the seat longer than others. The North will survive only until 721 B.C.E., when it is conquered by the Assyrians; the South only until 586 B.C.E., when it is conquered by the Babylonians. Between the two downfalls, the ancient Israelites will experience the "age of the prophets," whose gift to succeeding generations remains the finest religious-ethical literature in all of Western civilization.

THE MONARCHIES OF ISRAEL AND JUDAH, 924–722 BCE

Sidon

PHOENICIA

ARAM (SYRIA)

Zarephath

Damascus

Mt. Hermon

Tyre

The Great Sea
(Mediterranean Sea)

Kedesh

Hazor

GALILEE

BASHAN

Sea of Galilee

Mt. Carmel

Yarmuk River

Edrei

Shunem

Megiddo

Jezreel

Ramoth

Mt. Gilboa

GILEAD

ISRAEL

Samaria

Penuel

Jabbok River

Shechem

Succoth

Mahanaim

Joppa

Shiloh

AMMON

Bethel

Gilgal

Geba

Jericho

Rabbah

Ekron

Jerusalem

Heshbon

Ashdod

Ashkelon

Bethlehem

PHILISTIA

Libnah

Gaza

Gath

Lachish

Hebron

Dead Sea

Arnon River

Gath

JUDAH

Beersheba

Kir-Hareseth

N

MOAB

0   10   20   30 Miles
0   10   20   30 Kilometers

EDOM

Zered River

Map 2.3 The Monarchies of Israel and Judah, 924–722 B.C.E. Map from *The People's Bible* © 2009 Fortress Press

Social Structures of Ancient Israel

Charting the development of early Israelite social structures is no easy task, complicated all the more by the paucity of materials found directly in the Torah itself. Thus, much of our theoretical understandings are derived from comparisons to other cultures with whom the ancient Hebrews likely came into contact.

Patriarchal Structure

This much, however, does make sense to us: the overarching structure was that of the tribe, based on a patriarchal model. (Matriarchal modeling will come to the fore in the postbiblical or rabbinic period and continue to dominate Jewish identity up to and including the present day.) Originally, the tribes themselves were nomadic or seminomadic, their wanderings governed by the need to provide food for their herds, primarily sheep and cattle. Prior to the monarchy, probably for reasons of safety, security, and survival, the tribes were loosely governed by a council or councils of elders, elected from within their own tribes, whose own elevation was, in all likelihood, based on age, experience, and social-cultural status. Within their tribes, families were likewise patriarchal (alpha-male dominant); clusters of tribes—here we may

BOX 2.2

Prophets of Ancient Israel	
Abraham	Gen. 11:26—25:10
Isaac	Gen. 21:1—35:29
Jacob	Gen. 25:21—49:33
Moses	Exod. 2:1—Deut. 34:5
Aaron	Exod. 4:14—Num. 33:39
Joshua	Exod. 17:9-14, 24:13, 32:17-18, 33:11; Num. 11:28-29, 13:4—14:38, 27:18—27:23, Deut. 1:38, 3:28, 31:3, 31:7; Josh. 24:29
Pinchas	Exod. 6:25; Num. 25:7-11, 31:6; Josh. 22:13, 24:33 Judg. 20:28
Elkanah	1 Sam. 1:1—2:20
Eli	1 Sam. 1:9—4:18
Samuel	1 Sam. 1:1—25:1
Gad	1 Sam. 22:5; 2 Sam. 24:11-19; 1 Chron. 21:9-19, 29:29
Nathan	2 Sam. 7:2—17, 12:1-25
David	1 Sam. 16:1—1 Kings 2:11
Solomon	2 Sam. 12:24; 1 Kings 1:10—11:43
Iddo	2 Chron. 9:29, 12:15, 13:22
Michaiah son of Imlah	1 Kings 22:8-28; 2 Chron. 18:7-27
Obadiah	1 Kings 18; Obadiah
Ahiyah the Shilonite	1 Kings 11:29-30, 12:15, 14:2-18, 15:29
Jehu son of Hanani	1 Kings 16:1-7; 2 Chron. 19:2, 20:34

BOX 2.2 (CONT.)

Azariah son of Oded	2 Chron. 15
Jahaziel the Levite	2 Chron. 20:14
Eliezer son of Dodavahu	2 Chron. 20:37
Hosea	Hosea
Amos	Amos
Micah the Morashtite	Micah
Amoz	(the father of Isaiah)
Elijah	1 Kings 17:1—21:29; 2 Kings 1:10—2:15, 9:36-37, 10:10, 10:17
Elisha	1 Kings 19:16-19; 2 Kings 2:1—13:21
Jonah ben Amittai	Jonah
Isaiah	Isaiah
Joel	Joel
Nahum	Nahum
Habakkuk	Habakkuk
Zephaniah	Zephaniah
Uriah	Jer. 26:20-23
Jeremiah	Jeremiah
Ezekiel	Ezekiel
Shemaiah	1 Kings 12:22-24; 2 Chron 11:2-4, 12:5-15
Barukh	Jeremiah 32, 36, 43, 45
Neriah	(father of Barukh)
Seraiah	Jer. 51:61-64
Mehseiah	(father of Neriah)
Haggai	Haggai
Zechariah	Zechariah
Malachi	Malachi
Mordecai Bilshan	Esther
Oded	(father of Azariah)
Hanani	(father of Jehu)
Female Prophets	
Sarah	Gen. 11:29—23:20
Miriam	Exod. 15:20-21; Num. 12:1-15, 20:1
Deborah	Judg. 4:1—5:31
Hannah	1 Sam. 1:1—2:21
Abigail	1 Sam 25:1-42
Huldah	2 Kings 22:14-20
Esther	Esther

use the word *clans*—coming together and constituting the various tribes identified within the Hebrew Bible. According to *Bereshith*/Genesis 48–50, the patriarch Jacob fathered twelve sons, each of whom would then occupy his own territory within the Land of Israel, except for the tribe of Levi, who would serve as priests of the holy temple. In order of their birth, they were: Reuben, Simeon, Levi, Judah, Dan, Naphtali, Gad, Asher, Issachar, Zebulon, Joseph, and Benjamin. (After the destruction of the North by the Assyrians in 721 B.C.E., ten of the tribes would be lost, and the South would be inhabited by the tribes of Judah and Benjamin only. But we are getting somewhat ahead of ourselves in the story.)

Rise of Urbanization

The drive toward settlement brought with it more and more cultivation of the land itself, fruit trees and harvestable grains in particular, and new classes of craftspersons and artisans. Urbanization coupled with conquest saw the status of the ruling elders increase and, concomitantly, increase the importance both of the households and the smaller clan units. Out of such an evolving settled society came the monarchy, held in power by larger and larger landowning households, clans, and tribes, and within it the increasing social stratification known to us today: peasants and slaves (captives, residents, Israelites) to work the land; small landowners working the land themselves, possibly with the assistance of hired laborers; various governmental functionaries required for the success of the monarchy (e.g., administrators, scribes, accountants, military leaders and subordinates, and the like); Levitical religious leaders as worship comes to occupy more and more a central place in Israelite life; and artisans, merchants, and businesspersons.

It should be noted here that one of the threads that runs throughout the Hebrew Bible is an ambivalent attitude of the Israelites toward urban as opposed to pastoral life. Ironically, however, later Jewish safety, survival, and religious and cultural productivity will all be contingent on urban life, and it is only with the rise of the modern State of Israel in the twentieth century that we see a truly positive return and renewed celebration and valuation of pastoral life in the development of both the *kibbutzim* and the *moshavim,* Israel's collective farming settlements.

Before the Destruction
of the First Temple
to Alexander the Great

In the year 721 B.C.E., invaders from the north, known as Assyrians, journeyed southward and destroyed the loose confederation of the ten Israelite tribes in the area. Though the Temple of Solomon was in the south, in Jerusalem, the devastation caused by this destruction, both on those who remained and those who were spared, should not be minimized or underestimated. A formerly unified people, even if contentiously so, saw its majority severed from its body, and with it the rise of a religious myth that has endured even today: that of the so-called Ten Lost Tribes, some arguing for the peoples of the Alaskan peninsula, some for indigenous Native Americans, and some for the peoples of the Indian continent or China or Japan as well as other groups.[6] The historical reality of that loss is, however, the following: defeat in battle on earth mirrored defeat in battle in the realm of the gods, who themselves entered into the fray. Those who survived, willingly or unwillingly, surrendered their systems of belief, embraced those of the victors, and more often than not assimilated into the society of the conquerors. Thus, the God of Israel had seemingly been defeated by the gods of the Assyrians, as had the people themselves, and the northern tribes, within a few generations, assimilated themselves and their unique identity out of existence, nevermore to be seen or heard from again.

The Age of the Prophets

For the next 135 years, until the destruction of Solomon's temple by the Babylonians in 586 B.C.E., the southern kingdom, the tribes of Judah and Benjamin (and the Levites of course), struggled to maintain their existence, deflected enemy attacks, entered into treaty-alliances with their neighbors, and sought to create a nation-state of economic prosperity. And, according to the prophetic texts found in the second section of the Hebrew Bible, were reasonably successful in doing so—at a price.

Prophetic guilds in ancient Israel were not unique to the Hebrews. Both 1 Samuel and 1 and 2 Kings tell us of such Israelite groups—the so-called *B'nei Nevi'im* ("sons of the prophets")—who lived communally and were given to states of ecstasy prior to their public utterances. Samuel, Elisha, and Elijah may have initially been part of such groups.

The prophets of ancient Israel with whom we are most familiar—Isaiah, Jeremiah, Ezekiel, and "the Twelve," the minor prophets (Hosea, Joel, Amos, Obadiah, Jonah, Micah, Nahum, Habakkuk, Zephaniah, Haggai, Zechariah, Mala-

chi)—and who constitute this second section of the Hebrew Bible, were individuals of heightened moral sensitivity and devout religious sensibility who continually condemned their nation for what they regarded as catastrophically serious lapses of both ethical and religious responsibilities. Collectively, their goal was (1) to return their people and its leadership to the right path and (2) to prevent the physical destruction of their country and the annihilation of its population. On both counts, they failed, but in so doing, they bequeathed to subsequent generations a religious-ethical literature that continues to inspire Jews and Christians today and challenges both groups to engage in *tikkun olam*, repairing a damaged world. Their concern for the "the poor, the fatherless, the orphan, the widow," coupled with their critiques of both governmental and religious corruption, remain the yardstick by which we assess both institutions even today.

Babylonian Captivity

In 586 B.C.E., the Hebrew people found its very existence threatened by Babylonian invaders. It is the Babylonians who will breech the walls of Jerusalem, raze the Temple of Solomon to the ground,

---

BOX 2.3

The Lost Tribes of Israel

The quest for the Lost Tribes of Israel, like the quest for the Holy Grail, for Prester John or for the Ark of the Covenant, is one of the enduring motifs underlying western views of the wider world. It has spawned legends which have been used to explain the origin of myriad peoples in every part of the globe from ancient times until the present. The tribes disappeared from history before Christ but the Bible foretold that one day they would be reunited in the final redemption of the people of Israel. The belief persisted that they had been "lost" in some remote part of the world and there were countless suggestions and claims as to where, peddled by madmen, saints and eccentrics.

Tudor Parfitt, *The Lost Tribes of Israel: The History of a Myth* (London: Weidenfeld & Nicolson, 2002), back cover.

and carry off into captivity the governmental, religious, social, economic, and military leaderships, leaving behind devastation unparalleled in the people's history. (The word *holocaust*—with a lowercase *h*—may perhaps be appropriately used here to mark destruction beyond compare, both physical and religious.) Those who remained, in truth the lowest levels of their society, will literally have to confront the pieces of their shattered existence. If what happened in and to the southern kingdom were to parallel that of the northern, the story of the Hebrews would have ended, for obviously the God of Israel had now been defeated a *second* time. All that remained was for the people, once in captivity, to abandon their commitment to their God and their identity, and embrace that of the victors. But such was not to be the case.

Significantly, the Babylonians proved gracious in their victory, and allowed the Israelites to settle in their own neighborhoods and worship their own God—provided they themselves proved to be good captive citizens, paying their taxes and not engaging in subversive military activities. With their temple destroyed and their wounds still fresh, scholars believe that the origins of what would later become the synagogue were born here: with no central sanctuary, no sacrificial cultic priesthood to oversee the rituals and ceremonies of worship, the Israelites reinterpreted their defeat as part of God's plan to spread the word of his singular sovereignty. In order to do so, they embarked on a threefold religious regimen that became the foundation of postbiblical Judaism: First, they told and retold their stories, myths, and legends as initially manifested in their sacred writings ("religious study"). Second, they communicated with their God directly, without the necessity of animal sacrifice ("prayer process"). And, third, they gathered regularly, especially on the Sabbaths and the festivals as a community in worship, an *ekklesia* (Greek, "religious assembly").

Return to Palestine

Approximately 100 to 150 years after settling in Babylonia and making an uncomfortable peace with their reality (c. 438–400 B.C.E.), some Israelites, still stirred by longings to return to the land of their origins, began the journey home under the Aaronide priest Ezra, and the man who would govern them, Nehemiah. Their own books of the Torah tell us of both Ezra's success in getting those already resident in Israel to divorce their foreign wives, and Nehemiah's success in refortifying Jerusalem's walls and participating in the restoration and rededication of the Temple's foundation, though it will take several centuries before its rebuilding. Yet the texts themselves are strangely silent about whatever relationship, if any, existed between the two of them, and whether, in fact, they were there or not during the same period.

The Second Temple Period and the Conflicts with Hellenism and "Romanism"

With the advancing legions of Alexander the Great (356–332 B.C.E.), son of Philip of Macedon (382–336 C.E.), the hegemony of the Babylonians came to its end. After his own death, and without a designated successor, Alexander's conquered kingdom was divided between the Ptolemies of Egypt and the Seleucids of Syria, with Judea under the reign of the Ptolemies. They enforced their own pattern of city governance as they understood it, affecting both social and political life, with Judea ruled by a high priest who served both religious and political functions, and a council of elders validating his decisions. Constantly being battling over for dominant control, Judea changed hands and came under the rule of the Seleucids about a century after Alexander's death. Initially, little change was evident for the

Fig. 2.4 The Second Temple This scale model of Jerusalem and the Second Temple at the time of King Herod the Great (c. 20 B.C.E.) is located at the Holy Land Hotel in modern-day Jerusalem. Photo courtesy Creative Commons: http://commons.wikimedia.org/wiki/File:Second_Temple.jpg

people and leadership of Judea, until the ascension to the throne of Antiochus IV (215–163 B.C.E.), named *Epiphanies* ("the Great One") by those who supported him, and *Epimanes* ("the Mad One") by those who opposed him. He saw his responsibility as the imposition of all that was Greek on his subjects, forbidding Israelite religious practice on pain of death and desecrating the holy temple of Jerusalem.

Hasmonean Revolt and Rule

In 165 B.C.E., guerilla warfare broke out against the Seleucids, led by a family of Hasmonean priests from Modi'in. One year later, they had achieved victory over their hated enemies and consecrated and rededicated their temple with, according to Jewish religious tradition, enough oil to keep burning the eternal flame of God's presence for eight days until additional stores could be found. (The *minor* Jewish festival of Hanukkah emerges from this story.)

For the next 130 years, the Hasmoneans would remain central to the leadership of the peoples of Judea, with Aristobulus I (140–103 B.C.E.) taking upon himself the restoration of the monarchy in 104 B.C.E. Prior to his ascension, however, his Hasmonean predecessors, to solidify their leadership, had entered into an alliance with Rome, and by 67 B.C.E., Rome was very much in evidence in the region, and thus ultimately undermined his and their sovereignty.

Oppression under Roman Rule

This time, Judea was under the governorship of Syria, with limited autonomy and freedom to worship. Even the Roman political and military leader Julius Caesar (100–44 B.C.E.), who would later become emperor, initially viewed the province and its inhabitants most favorably. History, however, began to repeat itself with his death by assassination in 4 B.C.E.; without a designated successor, jockeying for power and position was the order of the day, with Judea itself buffeted about as a prize, until King Herod (74–4 B.C.E.) the Idumean assumed power in 37 B.C.E. His reign was marked by an iron hand, diminishing the power of both the *Sanhedrin*, the ruling religious council, and the high priesthood as well, despite the relative internal tranquility of the province. Most notably, however, prior to his death in 4 B.C.E., he had caused to be rebuilt the temple in Jerusalem. (Today's Western Wall in Jerusalem, Judaism's confirmed holiest site, is the last remaining structure of that ancient temple.)

Upon his death, Judea would be governed by a series of Roman procurators, including one of Judean origin (Julius Alexander Tiberias), who would restore some measure of authority to both the Sanhedrin and high priesthood. It is only with the procurator Pontius Pilate (26–36 C.E.) that things go from bad to worse, with Roman soldiers occupying the streets of Jerusalem, Roman supervision of temple practices, and oppressively heavy taxation.

It is during this period of oppression, and slightly before, that a Jew is born, according to the New Testament text, to a poor family in Bethlehem, grows up thoroughly grounded in his Jewish religious education, unusually adept at teaching through stories (i.e., parables), feels the pain of his people, and travels the region offering his wisdom and comfort, generating increasingly large crowds and interest primarily among the lower socioeconomic classes of Judean society. Misperceived by the Romans as a political insurrectionist, he is arrested and dies by crucifixion. That man, possibly named (in Hebrew) *Yeshua*, *Yehoshua*, or *Yeshu* (all meaning "God will save"), son of Joseph (Hebrew *Yosef*) and Miriam (not Mary, but, rather, *Miryam*) is known to us today as Jesus [the] Christ (Anglicized Greek for "Messiah," *Christos*). His death and subsequent theological understandings will ultimately give rise to Christianity, a nascent *minority* Jewish religious movement that will split from its parent centuries later and mark a two-thousand-year journey of tragedy for both Jews and Christians. (More on this in chapter 5.)

Destruction of the Second Temple

In 66 C.E., open rebellion against Rome finally breaks out, one which Emperor Nero (37–68 C.E.) simply cannot afford to ignore. He sends his most trusted general, Vespasian (9–79 C.E.), to quell the revolt, but Nero dies in 68 C.E. Vespasian will crown himself emperor in 69 C.E., and tasks his own son and general, Titus (39–81 C.E.), with the destruction of Roman-occupied Palestine. Titus besieges Jerusalem in 70 C.E. and, in his success, razes the Second Temple to the ground and with it ending all hopes for Jewish hegemony in the land until the birth of the Third Jewish Commonwealth, the modern State of Israel, on May 14, 1948.

Aftermath of the First Roman War

The religious and political devastation to the Jews wrought by the Roman destruction of Jerusalem and its temple were initially incalculable, as Jews now came to grips with horrors previously unknown. The Babylonian Talmud (more about which we will read in the next chapter), suggests that there were so many crucifixions and other deaths that the streets of Jerusalem ran red with the blood of those killed. Here again it appeared that the God of Israel and his chosen ones had been thoroughly vanquished yet a *third* time—were it not for the unsung savior of the Jewish people and the religion of Judaism, Rabbi Yochanan ben Zakkai.[7]

Legend has it that prior to the final military assault on besieged Jerusalem, Rabbi Yochanan had some of his students carry him out of the city in a coffin (the Roman soldiers being loathe to come into contact with those who died by means other than warfare). He then proceeded to the tent of the Roman general Vespasian (which says much about

Roman security!), where he informed him he would soon be named emperor of Rome, for which Rabbi Yochanan was promptly thrown into prison. When word came soon thereafter that such was indeed the case, Vespasian had him brought out of prison (shades of the Hebrew Bible story of Joseph!) and granted him one favor. Rabbi Yochanan asked for permission to found a rabbinical academy in the town of Yavneh (Jamnia). This wonderful tale of quasi-historical accuracy will support not only the canonization (fixity) of the Hebrew Scriptures—the process of which we know almost absolutely nothing and believed to have occurred in the year 90 C.E.—but also the dramatic change of religious Judaism from that of a cultic religion expressed through animal sacrifice and priestly ritual into a more democratic Judaism in which all, though initially only males, could participate, though changes were already occurring prior to the Roman debacle under the leadership of the Pharisees (perhaps the most misunderstood group in all of Judaic history).

Bar Kokhba Revolt

For the next century, the fortunes of Jews went up and down, depending on who occupied the seat of the emperor in Rome and who was the governor of

Fig. 2.5 Bar Kokhba coin Minted during the Bar Kokhba rebellion, these coins reflect the last gasp in the Jewish attempt to overcome the oppression experienced under their Roman overlords. Photo courtesy Creative Commons: http://commons.wikimedia.org/wiki/File:Barkokhba-silver-tetradrachm.jpg

Judea. The situation, however, was unstable enough that, in the year 132 C.E., revolt against Rome broke out once again, this time under one Simeon Bar Kokhba (or Bar Kosiba, literally "son of the star," and reference to a passage in the Book of *Bemidbar/* Numbers), and validated by the leading rabbi of the day, Akiba (50–135 C.E.). Thoroughly quashed by the emperor Hadrian (76–138 C.E.), it came to represent the dying gasp of a people for political sovereignty and hegemony over its own affairs. From that point on, the people and its land would be governed by others, more and less benignly, until the midpoint of the twentieth century, when the State of Israel would be declared.

Subsequent to the Bar Kohkba revolt, under the patriarchal leadership of the charismatic third-century rabbi, Rabbi Judah (135–219 C.E.), the internal laws governing the Jewish people were brought together, organized and codified in a document known as the *Mishnah* ("Second Torah"). Consisting of six major divisions—"Seeds," or agricultural and prayer matters; "Festivals," or the Sabbath and holidays; "Women," or marriage and divorce; "Damages," or civil and criminal matters; "Kodashim," or religious matters and the dietary system; and "Purities," or matters of purity for both the priesthood and the family—and based on the Hebrew Bible, its ongoing commentaries over the next centuries by both the rabbis in Roman Palestine and Babylonia would later be joined together in the authoritative Talmud of Babylonia and the lesser Talmud of Palestine.

Rise of Rabbinical Academies

Though terribly significant in the formative development of postbiblical Judaism, the Mishnah itself marked the end of Palestine as the center of Judaic life, and the scene shifted to Babylonia, where the Jewish population has been estimated to have been as high as 10 percent of the population, with political autonomy, religious freedom unrivalled by their compatriots in Palestine, and economic success far in excess of their southeastern relatives. As the Jewish population grew, its rabbinical academies grew, especially at Nehardea, Sura, and Pumbedita, and the learning itself became more and more advanced. Its own codification of Mishnah and Gemara (Talmudic commentaries) provided the foundation on which all subsequent Jewries would come to depend as the authoritative source of information, both religious and secular, for all Jewish communities, up to and including our own day.

Fig. 2.6 A page of the Talmud After the Torah/Hebrew Bible, the Babylonian Talmud, viewed here by this sample page, remains the authoritative heart of Jewish religious observance and addresses all manner of Jewish life during the initial five hundred years of its composition and the subsequent commentaries which surround both the law itself (Mishnah) and its rabbinic discussion (Gemara).

Fourth to Seventh Centuries

At the start of this period, the Jewish communities of both Babylonia and Palestine were large, the former more so than the latter, and flourishing economically as well. Jews were also well represented in the Roman cities of Alexandria in Egypt, Antioch in Greece, and Rome itself. Now that the destruction of the Second Temple had receded somewhat into history, western Jewish migration was becoming more and more of a reality.

Constantine, Christianity, and the Edict of Milan

Fortunes began to change significantly, however, in the year 313 C.E., when Emperor Constantine I (232–337) affirmed the Edict of Milan, which favored the growing religion of Christianity in his empire, and entered into an alliance with Christian leadership in what today we now refer to as the "Holy Roman Empire." While early on, both emperors and church leaders behaved ambivalently toward their Jewish populations, some supportive and well-intentioned, others restrictive and mean-spirited (e.g., the great orator John Chrysostom [309–407], Bishop of Syria and Constantinople, who attacked the Jews and the intellectual giant Augustine, Bishop of Hippo [354–430], who supported the Jews), the alliance saw Jewish communities in increasingly impoverished statuses, their religious and political freedoms restricted, and their now-diminished existence proof of the "truths" of Christianity.

Emergence of Islam

In the East, in the area known as the Arabian Peninsula, Jewish tribal communities had also lived reasonably well and successfully, interacting with the non-Jewish tribes in the region. In the seventh century, Muhammed (570–632) came forward, in response to what he (and his followers) accepted as a divine mandate, attempting to unite these tribes into a loose confederation and to share with them a revelation known as the *Qur'an*. Initially favorably disposed toward both Jews and Christians—to whom he gave the title "people of the Book" (i.e., Torah/Hebrew Bible and New Testament)—when the Jews rejected both his political leadership and his newer understanding of God's plan, he engaged them militarily, wiping out the Jews of Banu Qurayza, for example, in 627. From that point on, both Jews and Christian would be classed as *dhimmis*, "protected ones," with Jews, however, occupying a somewhat higher status than that of Christians. (The uneasy and ongoing relationship between all three groups remains problematic even today, further exacerbated by events in the Middle East with regard to the State of Israel, its own history, and that of its neighbors.)

Middle Ages:
Eighth to Fifteenth Centuries

The continuing success of Islam saw Arabs extending their empire from India to Spain and, as a byproduct, encompassing by the year 712 approximately 90 percent of the Jews then alive. (Jerusalem had already been retaken from the Christian West by 638.) Increasingly, Jews under Muslim hegemony gravitated toward cities and towns, away from their former occupation as farmers, and became traders, merchants, and craftspersons. Nowhere was their successful integration into the life of the empire more evident than in Spain in the lives of three truly remarkable individuals: Hasdai *ibn* (the Arabic equivalent of the Hebrew *ben*, "son of") Shaprut (915–970? or 990?), physician and diplomat; Samuel ibn Nagrela (993–1056), Talmudist, poet, soldier, and diplomat; and Solomon ibn Gabirol (1021–1058), poet and philosopher.

Communally, during this same period, two movements seemingly competed for the souls of the Jews: (1) the larger and more dominant one, which we may call "Rabbinism" or "Talmudism," was grounded in the Talmudic texts stretching back to the time of the Mishnah, of the third century, and (2) the smaller opposite, which we may call "Karaism," was conservative, more biblically literalist, rejecting the authority of the rabbis and their texts, and was not unlike their Palestinian predecessors, the Sadducees, in their controversies with the Pharisees, though they never claimed lineal descent from them.

The First Crusade

In the Christian West, however, the situation of the Jewish communities continued to deteriorate, experiencing a worsening of attitudes, economic impoverishments, increasing isolation, and forced ghettoizations. As Christians under the imprimatur of Pope Urban II (1042–1099) prepared to launch the First Crusade (1095/6–1099), whose objective was to recapture the city of Jerusalem and all of the Holy Land—and succeeded shortly before the pope's death—Jewish communities in the path of the crusaders found themselves particularly vulnerable. The rallying cry *Hep! Hep! Hierosolyma est perdita!* (Latin, "Jerusalem is/has been lost!") galvanized western Europeans to action. Led by knights and priests, the bulk of those who sallied forth to battle were largely illiterate peasants and needed little reminder and encouragement that the Jews found in their way were the descendants of those who supposedly killed their Christ and, thus, were infidels like the Muslims of Palestine. Jewish communities were destroyed, their populations decimated, including women and children, and their synagogues desecrated. Those who survived these onslaughts either fled to other locations or feebly attempted to reconstruct their lives, not always successfully.

Yet, even despite this picture of darkness and gloom, Jewish cultural and religious creativity did not diminish. The bright light of Jewish learning shone no more brightly than it did during this period in the person of Rabbi Solomon ben Isaac (1040–1105) of Troyes, France, where he established his own *yeshiva*, or academy of rabbinic and higher learning, in 1070. More known by his acronym *Rashi*, his commentaries on both Talmud and Torah/Hebrew Bible remain authoritative even today and are published together with those texts.

Later Crusades and Jewish Oppression

However, the Second Crusade (1146–1147) and the Third Crusade (1189–1190)—the latter under the imprimatur of Pope Innocent III (1161–1216)—saw repeated the very same reprehensible behaviors against Jews that marked the First Crusade a generation previous: destruction of Jewish communities and the murders of their inhabitants. As initiated, confirmed, and accepted by the Pope, the Fourth Lateran Council (1215) now saw the Jews (and Muslims) required to wear distinctive clothing to set them even further apart and lessen the contact between themselves and Christians. Also during this period, the notorious antisemitic charge of "blood libel"—using the blood of innocent Christian children during the Passover season in the making of the matzot or unleavened cakes required in celebration—began to surface. In addition, Jews found themselves expelled from England in 1290 and France in 1306.

On the continent, primarily in Italy, Jews again found themselves in an uncomfortably ambiguous position. With the rise of mercantilism and commerce, not only the church—which publicly condemned the charging of interest on loans ("usury")—but increasingly secular societies saw the need for larger and larger amounts of speculative capital and turned to the Jews for such monies. Equally, Jews saw such monies not only as forms of safety and security should quick exits from their places of residence present themselves, but as opportunities to ingratiate themselves into

the larger societies and make contributions to their growth and development, ideally reflecting back on them with goodwill from their hosts. Sadly, however, such was not to be the case, as usury was now added to the litany of deicide (i.e. killers of God/Christ) and blood libel/ritual murder in the antisemitic cacophony that marked the times.

A Golden Age

In Spain, the period from 900 to 1200 would be known among the Jews as a "golden age," when literary, cultural, and religious creativity was at its highest. Two of its more noteworthy representatives were the philosopher and poet Judah ha-Levi (1075–1141), born in Tudela, and physician, rabbi, and philosopher Moses ben Maimon (1135–1204), born in Córdoba and known today as Maimonides, perhaps the greatest figure in all Jewish history second only to Moses of the Torah. (Apocryphal lore has it that he once said of himself, "From Moses [of old] unto Moses [me], there is none like unto Moses!")

Initially, after the *Reconquista* (Christian retaking of Spain) proved successful during the twelfth and thirteenth centuries, Jews shared their knowledge of philosophy, science, mathematics, medicine, and even astrology with their old/new hosts. But all was not well. In 1263, in Barcelona, for example, the apostate and convert Dominican monk Pablo Christiani engaged in a public debate with Rabbi Moses ben Nachman, Nachmanides (1194–1270), in an unsuccessful attempt to humiliate the Spanish Jewish community. Earlier, in 1239, and again in 1244, Pope Gregory IV (1143–1291) and Pope Innocent IV (1195–1254) called for the confiscation and the burning of the Babylonian Talmud as a way to destroy Jewish communities. Conditions continued to worsen in Spain, with riots ultimately breaking out throughout the country beginning in 1391 and the expulsion of the entire Jewish community (estimated at more than 300,000 persons) under the royal edict of King Ferdinand II of

Aragon (1452–1516) and Queen Isabella (1451–1504)—with the imprimatur of her father confessor, the Dominican and Grand Inquisitor Tomás de Torquemada (1420–1498), who was himself responsible for a bloody attempt to root out all "insincere and false Christians" in the realm.

(As a sidebar, a rather unusual idea has surfaced about this period with regard to the rather mysterious Cristoforo Colon of Italy and Spain, known to us today as Christopher Columbus (1451–1506). Because his initial voyage coincided with the expulsion of the Jews, and his first interpreter, Luis de Torres (d. 1493), was known to be a Jew, and some financial support for his voyages came from wealthy members of the Jewish community, some have suggested that his mission was *not* a route to the East for spices and other valuables, but rather a mission to discover a safe haven for the departing Jews.[8])

Jewish Expulsions and Diasporas

In the so-called black death (i.e., bubonic plague), of 1348–1349, which saw the deaths of millions of Europeans, the Jews were again seen as guilty of making it happen, part of a conspiratorial plot to destroy their hated enemies. Because in their ghettos, Jews died in fewer numbers proportionately, and the illiterate peasantry observed this, they attributed their own misery to the Jews. The truth, however, was different: because Jewish ritual behaviors require both handwashing and full-body immersion at sacred times, these simple religious acts had a prophylactic effect, decreasing disease among the community, even if minimally. But for those without such knowledge, for whom Jewish religious practice was first and always dark magic and mysterious, their read of such things was negatively different.[9]

Thus, by the end of the fifteenth century, and continuing on into the sixteenth century, Jews had experienced expulsions from England, France, Italy, sporadically in Germany, and Bohemia-Moravia. Only in Poland-Lithuania was the situation reversed.

Middle Ages and Transition: Sixteenth to Seventeenth Centuries

With the expulsion of Jews from both Spain and, later, Portugal, Jews turned both east and west in their search for safe havens. In the East, in the Ottoman Empire, specifically Turkey and the Land of Israel, Jewish communities began to flourish both economically and religiously by the increase of their populations. In the West, in Germany, the Netherlands, and England (where they had been invited to return in 1655 after having been expelled in 1290), Jewish communities began to thrive. In Poland-Lithuania, where Jews had by and large avoided the calamities of expulsion and resettlement, the Jewish communities continued their positive ascendancy; prior to the time of the massacres initiated by the *Hetman* of the Ukrainian Cossacks, Bohdan Chmielnitski (1595–1657), in his successful attacks on the Polish aristocracy (1648–1654)—possibly as many as 100,000 Jews murdered there in 1648—the Jews were sufficiently well organized to convene the "Council of the Four Lands" (Heb. *Va'ad Arba Artzot*), dividing their lands of residence into four quadrants, with leaders from each sector meeting annually to discuss and finalize civil, political, economic, and religious matters.

Internal Jewish Dynamics

The Jews of The Netherlands also found a tolerant and safe port after fleeing Spain and Portugal. As the community itself began to grow and develop both economically and religiously, conservatizing elements began to assume control, so that by the time of the philosopher Benedict Spinoza (Baruch de Spinoza, 1632–1677), whose views were perceived as communally threatening, excommunication (Heb. *cherem*) was the only option.

In the East, in the Land of Israel, however, two significant events took place in the mountain city of Safed (Heb. *Tsefat*, "the city of mystics): Rabbi Joseph Karo (1488–1575), born in Turkey, had begun a reorganization with commentary of the legal materials of Judaism, *Bet Yosef* (Hebrew, " 'House' of Joseph"), which he completed and published in 1559. Realizing also the need for an abstracted version of his text for those whose education did not permit them the time to pour over such materials, he produced the *Shulchan Aruch* (Hebrew, "Set" or "Prepared Table") of the laws themselves, topically arranged, and which remains even today *the* code of Jewish law among the devout.[10] His larger work, however, was attacked by the leading Polish rabbi of the day, Moses Isserles (1532–1572), who regarded its commentaries as reflecting a Sephardic (i.e., Spanish) bias without taking into consideration the differences in customs and traditions of the Ashkenazic (i.e., Germanic) communities. Today, many Hebrew (and some English) editions of the *Shulchan Aruch* are published with both Karo's and Isserles's commentaries.

Further Christian Persecutions

The Protestant Reformation, of the sixteenth century, which ultimately resulted in a lessening of the political and religious power of the Roman Catholic Church and its splintering into various non-Catholic sects (e.g., Calvinists, Anabaptists, Anglican, and Lutheran), equally saw these various communities and their leaders ambivalent both about their relationship with Jews and the role, place, and function of Jewish communities and persons in this new European world. The case of Roman Catholic priest Martin Luther (1483–1546)—said to be the "father" of the Reformation with his protest nailing of his Ninety-five Theses to the door of the church in Wittenberg, Germany, in 1517—is an excellent

case in point. Initially, his attitude toward Jews was positive, attacking his own Catholic Church for its hateful and demeaning approach to the conversion of Jews. Fully expecting them to convert when a hand was proffered in love, his attitude toward them changed dramatically when they did not. In 1543, he published *Von den Juden und ihren Lügen* ("On the Jews and Their Lies"), considered today among the most antisemitic texts ever written, second only to that of Adolf Hitler's (1889–1945) *Mein Kampf,* and rivaled by the nineteenth-century Russian forgery *The Protocols of the Learned Elders of Zion*, which scurrilously attacks not only Jews, but religious Judaism, the Talmud, and synagogue buildings as well.

False Messiahs

Into the gloom, depression, and darkness of the Jewish communities of this period came those who offered a seeming way out, falsely however. It is no accident that Jewish historians refer to this period as the "Age of the False Messiahs," the two most well known being Sabbatai Sevi (1626–1676) and Jacob Frank (1726–1781). The former was said to have been born in Turkey, hailed by both Sephardic and Ashkenazic Jews as the long-awaited *mashiach* (Heb. "messiah"), many of whom surrendered their earthy goods to join him on his trek back to the Holy Land. Arriving back in Turkey, he was at first welcomed by the sultan as leader of the Jews, but when informed that his supposed "true agenda" was the sultan's overthrow, most likely by a dissident in Sevi's own ranks, he was cast into prison where he languished, until given the choice of conversion to Islam or the sword. He chose Islam and wrote himself out of Jewish history. (Many among his followers saw "the hand of God" in his decision, and followed him into Islam while retaining much of their Jewish religious practices. Their descendants are said to have existed in the Crimea up until the 1800s.)

More ignominious was Jacob Frank (1726–1781), who convinced some that he was the reincarnation of both Sevi and King David. Offering an interpretation of both Judaism and Christianity, he tried to merge them, attempted to incorporate the New Testament into the world of the Jews, and together with his followers suggested that the way to God was through sin. Excommunicated by the Jews, his followers were later absorbed into the Catholic Church after his death.

By the end of this period, various Western nations, to the degree to which the "plight of the Jews" was part of their political thinking and agenda, began to address issues of toleration and interaction with the Jewish communities resident in their midst. In France, Germany, England, and The Netherlands, conversations were beginning to take place about the Jews as the movement toward modernity continued.

Pre- and Early Modernity: The Eighteenth and Nineteenth Centuries

A simple division of Jewish history is the following: (1) the prebiblical and biblical period (to 70 C.E.), (2) the postbiblical or rabbinic period (to 1791), and (3) the modern period (1791 to the present). Why so? Because the year 1791, coincident with the French Revolution (1789–1799) saw the Jews of France granted the right to vote, and with it status as citizens for the first time since leaving their ancestral homeland. A revolution in the West, even if not of their own making, had truly begun.

Citizenship, however, does not equate with either integration or assimilation, and it remains worrisome, even today, for Jews of all persuasions in enlightened, democratic societies, who seek the preservation of a unique parochial identity versus participating in the larger society. In 1806, Emperor Napoléon Bonaparte (1769–1821) convened an "Assembly of Jewish Notables" out of

which grew a "Sanhedrin," convened in 1807, both of which effectively rendered null and void any notion of Judaism as a *national* rather than a *religious* identity, and enabled the Jews of France to see themselves as part of the French Republic. (Other Jewish communities in both Europe and the United States would, and continue to, follow this model.)

Period of Jewish Emancipation

With the ghetto walls down after many centuries of isolation and closed-off existence, Jews now found themselves admitted to universities and entering into professions heretofore denied them. For some, the heady excitement proved too much and, during the eighteenth century, it is estimated that more than 200,000 Jews renounced the specifics of their Jewish identity in favor of the larger, and largely Christian, world of Western society.

Though emancipation of the Jews, hastened by the European Enlightenment of the eighteenth century, which was in many ways the final blow to the political power of the Roman Catholic Church, would not come to Germany or England until the 1850s, one truly outstanding Jew who saw the possibilities of successfully bridging the gulf was the philosopher Moses Mendelssohn (1729–1786) of Berlin. For him and others like him, it was possible to be a devout and religiously practicing Jew at home and an intellectual man of the world outside. Though somewhat deformed by his hunchback, the brilliance of his intellect and oratory caused those who interacted with him to pay it little mind. His own children, however, were unable to carry this dual torch; they *all* converted to Christianity.

The great Jewish community of Poland-Lithuania suffered from the breakup of the land by Austria in 1772, Czarist Russia in 1793, and Prussia in 1795. What had been a thriving and united population was now divided; its communal and organizational structures shrunken and dramatically reorganized on a far smaller scale. Czarist Russia, which annexed the largest land area, also annexed the largest Jewish population, for which it was neither desirous nor prepared. Its monarchy, its peasantry, and its Russian Orthodox Church vacillated between limited acceptance and outright hostility. Ultimately, hostility won out, and by the end of the period, Jewish residence had been restricted to what became known as the "Pale of Settlement." The vast majority of Russia's Jews found themselves unable to travel great distances for their livelihood, occupationally restricted, economically deprived, and threatened by an antisemitism that, by and large, they had not experienced in old Poland-Lithuania.

Four Jewish Movements

Yet, despite these various deprivations, four remarkable, and remarkably unique, movements arose during this period: (1) *Hasidism*, an Eastern religious movement, (2) *Reform Judaism*, a Western religious movement; (3) Haskalah, an Eastern secular movement, and (4) *Zionism*, a Western secular movement. While these identifiers should not be understood as hard and fast distinctions, collectively, they established the foundational pattern for Jewish life today and set the stage for it tomorrow.

In the late 1770s, traditional Jewish religious life and practice were perceived by many, especially the lower socioeconomic classes, as rigidly authoritarian (read "Orthodox") and joyless. Into this scene came a pietistic Polish rabbi named Israel ben Eliezer (1698–1760), whose approaches to God are filled with joyous singing and (segregated male) dancing, respect for all, especially the lower classes, optimism toward the future, embracing of certain mystical aspects of the Jewish religious tradition, and a rejection of ascetic religious life. Though not without opposition from those already in authority—the so-called *Mitnagdim* (Hebrew, "opponents")—he and his followers survived the challenge, and today the various offshoots of his original understandings are known for their distinctive garb, modeled on the eighteenth-century Polish nobility, and their primary use of Yiddish (a folk and literary language akin to Hebrew) as the language of discourse, as well as their self-imposed residence restrictions.

Fig. 2.7 Hasidism These worshippers, some in Sabbath dress, are praying at the Western Wall in Jerusalem. Photo: Alinari / Art Resource, N.Y.

One-half century later, 1810 to be exact, in Sessen, Germany, wealthy Jewish landowner Israel Jacobson (1768–1828) built a beautiful synagogue on the grounds of the school he had built a decade earlier, to which he added musical instrumentation and invited prominent liberal and university-educated rabbis to deliver sermons in the vernacular (i.e., German rather than Yiddish). From such a beginning came Reform Judaism, a liberal and progressive alternative to the legalistic Orthodox Judaism of the day. Like many upstart movements, it initially went too far and, in the 1850s, Positive-Historical Judaism (modern Conservative Judaism) also arose in Germany, not as a challenge to Orthodoxy but a reaction to the too-liberal-fast-becoming-radical Reform Judaism, whose own initial goals were the *reforming* or changing of the liturgy, stemming the tide of assimilation, and integration into the larger society while maintaining positive Jewish identity. (It is today, in the United States where it continues to flower, the largest Jewish religious movement of all the denominations.)

Impact of Secularization

By the late eighteenth century, Czarist Russia was in the throes of political and revolutionary chaos as movements sprang up that sought new forms of governmental models. Jews, too, participated in these calls for change, feeling that their participation could only redound positively for their discriminated-against communities. Internally, however, the impact of Western European secularism had already begun to intrude into those same communities. For the first time, Jewish thinkers and writers began to draw on the university educations of others and their own thoughts to critically assess the Torah/Hebrew Bible but, more importantly, to see in the Hebrew language a means of discourse not confined to the religious realm. Plays, novels, short stories, essays, newspapers, all manner of written texts, began to pour forth. Among those associated with the Jewish Haskalah (Hebrew, "enlight-

enment") movement were Chaim Nachman Bialik (1873–1934), "the Father of Modern Hebrew Literature"; writer of humorous stories Sholom Aleichem (born Sholem Rabinowitz, 1859–1916); poet Saul Tchernichov-sky (1875–1943), and too, too many others to cite here. Unbeknownst to themselves, or perhaps pres-cient nonetheless, their work set the foundation for the cultural life of the modern State of Israel.

In 1894, in Paris, France, a Jewish army officer named Captain Alfred Dreyfus (1859–1935) stood trial accused of treason (for which he was ultimately acquitted twelve years later). Covering the trial for the *New Free Press* of Vienna was Jewish journalist Theodor Herzl (1860–1904). So shocked was he

Fig. 2.8 Theodor Herzl (1860–1944) This "father of modern political Zionism" was a Viennese journalist who rallied Jews to translate their ancient dream of a return to Zion into a living reality. Photo: Jewish Chronicle Archive/HIP/ Art Resource, N.Y.

BOX 2.4

From "The Pond" (1908)

I know a forest, and in the forest
I know a hidden pool:
In the density of the thicket, secluded from the
    world,
In the shadow of a lofty oak, blessed of light and
    accustomed to storm,
Alone she dreams for herself a dream of an
    inverted world
And quietly keeps for herself her golden fish—

In the morning,
When the sun bathes the braids of the forest's
    splendor
Pouring out a sea of brilliance upon his ringlets;
And he, the steadfast one, stretching out all his
    golden nets,
As is his want, like Samson in Delilah's hands,
    stands captured,
With an easy laughter and the light of a lover's
    face who feels his strength,
With a golden net of his own, receives his shack-
    les in love,
And raises his crowned head beneath the sun's
    might

As if saying to her: Wash me away, cherish me or
    bind me up
And do with me that which your heart desires—

The pond at this moment, if she be awarded
    with
A single ray from on high—
Swoons in the shadow of her shield of many
    boughs,
Silently suckles his roots and her waters are
    calm;
As if she silently rejoices in her portion
That she merited to be a mirror for the strong
    one of the forest.
And who knows, perhaps she dreams secretly,
That not only his image together with his young
    shoot are in her—
But all of him grows up within her.

Excerpt from Steven Leonard Jacobs, trans.,
*Shirot Bialik: A New and Annotated Translation of
Chaim Nachman Bialik's Epic Poems* (Columbus,
Ohio: Alpha Publishing, 1987), 169–70.

at the daily evidence of antisemitism, including the rightist Catholic and monarchist newspapers, that he quickly realized the successful integration of Jews into European life was all but impossible, and upon his return home in 1895–1896, he published *Der Judenstaat* ("The Jewish State"), forcefully arguing that antisemitism would cease when Jews, too, had a state of their own and could enter into relationships with other groups as equal players. By virtue of his passionate and charismatic personality and his prodigious energy, he gathered Jews together in the First Zionist Congress in Basel, Switzerland, in 1897, and met with leaders through Europe and the Middle East to campaign for a homeland for Jews.

At his death in 1904, this "father of modern political Zionism" is said to have remarked, "In fifty years, there *will* be a Jewish state!" (The State of Israel declared its sovereignty on May 14, 1948. Herzl's body is interred in Israel and is continually visited by Jews worldwide.) Sadly and ironically, Herzl's dream has yet to be realized: with the creation of the State of Israel, the world has not yet accorded Jews equal status, antisemitism has not decreased, and the troubles and tragedies of the Middle East continue to play out on a far larger canvas.

At the start of the twentieth century, however, the worlds of the Jews seemed poised to advance positively, at least in the West, with an estimated

BOX 2.5

Herzl's Jewish State
The Jewish State (from chapter 2, "The Jewish Question")

The whole plan is in its essence perfectly simple, as it must necessarily be if it is to come within the comprehension of all.

Let the sovereignty be granted us over a portion of the globe large enough to satisfy the rightful requirements of a nation; the rest we shall manage for ourselves.

The creation of a new State is neither ridiculous nor impossible. . . . The Governments of all countries scourged by Anti-Semitism will be keenly interested in assisting us to obtain the sovereignty we want.

The plan, simple in design, but complicated in execution, will be carried out by two agencies: The Society of Jews and the Jewish Company.

The Society of Jews will do the preparatory work in the domains of science and politics, which the Jewish Company will afterwards apply practically. The Jewish Company will be the liquidating agent of the business interests of departing Jews, and will organize commerce and trade in the new country. . . .

Let all who are willing to join us, fall in behind our banner and fight for our cause with voice and pen and deed.

Those Jews who agree with our idea of a State will attach themselves to the Society, which will thereby be authorized to confer and treat with Governments in the name of our people. The Society will thus be acknowledged in its relations with Governments as a State-creating power. This acknowledgement will practically create the State. . . .

The Society of Jews will treat with the present masters of the land, putting itself under the protectorate of the European Powers, if they prove friendly to the plan. We could offer the present possessors of the land enormous advantages, assume part of the public debt, build new roads for traffic, which our presence in the country would render necessary, and do many others things. The creation of our State would be beneficial to adjacent countries, because the cultivation of a strip of land increases the value of its surrounding districts in innumerable ways.

Theodor Herzl, *The Jewish State*,
trans. Sylvie D'Avigdor (New York:
American Zionist Emergency Council, 1946)

population of more than 7.5 million persons. Horrifically, such would not prove to be the case.

Modernity:
The Twentieth Century
and Beyond

Already in the early 1800s, increasing antisemitism in Russia led her Jews to consider the option of mass emigration to either Arab-controlled Palestine (Herzl's Zionist movement found a far more willing and receptive audience in the East than in the West) or the United States. By the 1880s, massive and continuous pogroms were no longer idle conversation. More and more, Jews fled, the vast majority coming to an American Jewish community already resident and successfully integrated for 250 years, the first Jews having arrived in the Dutch colony of New Amsterdam in 1654. Portuguese émigrés from Recife, Brazil, had arrived more than a century earlier, the descendants of those who originally fled Spain and Portugal.

Immigration and Emigration

The American Jewish story may be characterized historically as successive *waves* of immigration, though this first group was, in truth, more of a trickle than an actual wave. The Jews who did come, however, settled mainly in the larger cities, including the American South, and by the time of the American Revolutionary War (1776) numbered approximately 200,000 persons, primarily Jews of Sephardic background. After that, and prior to the American Civil War (1861–1865) and after, until the First World War (1914–1918), the Jews who came and established the organizational pattern of American Jewish life were Ashkenazim, primarily from Germany and Austria. In the aftermath of both World War I and the Russian Revolution (1917), the Jews who came were Eastern Europeans who brought with them their religious ways, especially Hasidism, which was something of an anathema to their co-religionists who had already established Reform Judaism as a very much Westernized American reinterpretation of traditional

Jewish religious thought and practice. After World War II (1939–1945) and Israel's War for Independence (1948), the Jews who came, primarily from a devastated Europe, were both Ashkenazim and Sephardim. Today, the Jewish communities of both the United States and the State of Israel are the largest in the world.

Antisemitism in Europe

During the early part of the twentieth century, Jews found themselves active in both the First World War on both sides of the battlefront and in the Russian Revolution. While antisemitism was a fixture of both, it would not truly rear its ugly head to any appreciable degree until both events were over. In what had become Soviet/Communist Russia, Jewish distinctiveness and parochial uniqueness remained a hindrance to universal identity. For both the Leninists (followers of Vladimir Lenin, 1870–1924) and the Stalinists (followers of Joseph Stalin, 1878–1953), more so the latter than the former and especially Stalin himself, the Jews remained a cos-

Fig. 2.9 American Judaism These children are studying the Torah in synagogue. Photo: Lawrence Migdale/ Stone/Getty Images

mopolitan enemy, unassimilable and unintegratable. Liquidation and imprisonment of Jewish religious leaders and other professionals (e.g., Stalin's notorious "Doctors' Plot," 1953), and the destruction of Jewish religious and cultural life became the norm rather than the exception under the Communists. It was only in the 1970s, when cracks appeared in the so-called Iron Curtain, that the failure to destroy Jewish identity totally and completely was realized to have significantly failed; in the twenty-first century, the former Soviet Union (Communist rule ended in 1991) is experiencing a revitalization of Jewish life on many fronts, cultural as well as religious.

Germany and the Holocaust/Shoah

Not so for Germany, however, in the chaotic days after the First World War. Economic, political, and social dislocation were the order of the day as political parties on both the right and the left attempted to bring stability to a country made to pay heavily for its sins by the Versailles Treaty of 1919. Even the failed Weimar Republic (1919–1933) could do little to lessen the chaos, made all the more dra-

matic by the worldwide Depression of 1929. Into the breech stepped an unknown Austrian who had served in the German army as a corporal, was temporarily blinded by mustard gas and hospitalized, remained in the army upon his discharge, only to quit, join, and reorganize the National Socialist German Workers Party and become chancellor of Germany on January 30, 1933.

Adolf Hitler (1889–1945) was born in Braunau-am-Inn, Austria, the son of Klara and Alois Hitler, a minor civil servant. According to his own accounts in his political autobiography *Mein Kampf* (German, "My Fight" or "My Struggle"), he was underappreciated for his intellectual abilities in school and later unappreciated for his artistic and architectural talents in Vienna, where he lived prior to World War I. Absorbing both the public antisemitism and pan-Germanism that were rife in Austria, he would make use of both in his political ambitions as a skilled orator and organizer. Once in power, he was able to exploit both, first to remilitarize Germany—despite violating the Versailles Treaty—and second to implement a master plan, nearly successful, to exterminate and annihilate the eleven million Jews of Europe.

BOX 2.6

The Riegner Telegram

In August of 1942, Gerhard M. Riegner (1911–2001), office manager of the Geneva, Switzerland, office of the World Jewish Congress received information from German industrialist Eduard Schulte (1891–1966) concerning the Nazi plans for the "Final Solution to the Jewish Question" (German, "die Endlösung der Judenfrage"). Riegner, in turn, sent the following telegram to both the British Foreign Office and the United States State Department:

"Received alarming report about plans being discussed and considered in Führer headquarters to exterminate at one fell swoop all

Jews in German-controlled countries comprising three and a half to four million after deportation and concentration in the east thus solving Jewish question once and for all—stop—campaign planned for autumn methods being discussed including hydrocyanic acid—stop."

While initially met with disbelief by officials in both quarters, it would take a few months before reaching Rabbi Stephen S. Wise (1874–1979), president of the World Jewish Congress, who would then bring it to the attention of the American president Franklin Delano Roosevelt (1882–1945).

The *Holocaust*, as it has come to be called in English (from the Greek for "a totally burnt offering to God," and based on the cultic sacrificial system of the Hebrew Bible)—though the currently preferred term is the Hebrew *Shoah* ("Devastation" or "Destruction")—saw the murderous deaths of almost 6,000,000 Jewish men, women, and children (one million of whom were twelve years old or younger, and one-half million of whom were between the ages of twelve and eighteen) between the years 1939 (the start of World War II) and 1945 (Hitler's suicide together with his mistress-wife Eva Braun). The manner of these Jewish deaths in ghettoes, rounded-up villages, and concentration and death camps is filled with horror and terror and well known to most if not all readers of this text. The meaning and implications of those deaths, however, is yet another matter.

For one thing, at the beginning of the Second World War, the Jewish population of the world was estimated to be approximately 16,000,000 persons. Among those who were murdered were young females, those who never married, those who married but had no children, and those who mar-

ried and had children but not the number they had dreamed or planned. Using the statistical tools of the demographer, such deaths in total are said to *represent* a net collective loss to the Jewish people approximately two and a half times their number. Thus, the reality of the deaths of the Jews in the Holocaust/Shoah equals 15,000,000 persons (i.e., 6,000,000 x 2.5 = 15,000,000). With a post–World War II population of approximately the same as that before the war, the Holocaust destroyed a present and future by 50 percent, a loss from which Jews may very well never recover in terms of what could have been and will never be.

Second, as the revelations of what was done to the Jewish people by the Nazis and their allied minions became more and more public, it caused a frightening divide among religious Jews as to how to make sense of their Judaism in its aftermath. At the same time, it also caused a reappraisal on the part of some in the Christian world as to how such a thing could have happened in the very heart of a Christianized Europe. These latter investigations led to a rethinking of the relationship between Jews and Christians and Judaism and Christianity, not

Fig. 2.10 The Holocaust, or Shoah
This clothing was worn by imprisoned Jews in Nazi concentration camps during World War II and is on display at Yad Vashem in Jerusalem.
Photo: Cosmo Condina/The Image Bank/ Getty Images

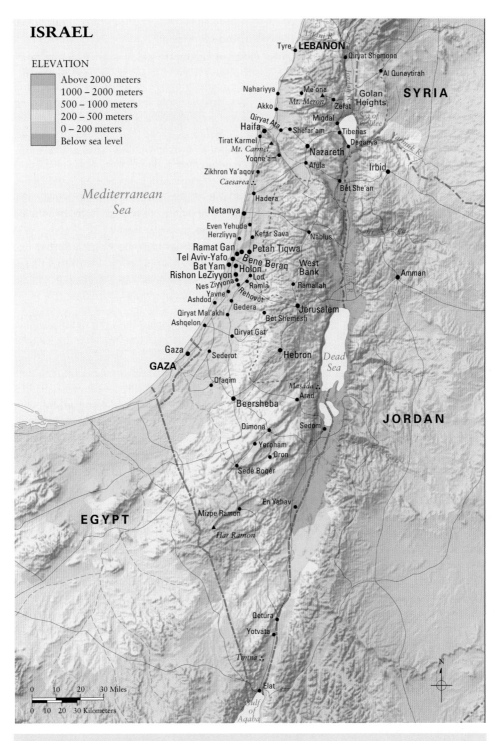

ISRAEL

ELEVATION

Above 2000 meters
1000 – 2000 meters
500 – 1000 meters
200 – 500 meters
0 – 200 meters
Below sea level

Litani R.

Tyre **LEBANON**

Qiryat Shemona

Al Qunaytirah

Nahariyya
Me'ona
Golan
Heights

SYRIA

Akko
Mt. Meron
Zefat

Qiryat Ata
Migdal
Sea of Galilee

Haifa
Shefar'am
Tiberias

Tirat Karmel
Mt. Carmel
Deganya

Yoqne'am
Nazareth

Zikhron Ya'aqov
Afula
Irbid

Caesarea

Bét She'an

*Mediterranean
Sea*

Hadera

Yarmuk R.

Netanya

Even Yehuda
Herzliyya
Kefar Sava
Nablus

Ramat Gan
Petah Tiqwa
Tel Aviv-Yafo
Bene Beraq

Bat Yam
Holon
**West
Bank**

Rishon LeZiyyon
Lod

Nes Ziyyona
Ramla
Ramallah

Yavne
Rehovot

Ashdod
Gedera
Jerusalem

Qiryat Mal'akhi
Bét Shemesh

Ashqelon

Qiryat Gat

Gaza
Hebron

GAZA
Sederot
*Dead
Sea*

Ofaqim

Masada
Arad

Beersheba

Dimona
Sedom
JORDAN

Yeroham
Oron

Sedé Boqer

En Yahav

EGYPT
Mizpe Ramon

Har Ramon

Qetura

Yotvata

Timna

N

Elat

0   10   20   30 Miles

0   10   20   30 Kilometers

*Gulf
of
Aqaba*

Map 2.4 Modern Israel Map © 2010 Fortress Press

BOX 2.7

Israel's Declaration of Independence

Eretz-Israel [Land of Israel] was the birthplace of the Jewish people. Here their spiritual, religious and political identity was shaped. Here they first attained to statehood, cultural values of national and universal significance and gave the world the eternal Book of Books.

After being forcibly exiled from their land, the people kept faith with it throughout their Dispersion and never ceased to pray and hope for their return to it and for the restoration in it of their political freedom.

Impelled by this historic and traditional attachment, Jews strove in every successive generation to reestablish themselves in their ancient homeland. In recent decades they returned to their masses. Pioneers, ma'apilim [immigrants], and defenders, they made deserts bloom, revived the Hebrew language, built villages and towns, and created a thriving community controlling its own economy and culture, loving peace but knowing how to defend itself, bringing the blessings of progress to all the country's inhabitants, and aspiring towards independent nationhood.

In the year 5667 (1897), at the summons of the spiritual leader of the Jewish State, Theodor Herzl, the First Zionist Congress convened and proclaimed the right of the Jewish people to national rebirth in its own country.

This right was recognized in the *Balfour Declaration* of the 2nd November, 1917, and re-affirmed in the *Mandate of the League of Nations*, which, in particular, gave international sanction to the historic connection between the Jewish people to rebuild its National Home.

The catastrophe which recently befell the Jewish people—the massacre of millions of Jews in Europe—was another clear demonstration of the urgency of solving the problem of its homelessness by re-establishing in Eretz-Israel the Jewish State, which would open the gates of the homeland wide to every Jew and confer upon the Jewish people the status of a fully privileged member of the comity of nations.

Survivors of the Nazi holocaust in Europe, as well as Jews form other parts of the world, continued to migrate to Eretz-Israel, undaunted by difficulties, restrictions and dangers, and never ceased to assert their right to a life of dignity, freedom and honest toil in their national homeland.

In the Second World War, the Jewish community of this country contributed its full share to the struggles of the freedom- and peace-loving nations against the forces of Nazi wickedness and, by the blood of its soldiers and its war effort, gained the right to be reckoned among the peoples who founded the United Nations.

On the 29th of November, 1947, the United Nations General Assembly passed a resolution calling for the establishment of a Jewish State in Eretz-Israel, the General Assembly required the inhabitants of Eretz-Israel to take such steps as were necessary on their part for the implementation of that resolution. This recognition by the United Nations of the right of the Jewish people to establish their State is irrevocable.

This right is the natural right of the Jewish people to be masters of their own fate, like all other nations, in their own sovereign State.

Accordingly, we members of the People's Council, representatives of the Jewish community of Eretz-Israel and of the Zionist movement, are here assembled on the day of the termination of the British mandate over Eretz-Israel and, by virtue of our natural and historic right and on the strength of the Resolution of the United Nations General Assembly, hereby declare the establishment of the Jewish State in Eretz-Israel, to be known as the State of Israel.

only by Roman Catholics but by Protestants as well, which has not abated even today.

Third, the tragedy of the Holocaust/Shoah caused a reuniting and resolidification of Jews worldwide, most often expressed in unwavering support for the nascent State of Israel, for while the events of World War II did not bring about its rebirth—a myth exploited by its enemies—Jews having been politically active in realizing this dream since the late 1800s, it did cause the nations of the world to be more open and receptive to its possibility. Even this tragedy, however, has not caused the nations of the world, particularly Israel's neighbors, to welcome Jews into the world community of peoples and nations; tensions and worse in that region continue to remain high, and needless and wanton deaths, stridently negative political decisions, and costly military operations on both sides remain the order of the day.

Conclusion

The last decades of the twentieth century find Jews safely ensconced in Western democratic societies such as the United States, Australia, and Canada, less so in Germany, Great Britain, and France, and facing hostile enemies inside Israel and nations under Arab and Muslim control. At the start of the twenty-first century, however, Jews remain troubled by their existence; too many continue to perceive themselves as the world's "pariah people."

The ongoing issues of safety and security and a meaningful survival continue to dominate the Jewish landscape worldwide and not just in locations of danger.

IN REVIEW

In this chapter, we surveyed the history of the Jewish people from their prebiblical origins approximately four thousand years ago until the present moment. In that first period—prebiblical and biblical—we focused on their nomadic origins; the two kingdoms of Judah and Israel; the monarchies of Saul, David, and Solomon; and the "age of the prophets." In the second period—the postbiblical or rabbinic period—we began with the destruction of the Second Temple by the Romans (70 C.E.), saw the emergence of both Christianity and Islam, and witnessed the lengthy period of Jewish persecutions for over four hundred years. In the third period of Jewish history—the Pre-Modern and Modern period to the present—we focused on the Enlightenment, new Jewish movements, the American Jewish story, the Holocaust/Shoah, and the founding of the State of Israel and implications for Jewish survival.

KEY TERMS

antisemitism

Ashkenazim

Babylonian Talmud

Baruch de Spinoza

B.C.E. (Before the Common Era)

C.E. (Common Era)

deicide

Der Judenstaat

Edict of Milan

Gemara

continues on following page

Hasidism

Haskalah

Hasmoneans

Hebrew Bible

Holocaust/Shoah

Holy Land

Holy Roman Empire

Israelites

Jews

Judaism

Karaism

Kingdom of Israel

Kingdom of Judah

Land of Canaan

Land of Israel

messiah

Moses ben Maimon (Maimonides)

Mishnah (Second Torah)

Pale of Settlement

Palestinian Talmud

Pharisees

Positive-Historical (Conservative) Judaism

postbiblical or rabbinic period

prebiblical and biblical period

Rabbinism or Talmudism

Reconquista

Reform Judaism

Sadducees

Sanhedrin

Shulchan Aruch (Prepared Table)

Simeon bar Kokhba

State of Israel

synagogue

Temple of Solomon (Second Temple)

Ten Lost Tribes

Theodor Herzl

Theophany at Sinai (Giving of the Torah)

Tikkun Olam (Repairing the World)

Torah

usury

Y'tziat Mitzrayim (Going forth from Egypt)

Yochanah ben Zakkai

Zionism

Questions for Review, Study, and Discussion

1. Do you think the metaphor of *cycles* is the appropriate term to address the recurrent historical events discussed in this chapter? Why or why not? If not, what term would you use and why?

2. What events would you consider as the most important in the overall Jewish historical journey? Why so?

3. In each of the three historical periods, what single event would you label the most important? Why so?

4. Consulting either edition of the *Encyclopedia Judaica* (1972 or 2007), look up the entry "Messiah," and compare the Jewish and Christian understandings of the term. Do you see any arena of agreement between these two religious communities and traditions regarding this central concept?

5. The Israeli–Arab/Palestinian Middle East conflict remains unresolved, as it has since the creation of the State of Israel on May 14, 1948. What are your thoughts regarding the resolution of this ongoing crisis?

Suggested Readings

Prebiblical and Biblical Period

Aageson, James W. *In the Beginning: Critical Concepts for the Study of the Bible*. Boulder: Westview, 2000.

Berlin, Adele, and Marc Zvi Brettler, eds. *The Jewish Study Bible*. New York: Oxford University Press, 2004.

Brettler, Marc Zvi. *How to Read the Bible*. Philadelphia: The Jewish Publication Society, 2005.

Collins, John J. *A Short Introduction to the Hebrew Bible*. Minneapolis: Fortress Press, 2007.

Gottwald, Norman K. *The Hebrew Bible: A Brief Socio-Literary Introduction*. Minneapolis: Fortress Press, 2009.

Greenspan, Frederick E., ed. *The Hebrew Bible: New Insights and Scholarship*. New York: New York University Press, 2008.

Kugel, James L. *The Bible as It Was*. Cambridge, Mass.: Harvard University Press, 1997.

———. *How to Read the Bible: A Guide to Scripture, Then and Now*. New York: Free Press, 2007.

———. *Traditions of the Bible: A Guide to the Bible as It Was at the Start of the Common Era*. Cambridge, Mass.: Harvard University Press, 1998.

Rosenbaum, Stanley Ned. *Understanding Biblical Israel: A Reexamination of the Origins of Monotheism*. Macon, Ga.: Mercer University Press, 2002.

Sanders, E. P. *Jesus and Judaism*. Minneapolis: Fortress Press, 1985.

Sparks, Kenton L. *Ancient Texts for the Study of the Hebrew Bible: A Guide to the Background Literature*. Peabody, Mass.: Hendrickson, 2005.

Vermes, Geza. *Jesus the Jew: A Historian's Readings of the Gospels*. Minneapolis: Fortress Press, 1998.

Postbiblical and Rabbinic Period

Brody, Robert. *The Geonim of Babylonia and the Shaping of Medieval Jewish Culture*. New Haven, Conn.: Yale University Press, 1998.

Davidson, Herbert A. *Moses Maimonides: The Man and His Work*. New York: Oxford University Press, 2005.

Fonrobert, Charlotte Elisheva, and Martin S. Jaffee, eds. *The Cambridge Companion to the Talmud and Rabbinic Literature*. New York: Cambridge University Press, 2007.

Kraemer, Joel L. *Maimonides: The Life and World of One of Civilization's Greatest Minds*. New York: Doubleday, 2008.

Nadler, Steven. *Spinoza: A Life*. New York: Cambridge University Press, 1999.

Neusner, Jacob. *Introduction to Rabbinic Literature*. New York: Doubleday, 1994.

———. *Rabbinic Judaism: Structure and System*. Minneapolis: Fortress Press, 1995.

Rubenstein, Jeffrey L. *The Culture of the Babylonian Talmud*. Baltimore: Johns Hopkins University Press, 2003.

Modern Period

Crowe, David M. *The Holocaust: Roots, History, and Aftermath*. Boulder: Westview, 2008.

Gelvin, James L. *The Israel–Palestine Conflict: One Hundred Years of War*. New York: Cambridge University Press, 2007.

Hilberg, Raul. *The Destruction of the European Jews*. New Haven, Conn.: Yale University Press, 2003.

Lewis, Bernard. *The Middle East: A Brief History of the Last 2,000 Years*. New York: Scribner, 1995.

Lindemann, Albert S. *Esau's Tears: Modern Anti-Semitism and the Rise of the Jews*. New York: Cambridge University Press, 1997.

Miller, Aaron David. *The Much Too Promised Land: America's Elusive Search for Arab-Israeli Peace*. New York: Bantam Dell, 2008.

Poliakov, Léon. *The History of Anti-Semitism*. 1975. Reprint, Philadelphia: University of Pennsylvania Press, 2003 (1975).

Sachar, Howard M. *A History of the Jews in America*. New York: Vintage, 1993.

Sarna, Jonathan. *American Judaism: A History*. New Haven, Conn.: Yale University Press, 2005.

Schäfer, Peter. *Judeophobia: Attitudes toward the Jews in the Ancient World*. Cambridge, Mass.: Harvard University Press, 1997.

Schoenberner, Gerhard. *The Yellow Star: The Persecution of the Jews in Europe, 1933–1945*. New York: Fordham University Press, 2004.

Wistrich, Robert S. *Antisemitism: The Longest Hatred*. New York: Pantheon, 1991.

A Timeline of Jewish History

c. 6000–5500	Origins of the Hebrew/Israelite peoples (?)
1750–1250	*Y'tziat Mitzrayim*/"Going forth from Egypt"/Exodus
1100	Settlement in the promised land/Beginnings of the monarchy
1101–971	Reign of King David
970–928	Reign of King Solomon
721	Destruction of the northern kingdom of Israel by the Assyrians ("Ten Lost Tribes")
c. 721–586	"Age of the Prophets"
586	Destruction of the southern kingdom of Judah by the Babylonians (Tribes of Judah and Benjamin)
c. 438–400	*Some* Israelites return to the Holy Land under Ezra and Nehemiah
165	Hasmonean revolt against the Seleucids
104	Restoration of the monarchy under Aristobulus I
37	Herod the Idumean assumes the throne

66–70	Rebellion against Roman-occupied Palestine
70	Destruction of Jerusalem and the Second Temple
90	Canonization of the Torah/Hebrew Bible
132	Bar Kokhba revolt
220	Codification of the Mishnah under Rabbi Judah
220–700	Construction of the Talmuds of Babylonia and Palestine
900–1200	Golden Age of Spanish Jewry
1095/6–1099	First Crusade to retake Jerusalem from the Muslims
1146–1147	Second Crusade to the East
1189–1190	Third Crusade to the East

1290	Expulsion of Jews from England
1306	Expulsion of Jews from France
1492	Expulsion of Jews from Spain
1543	Publication of Martin Luther's *On the Jews and Their Lies*
1648	Chmielnitski massacres in Poland
1654	First Jews arrive in New Amsterdam from Recifé, Brazil
1655	Jews return to England
1791	Jews given the right to vote as citizens in France
1806	"Assembly of Jewish Notables" convened in France by Emperor Napoleon
1807	"Sanhedrin" convened in France by Emperor Napoleon
1810	Beginnings of Reform Judaism under Israel Jacobson in Germany
1850s	Beginnings of Positive-Historical (Conservative) Judaism in Germany
1894	Espionage trial of French army captain Alfred Dreyfus
1896	Theodor Herzl publishes *Der Judenstaat* ("The Jewish State")
1897	First Zionist Congress convened in Basel, Switzerland
1914–1917	World War I, with Jewish participation on both sides
1917	Russian Revolution with Communist antisemitic elements
1933	Adolf Hitler becomes chancellor of Germany
1939–1945	World War II and the Holocaust/Shoah and the deaths of six-million-plus Jews
1948	State of Israel reborn (with subsequent wars in 1956, 1967, 1973, 1981, 2005)
End of 20th century	Jews thrive in the United States and Israel; Begin leaving the Soviet Union in increasingly large numbers
Beginning of 21st century	Revival of antisemitism in the Middle East and on the European continent

CHAPTER 3

Cycles *of* TEXTS

Building the Foundation

OVERVIEW

In this somewhat longer chapter, we will examine the central literatures of the Jewish people: the Hebrew Bible/Torah (composed of the First Five Books of Moses), the Prophets, and the Writings; the Mishnah; the Talmuds of Palestine and Babylonia; Midrash; *Zohar*; and Codes and *Responsa*. Along the way, we will read representative selections of each and, in so doing, come to realize that this literary tradition remains at the very heart of the Jewish journey not only for Jews but for Judaism as well.

Introduction

Almost from its inception, certainly from the time of its return to the *Eretz Havtakha* (Hebrew, either "the Promised Land" or "the Land of Promise"), more than 2,500 years ago, the Jewish people was well on its way toward becoming a literate people

and society, a supreme value—along with family and religion—which manifests itself even today in many arenas: high rates of post–high school and otherwise required education of its young, numerous, and diverse literary productions (novels, short stories, journalistic articles, scholarly tomes), valuing professions that require intense education (e.g., medicine, law, the academy, the rabbinate), and the like. This orientation to becoming "well read" has been historically understood to mean *well-read in classical Jewish texts*—Torah/Hebrew Bible, Talmud, Midrash—but has more and more come to mean well read in the literatures of, primarily, Western civilization, as well as one's own field of specialization. Without, however, a foundational grounding in Jewish sources, neither the Jewish people nor Judaism itself will survive beyond the present generation. Corollary to this concern, at least in some quarters, is the inability of many of today's Jews to read the literatures of Judaism in the original Hebrew. The growth of published translations of Jewish texts, especially in English, requires no or very little knowledge of the Hebrew language. Somewhat ironically, at the very same time that knowledge of Hebrew has declined in the rest of the world, the State of Israel has commendably pioneered Hebrew language education—of necessity during its founding—by continuously welcoming Jewish immigrants via its *ulpan* system of immersion learning. However, this knowledge of Hebrew is not yet truly exportable. It is to these texts to which we now turn.

Fig. 3.1 A Hebrew script Looking beyond the candle and flame, we see the beautiful calligraphy that characterizes Hebrew printing, whether it is in the Torah/Hebrew Bible or the Talmud. Specially trained scribal artists, called *soferim*, practice their craft throughout the Jewish world and reflect an ancient Jewish tradition. Photo: © Corbis

Torah/Hebrew Bible

The foundation upon which all Jewish learning rests is that of the Torah/Hebrew Bible. While we know next to nothing regarding its canonization or coming together as a unified text (believed to have taken place in the year 90 C.E. in Yavneh under the aegis of Rabbi Yochanan ben Zakkai), and are comfortable with the origins of its various components at least one thousand or more years previous, it is as it has always been the *central sacred document* of the Jewish people throughout its journey. And, regardless of the modern science of higher biblical criticism (which the nineteenth-century Jewish thinker Solomon Schechter [1847–1915] once referred to as "higher antisemitism"), or missing texts or texts excluded yet coterminous, or religious denominational differences, the Torah/Hebrew Bible of the Jews is that collection venerated by Jews as most precious, and the basis from which Jewish life derives its ultimate meaning.

Evidence of that veneration is maintained by the simple fact that the First Five Books of Moses (*Bereshith*/Genesis, *Shemot*/Exodus, *Vayyikra*/Leviticus, *Bemidbar*/Numbers, and *Devarim*/Deuteronomy) are still most carefully copied by hand by

BOX 3.1

What Makes a Jewish Thought Jewish?

An intriguing question, sometimes asked by more than one inquirer, is "What makes a Jewish thought Jewish?" That is to say, if someone who is already acknowledged as a Jewish person has a particular thought about some particular thing, does that make it *by definition* "Jewish"? And, by extension, does that thought then become representative of Judaic thinking across the board if it mirrors the majority of Jews who then share that view?

For this writer—and others—*an authentically Jewish thought is one that results from a confrontation with the classical sources of the Jewish religious tradition, whether one accepts or rejects what appears to be the dominant view, or in some cases, the voice of the minority.* And, because, over the generations, Jews have adamantly refused to succumb to a monolithic stance on thinking, diverse and often contentious differences on just about every issue affecting Jews and/or Judaism have become the norm. This perspective *does*, however, exclude the one who is not a Jew from having an *authentically* Jewish thought, even if he or she is well acquainted with the texts of Judaism. Internally, Jewish civil discourse, at its best, results from various thinkers engaged in serious conversations, all of whom are themselves knowledgeable in these sources, but who bring to the table strong differences of opinion based on their own reading, learning, and experience. This "give and take" among Jews is mirrored in such phrases as *makhlokot l'shem Shamayim* (Hebrew, "controversies for the sake of Heaven") and *elu v'elu divrei Elohim hayyim* (Hebrew, "these [words] and these [words] are the words of the Living God").

Torah *soferim*/scribes on sewn parchment sheets (as they have done for generations), wrapped around *Atzai Hayyim* (wooden rollers, Hebrew, "trees of life"), and housed in the Aron Kodesh/"holy ark" in the sanctuaries of all Jewish congregations, and facing Jerusalem. And, during periods of antisemitic stress and worse, when the enemies of the Jewish people invaded these sanctuaries and attempted to destroy these sacred scrolls, reports of Jews surrendering their lives to ward off these desecrations are legion.

With the rise of modern publishing à la Johannes Gutenberg's (1398–1468) innovative printing press in circa 1450, Torah/Hebrew Bibles, too, became standardized, and the best editions are those, whether solely in Hebrew or Hebrew-local languages, which are replete with the commentaries of countless generations of rabbis and Jewish thinkers, making these texts come "Jewishly alive."

Fig. 3.2 A Torah scroll This is a copy of the Torah located in the former Glockengasse synagogue in Cologne, Germany. Photo courtesy Creative Commons: http://commons .wikimedia.org/wiki/File:K%C3%B6ln-Tora-und-Innenansicht-Synagoge-Glockengasse-040.JPG

One further note: The Torah/Hebrew Bible of the Jews is *not* the same as the "Old Testament" of either Roman Catholic or Protestant Christian traditions. Both non-Jewish groups read the texts of Torah/Hebrew Bible differently from Jews, historically mining each and every sentence contained within and seeking out affirmations of the central personage of Christianity, Jesus Christ. Additionally, after the five initial texts, Roman Catholic tradition *reordered* the remaining texts according to its own historical understanding and added to its *Bible*

(from the Greek *ta biblia*, "the Bible," or *biblos*, "the books") additional Jewish texts not included by Jews, which, over time, have acquired the name *Apocrypha*.[1] After the Protestant Reformation of the sixteenth century, one further divisive result intended to differentiate these various newer groups from Roman Catholics was a further reordering of the initial texts, again after the first five, not so much to separate from the Torah/Hebrew Bible of the Jews, but to separate from the Old Testament of the Catholics.[2]

Fig. 3.3 A Torah scribe at work Jewish law requires the Torah to be written out by hand rather than mechanically reproduced. Scribes, or *sofers*, such as Bernard Nuremberg (here), are specially trained for this and can take up to one year to produce a complete Torah. Photo: Jewish Chronicle Archive/HIP/Art Resource, N.Y.

Chumash: The First Five Books of the Torah and of Moses

Among the terms Jews have used to title this first set of texts is the Hebrew word *Chumash*, derived from the word *hamash*, or "five," and is the commonly accepted reference for texts that describe not only the story of creation but the creation of the Israelite/Hebrew/Jewish people as well, most especially the journeys of its primary patriarchs and legendary leaders *Avram/Avraham/*Abraham, *Yitschaq/*Isaac, *Ya'aqov/*Jacob, *Yosef/*Joseph, *Moshe/*Moses, *Sha'ul/*Saul, *Dawid/*David, and *Shelomo/*Solomon.[3] Editor Barry W. Holz, in his excellent introduction in English to Judaic texts *Back to the Sources: Reading the Classic Jewish Texts*,[4] divides the genres of the Hebrew Bible into three categories: biblical narrative(s), biblical law(s), and biblical poetry. Two brief examples of the first would be the following, first with regard to patriarch Abraham, the "father of monotheism."

While offering not a murmur of protest with regard to the near sacrifice of his son *Yitschaq/*Isaac (from the Hebrew verb *tzachaq*, "to laugh," referencing Sarah's response when, in her advanced years, informed of her forthcoming pregnancy, "she laughs") in *Bereshith/*Genesis 22, Abraham remonstrates loudly with God in the following dialogue from *Bereshith/*Genesis 18 (box 3.2) concerning the fate of the "sinners" of Sodom (and Gomorrah), thus communicating to the hearers/readers a marvelous intimacy between one of God's creatures and God himself (as the ancients understood divine gender).

The second example, also from *Bereshith*/Genesis, but this time from chapter 32 (box 3.3), is that of the wrestling match between *Ya'akov*/Jacob and the *ish* (Hebrew, "man," who has been understood at various times and in various generations by both Jews and Christians to have been a human colleague but divine representative, a *mal'ak* or "angel," *Ya'akov*/Jacob himself, God himself, or Christ). *Ya'akov*/Jacob will emerge scathed from the encounter—perhaps ultimately symbolic of the journey his Jewish successors are about to undergo—but enabled to go on nonetheless.

Both texts, among countless others, have proven rich sources of rabbinic commentaries up to

---

BOX 3.2

Bereshith/Genesis 18:16-33

When the men got up to leave, they looked down toward Sodom, and Abraham walked along with them to see them on their way. Then the Lord said, "Shall I hide from Abraham what I am about to do? Abraham will surely become a great and powerful nation, and all nations on earth will be blessed through him. For I have chosen him, so that he will direct his children and his household after him to keep the way of the Lord by doing what is right and just, so that the Lord will bring about for Abraham what he has promised him."

Then the Lord said, "The outcry against Sodom and Gomorrah is so great and their sin so grievous that I will go down and see if what they have done is as bad as the outcry that has reached me. If not, I will know."

The men turned away and went toward Sodom, but Abraham remained standing before the Lord. Then Abraham approached him and said: "Will you sweep away the righteous with the wicked? What if there are fifty righteous people in the city? Will you really sweep it away and not spare the place for the sake of the fifty righteous people in it? Far be it from you to do such a thing—to kill the righteous with the wicked, treating the righteous and the wicked alike. Far be it from you! Will not the Judge of all the earth do right?"

The Lord said, "If I find fifty righteous people in the city of Sodom, I will spare the whole place for their sake." Then Abraham spoke up again: "Now that I have been so bold as to speak to the Lord, though I am nothing but dust and ashes, what if the number of the righteous is five less than fifty? Will you destroy the whole city because of five people?"

"If I find forty-five there," he said, "I will not destroy it."

Once again he spoke to him, "What if only forty are found there?"

He said, "For the sake of forty, I will not do it." Then he said, "May the Lord not be angry, but let me speak. What if only thirty can be found there?"

He answered, "I will not do it if I find thirty there."

Abraham said, "Now that I have been so bold as to speak to the Lord, what if only twenty can be found there?"

He said, "For the sake of twenty, I will not destroy it."

Then he said, "May the Lord not be angry, but let me speak just once more. What if only ten can be found there?"

He answered, "For the sake of ten, I will not destroy it."

When the Lord had finished speaking with Abraham, he left, and Abraham returned home.

and including our own day for those who read and re-read them as full evidence of God at work in the world and in the lives of the Jewish people.[5]

The second rubric of biblical law is no better found, first of all, in the twin presentations of the *Aseret Hadibrot* (Hebrew, "Ten Essential Statements," usually translated as "Ten Commandments"), appearing in both *Shemot*/Exodus 20:2-17 and *Devarim*/Deuteronomy 5:6-21, and the nineteenth chapter of *Vayyikra*/Leviticus, the "Holiness Code."

Perhaps the most enduring of the Jewish people's contributions to the civilizing and humanizing of humanity, the "Ten Commandments" remain central to a Judaic and a Christ-centered worldview, as well as an Islamic perspective. What we do not know is why the Torah/Hebrew Bible presents us with not one text but two such texts, the Deuteronomic version only slightly modified from the exilic one. Long understood by Jews, and commented on by generations of scholars, these short texts embody

the very foundations of any civil society to endure beyond its own initial creation. The text from Exodus is in box 3.4.

A different rendering of biblical law, however, is found in *Vayyikra*/Leviticus 19, the "Holiness Code," which has been understood by countless generations of Jews as central to the development of the entire Judaic ethical system. Important to note in this text is that the very notion of *qiddusha* (Hebrew, "holiness") is defined by ethical behavior *in a societal context*, not holiness removed from living in community. Also, when asked to rank-order the ritual-ceremonial obligations of the Jewish religious tradition as superior to or inferior to the moral-ethical obligations, the early rabbis responded that all are equal (that is to say, the ritual-ceremonial contains within it the seeds of the moral-ethical, and the reverse, the classic example of which was the preparation for the celebration of the Sabbath, not only for the landowner but also for his slaves and animals and livestock, which required allocating the

---

BOX 3.3

Bereshith/Genesis 32:22-32
(NIV, with slight Hebraic modifications)

That night *Ya'akov*/Jacob got up and took his two wives, his two maidservants and his eleven sons and crossed the ford of the Yabbok. After he had sent them across the stream, he sent over all his possessions. So *Ya'akov*/Jacob was left alone, and a man [*ish*] wrestled with him till daybreak. When the man saw that he could not overpower him, he touched the socket of *Ya'akov*/Jacob's hip so that his hip was wrenched as he wrestled with the man. Then the man said, "Let me go, for it is daybreak."

But *Ya'akov*/Jacob replied, "I will not let you go unless you bless me."

The man asked him, "What is your name?"

"*Ya'akov*/Jacob," he answered. Then the man said, "Your name will no longer be *Ya'akov*/

Jacob, but *Yisra'el*/Israel, because you have struggled with God and with men and have overcome."

Ya'akov/Jacob said, "Please tell me your name."

But he replied, "Why do you ask my name?" Then he blessed him there.

So *Ya'akov*/Jacob called the place Peni'el, saying, "It is because I saw God face to face, and yet my life was spared."

The sun rose above him as he passed Peni'el, and he was limping because of his hip. Therefore to this day the Israelites do not eat the tendon attached to the socket of the hip, because the socket of *Ya'akov*/Jacob's hip was touched near the tendon.

BOX 3.4

Shemot/Exodus 20:2-17[6]

I am the LORD your God, who brought you out of Egypt, out of the land of slavery.

You shall have no other gods before me.

You shall not make for yourself an idol in the form of anything in heaven above or on the earth beneath or in the waters below. You shall not bow down to them or worship them; for I, the LORD your God, am a jealous God, punishing the children for the sin of the fathers to the third and fourth generation of those who hate me, but showing love to a thousand {generations} of those who love me and keep my commandments.

You shall not misuse the name of the LORD your God, for the LORD will not hold anyone guiltless who misuses his name.

Remember the Sabbath day by keeping it holy. Six days you shall labor and do all your work, but the seventh day is a Sabbath to the LORD your God. On it you shall not do any work, neither you, nor your son or daughter, nor your manservant or maidservant, nor your animals, nor the alien within your gates. For in six days the LORD made the heavens and the earth, the sea, and all that is in them, but he rested on the seventh day. Therefore the LORD blessed the Sabbath day and made it holy.

Honor your father and your mother, so that you may live long in the land the LORD your God is giving you.

You shall not murder.

You shall not commit adultery.

You shall not steal.

You shall not give false testimony against your neighbor.

You shall not covet your neighbor's house. You shall not covet your neighbor's wife, or his manservant or maidservant, his ox or donkey, or anything that belongs to your neighbor.

---

proper amounts of food and protection prior to this twenty-four-hour period of rest). Hence *Vayyikra/*Leviticus 19 (see box 3.5).

While each of these laws are themselves worthy of an extended commentary, and have been so over the generations, the ordering of such texts remains a puzzlement. Perhaps the reasons were known to the original author(s) and/or audience, but are now lost in the sands of time.

The last category of text in the first five books of the Torah/Hebrew Bible using Holz's tripartite division is that of biblical poetry, of which *Shirat Moshe* (Hebrew, "Song of Moses") or *Shirat Hayam* (Hebrew, "Song of the Sea"), celebrating the children of Israel's narrow escape from their Egyptian slave masters and pursued by an Egyptian military bent on their annihilation, is found in the sublime poetry of *Shemot/*Exodus 15 (see box 3.6).

Significantly, when this passage is copied by the *soferim*, Jewish Torah scribes, its poetic formatting is retained, in contradistinction to the rest of the Torah/Hebrew Bible, which appears to be in a narrative paragraph style. Also, the opening line of verse 11—*mi-chamochah ba'elim Adonai/*"Who is like You *among the gods*, Adonai"—was understood to be a recognition of the *reality* of other gods for other nations, but as far as the ancient Israelites were concerned, uncompromisingly, only the God of Israel mattered for them.

As noted, the narrative texts throughout the Torah/Hebrew Bible—many if not most of which are known throughout Western Christian civilization, and certainly within the Jewish people and communities—are wonderfully told, are literarily well constructed, and possess uncanny psychological and sociological insights. As such, they have been

BOX 3.5

Vayyikra/Leviticus 19:1-37

The Lord said to Moses, "Speak to the entire assembly of Israel and say to them: 'Be holy because I, the Lord your God, am holy.

"'Each of you must respect his mother and father, and you must observe my Sabbaths. I am the Lord your God.

"'Do not turn to idols or make gods of cast metal for yourselves. I am the Lord your God.

"'When you sacrifice a fellowship offering to the Lord, sacrifice it in such a way that it will be accepted on your behalf. It shall be eaten on the day you sacrifice it or on the next day; anything left over until the third day must be burned up. If any of it is eaten on the third day, it is impure and will not be accepted. Whoever eats it will be held responsible because he has desecrated what is holy to the Lord; that person must be cut off from his people.

"'When you reap the harvest of your land, do not reap to the very edges of your field or gather the gleanings of your harvest. Do not go over your vineyard a second time or pick up the grapes that have fallen. Leave them for the poor and the alien. I am the Lord your God.

"'Do not steal.

"'Do not lie.

"'Do not deceive one another.

"'Do not swear falsely by my name and so profane the name of your God. I am the Lord.

"'Do not defraud your neighbor or rob him.

"'Do not hold back the wages of a hired man overnight.

"'Do not curse the deaf or put a stumbling block in front of the blind, but fear your God. I am the Lord.

"'Do not pervert justice; do not show partiality to the poor or favoritism to the great, but judge your neighbor fairly.

"'Do not go about spreading slander among your people.

"'Do not do anything that endangers your neighbor's life. I am the Lord.

"'Do not hate your brother in your heart.

Rebuke your neighbor frankly so you will not share in his guilt.

"'Do not seek revenge or bear a grudge against one of your people, but love your neighbor as yourself. I am the Lord.

"'Keep my decrees.

"'Do not mate different kinds of animals.

"'Do not plant your field with two kinds of seed.

"'Do not wear clothing woven of two kinds of material.

"'If a man sleeps with a woman who is a slave girl promised to another man but who has not been ransomed or given her freedom, there must be due punishment. Yet they are not to be put to death, because she had not been freed. The man, however, must bring a ram to the entrance to the Tent of Meeting for a guilt offering to the Lord. With the ram of the guilt offering the priest is to make atonement for him before the Lord for the sin he has committed, and his sin will be forgiven.

"'When you enter the land and plant any kind of fruit tree, regard its fruit as forbidden. For three years you are to consider it forbidden; it must not be eaten. In the fourth year all its fruit will be holy, an offering of praise to the Lord. But in the fifth year you may eat its fruit. In this way your harvest will be increased. I am the Lord your God.

"'Do not eat any meat with the blood still in it.

"'Do not practice divination or sorcery.

"'Do not cut the hair at the sides of your head or clip off the edges of your beard.

"'Do not cut your bodies for the dead or put tattoo marks on yourselves. I am the Lord.

"'Do not degrade your daughter by making her a prostitute, or the land will turn to prostitution and be filled with wickedness.

"'Observe my Sabbaths and have reverence for my sanctuary. I am the Lord.

"'Do not turn to mediums or seek out spirits, for you will be defiled by them. I am the Lord your God.

continues on following page

BOX 3.5 (CONT.)

"'Rise in the presence of the aged, show respect for the elderly and revere your God. I am the Lord.

"'When an alien lives with you in your land, do not mistreat him. The alien living with you must be treated as one of your native-born. Love him as yourself, for you were aliens in Egypt. I am the Lord your God.

"'Do not use dishonest standards when measuring length, weight or quantity. Use honest scales and honest weights, an honest ephah and an honest hin. I am the Lord your God, who brought you out of Egypt.

"'Keep all my decrees and all my laws and follow them. I am the Lord.'"

BOX 3.6

Shemot/Exodus 15:1-21

Then Moses and the Israelites sang
    this song to the Lord:
"I will sing to the Lord,
for he is highly exalted.
The horse and its rider
he has hurled into the sea.
The Lord is my strength and my
    song;
he has become my salvation.
He is my God, and I will praise him,
my father's God, and I will exalt
    him.
The Lord is a warrior;
    the Lord is his name.
Pharaoh's chariots and his army
he has hurled into the sea.
The best of Pharaoh's officers
are drowned in the Red Sea.
The deep waters have covered
    them;
they sank to the depths like a stone.

"Your right hand, O Lord,
was majestic in power.
Your right hand, O Lord,
shattered the enemy.
In the greatness of your majesty
you threw down those who opposed
    you.
You unleashed your burning anger;
it consumed them like stubble.
By the blast of your nostrils
the waters piled up.
The surging waters stood firm like
    a wall;

the deep waters congealed in the
    heart of the sea.

"The enemy boasted,
'I will pursue, I will overtake them.
I will divide the spoils;
I will gorge myself on them.
I will draw my sword
and my hand will destroy them.'
But you blew with your breath,
and the sea covered them.
They sank like lead
in the mighty waters.

"Who among the gods is like you,
    O Lord?
Who is like you—
majestic in holiness,
awesome in glory,
working wonders?
You stretched out your right hand
and the earth swallowed them.

"In your unfailing love you will lead
the people you have redeemed.
In your strength you will guide them
to your holy dwelling.
The nations will hear and tremble;
anguish will grip the people of
    Philistia.
The chiefs of Edom will be terrified,
the leaders of Moab will be seized
    with trembling,
the people of Canaan will melt
    away;

terror and dread will fall upon
    them.
By the power of your arm
they will be as still as a stone—
until your people pass by, O Lord,
until the people you bought pass by.
You will bring them in and plant
    them
on the mountain of your inheri-
    tance—
the place, O Lord, you made for your
    dwelling,
the sanctuary, O Lord, your hands
    established.
The Lord will reign
for ever and ever."

When Pharaoh's horses, chariots and horsemen went into the
sea, the Lord brought the waters
of the sea back over them, but the
Israelites walked through the sea
on dry ground. Then Miriam the
prophetess, Aaron's sister, took a
tambourine in her hand, and all the
women followed her, with tambou-
rines and dancing. Miriam sang to
them:

"Sing to the Lord,
for he is highly exalted.
The horse and its rider
he has hurled into the sea."

the subject of vast commentaries over the last two thousand years. Combined, these texts and commentaries are a treasure house of worldwide Judaic culture over the generations. The biblical laws contained within these First Five Books of Moses are themselves foundational to the whole of the Western legal tradition and are reflected throughout the various legal systems at work today. Moreover, the poetry and poetic language of the Torah/Hebrew Bible, rendered almost but not quite in translation because of the nature of its idiomatic and creative use of language, reveals generations of literarily creative persons whose love for their people and their God manifested itself in inspired texts second to none.

Nevi'im:
The Prophetic Literature

Not strictly speaking prophetic texts, the books of *Yehoshua*/Joshua, *Shofetim*/Judges, *Shemu'el*/Samuel 1 and 2 and *Melachim*/Kings 1 and 2, which introduce this second section of the Torah/Hebrew Bible, may perhaps best be understood as "preclassical" or "preliterary" texts that continue the journey of the Israelites and pave the way for the period in which the *major* prophets, Isaiah, Jeremiah, and Ezekiel, and the twelve *minor* prophets address the Israelite people in public arenas. The central characters of each are not strictly speaking or primarily prophets as such, though some, such as Deborah and Gideon in the Book of Judges, are known to engage in this work also. They are generals and administrators, priests, judges, and kings; and as such, we do not find within these texts the words of God spoken through his spokespersons, nor the literary and oratorical flourishes that mark the prophets themselves and their texts.

Yehoshua/Joshua, Moses' designated successor, is a man who shares the attributes of Moses himself—administrative and organizational skills, religious and spiritual sensitivities, and in his case, military acumen. His succession is relatively unique

among the ancient world's rulers: he shares no biological relationship to Moses whatsoever, whose own firstborn, *Gershom* (Hebrew, "I was a stranger there," referencing Moses' fleeing to Midian after killing an Egyptian slave master and marrying the daughter of the Midianite priest *Yitro*/Jethro), is further written out of the story of Israel. Today, we best understand Joshua's succession as a radical counterstatement against prevailing norms. In taking over from the great leader, he is "almost Moses" (to wit, in *Sefer Devarim*/Book of Deuteronomy, Moses dies at age 120; in *Sefer Yehoshua*/Book of Joshua, Joshua dies at

Fig. 3.4 The Book of Joshua From the Lisbon Bible (1482). Unique among the ancients, Moses' successor Joshua, the son of Nun, was not a member of his family but chosen because he possessed the spiritual, military, and administrative gifts necessary to lead the Children of Israel into the Promised Land. Photo: British Library/HIP/Art Resource, N.Y.

110) and fulfills Moses' dream of leading the people of Israel in their return to the promised land, and with it, the dividing of the land itself into eleven tribal areas, the Levites responsible for religious matters having no area to specifically call their own, other than so-called Levitical cities and cities of refuge, for those who unintentionally commit murders.

Joshua, however, dies without a designated successor, and thus we enter the period of the *Shoftim/* **Judges**—military, governmental, and religious leaders who attempt to keep the tribal communities at peace with each other and organize the defense of the land against external threats and enemies—at the same time serving as transitional figures from great leaders (i.e., Moses and Joshua) to great kings (Saul, David, and Solomon). Somewhat like the prophets, we could perhaps classify them as "major judges," about whom we know more—Ehud, Deborah, Gideon, Jephthah, and Samson—and "minor judges," about whom we know very little—Shamgar, Tola, Yair, Ibzan, Elon, and Abdon. Like the Book of Joshua, which precedes it, and the books of Samuel and Kings, which succeed it, Judges is primarily an historical text.

It will fall to the beloved priest of ancient Israel *Shemu'el/* **Samuel** in the two books that bear his name (though the division is somewhat artificial; scholars understand the text to have originally been one text divided much later by an unknown editor) to seek God's affirmation for his people's desire for a ruler (i.e., king) like that of other nations, though he himself is uncomfortable with the decision, preferring the judge model and God as divine king. Nonetheless, he crowns the soldier *Sha'ul/* Saul, who dies in battle, who is succeeded in turn by *Dawid/* David, who dies in old age, as does his own son and successor, by his wife *Bathsheva/* Bathsheba, *Shelomo/* Solomon. Thus, his two books advance the story of Israel's monarchy, which unfortunately does not fare well and goes from bad to worse.

Between approximately 932 and 597 B.C.E., thirty-nine kings will reign over the Israelite people as presented in the *Sifrei Melachim /* **Books of Kings**: twenty over the southern kingdom of Judah and nineteen over the northern kingdom of Israel. Some will reign as little as seven days (Zimri in the north) or as long as fifty-five years (Manassah in the south). For three-and-a-half centuries, this people will be subject to chaos at the highest levels of leadership and the inevitable corruptions that accompany it. It is into this world that the true giants of Israel's moral-ethical literature will emerge, the *nevi'im/* prophets of ancient Israel.

Unequally divided between the so-called major prophets (*Yesha'yahu/* Isaiah, *Yiremeyahu/* Jeremiah, and *Yehezkel/* Ezekiel) and the minor prophets (the remaining twelve)—a distinction based on the size of their texts and *not* on their moral stance or the issues with which they concerned themselves—we who are their readers have been gifted with the most sublime religio-ethical literature in all of Western and Judaic civilizations. And, while scholarly questions abound—for example, are there other sermons/addresses from these singularly rare and unique individuals waiting to be discovered? Did they undergo some kind of editorial process at their own hands or those of their secretaries or devoted disciples before or during canonization? Were they all given voice or were some of them solely written texts? If selections were made of their oral discourses, why these and no others?—they do not take away from the literature itself.

Then, too, what of their own individual stories? Some reveal insightful biographical material; others not at all. Collectively, how and why did Israel's God choose these particular persons, whose careers range from priests to agriculturalists, and not others? And why these males only—though in the Book of Judges Deborah is understood to have been a "prophetess"? What of the process of "divine selection"—how did it happen (in a dream? in a vision? the result of direct divine speech?), transforming morally righteous men into loving but nonetheless harsh critics of their people and society, who ultimately failed to achieve the desired result of bringing their people back onto the straight and narrow path of proper ritual observance and ethical responsibility for "the widow, the poor, the orphan," and alleviating the perceived corruption in their midst?

The "age of the prophets" of ancient Israel coincides roughly with the time between the destruction of the northern kingdom by the Assyrians in 721 B.C.E. and the destruction of the southern kingdom in 586 B.C.E. Thus, within only about 135 years, the Jewish people gave birth and voice to these fifteen (or more) remarkable persons who saw themselves both as speaking for God to their people and speaking for their people to God. Let us, therefore, briefly examine some but not all of them.

Yesha'yahu/Isaiah Scholarly consensus, at variance in both the Jewish and the Christian religious communities to be sure, is that there was not one but at least two and perhaps even three such persons, all subsumed under the same name, for the concerns of the first thirty-nine chapters appear to be significantly different from those of the remaining twenty-seven chapters; and some scholars equally see differences even in the second part. Greatly affected by the tribulations associated with the Assyrian invasion, "First Isaiah" condemns both the North and the South for their corruption, awaits a messianic redeemer, and lauds King Hezekiah, who reigned from 716/715–687 B.C.E. as a faithful servant of God. "Second Isaiah" (sometimes called "Deutero-Isaiah") appears to be more of a comforter of a hurting and grieving people than a condemner of a corrupt community, and one whose messages are directed toward the South after the North had been vanquished. "Third Isaiah" (sometimes referred to as "Trito-Isaiah") returns the text and the people to future hope by addressing the glories which yet await them, for God will restore them to his good graces as he has always done.

Whether one accepts or rejects the scholarly perspective of multiple Isaiahs or the religious perspective of a solitary Isaiah, the text is one text, and the voice heard regularly from the pulpit is one voice. Witness, for example, the following from the opening chapter (see box 3.7).

One hears quite easily the condemnation of Isaiah toward his people for their corruptions and violations of their covenantal responsibilities not only to their God but to each other as well.

Yiremeyahu/Jeremiah For *Yiremeyahu*/Jeremiah (sometimes referred to as the "prophet of doom" or the "reluctant prophet"), it is not the Assyrian tragedy that will mark his service to his people but the Babylonian one. Born to a priestly family, he will travel with them into exile and experience the trauma of dislocation and resettlement, though he will also instruct others to make their peace with their new reality and see, even in this tragedy, God's hand still at work. In the fourth chapter, his anguish not only for what he and his people are experiencing, but his own predicament at having to address it shines through (see box 3.8).

Yehezkel/Ezekiel Radically different from his two predecessors, as evidenced by this first chapter, *Yehezkel*/Ezekiel's phantasmagoric visions will ultimately provide the foundation for the later Jewish mystical tradition that will derive one of its many titles—*merkava* (Hebrew, "chariot") *mysticism*—from the reference to a "divine chariot" shown here. While little is known of his life, his opening autobiographical comment tells us he was a priest who traveled with his people into exile in Babylonia and through his visions found himself both condemner (not only of Israel but also of those nations who have afflicted her) and comforter. His text both opens (chapter 1; see box 3.9) and closes with his visions (chapter 40).

Trei Asar: "The Twelve" (Minor Prophets) In comparison to Isaiah, Jeremiah, and Ezekiel, these twelve prophets are *minor* in the size of their texts only (i.e., the number of chapters or individual "sermons" included), and *not* in terms of their lofty ideals, moral critiques, or the beauty of their language. While some are known, and known quite well to both Jewish and Christian readers, others are less well known, if at all. Hosea, Amos, and certainly Jonah have had their stories retold numerous times and their words incorporated into the liturgies of

BOX 3.7

Yesha'iyahu/Isaiah 1:1-31[7]

The vision concerning Judah and Jerusalem that Isaiah son of Amoz saw during the reigns of Uzziah, Jotham, Ahaz and Hezekiah, kings of Judah.

Hear, O heavens! Listen, O earth!
For the LORD has spoken:
"I reared children and brought them up,
but they have rebelled against me.
The ox knows his master,
the donkey his owner's manger,
but Israel does not know,
my people do not understand."

Ah, sinful nation,
a people loaded with guilt,
a brood of evildoers,
children given to corruption!
They have forsaken the LORD;
they have spurned the Holy One of
    Israel
and turned their backs on him.

Why should you be beaten anymore?
Why do you persist in rebellion?
Your whole head is injured,
your whole heart afflicted.
From the sole of your foot to the top of
    your head
there is no soundness—
only wounds and welts
and open sores,
not cleansed or bandaged
or soothed with oil.

Your country is desolate,
your cities burned with fire;
your fields are being stripped by
    foreigners
right before you,
laid waste as when overthrown by
    strangers.
The Daughter of Zion is left
like a shelter in a vineyard,
like a hut in a field of melons,
like a city under siege.
Unless the LORD Almighty
had left us some survivors,
we would have become like Sodom,
we would have been like Gomorrah.

Hear the word of the LORD,
you rulers of Sodom;
listen to the law of our God,
you people of Gomorrah!
"The multitude of your sacrifices—
what are they to me?" says the LORD.
"I have more than enough of burnt
    offerings,
of rams and the fat of fattened animals;
I have no pleasure
in the blood of bulls and lambs and
    goats.
When you come to appear before me,
who has asked this of you,
this trampling of my courts?
Stop bringing meaningless offerings!
Your incense is detestable to me.
New Moons, Sabbaths and
    convocations—
I cannot bear your evil assemblies.
Your New Moon festivals and your
    appointed feasts
my soul hates.
They have become a burden to me;
I am weary of bearing them.
When you spread out your hands in
    prayer,
I will hide my eyes from you;
even if you offer many prayers,
I will not listen.
Your hands are full of blood;
wash and make yourselves clean.
Take your evil deeds
out of my sight!
Stop doing wrong,
learn to do right!
Seek justice,
encourage the oppressed.
Defend the cause of the fatherless,
plead the case of the widow.

"Come now, let us reason together,"
says the LORD.
"Though your sins are like scarlet,
they shall be as white as snow;
though they are red as crimson,
they shall be like wool.
If you are willing and obedient,
you will eat the best from the land;
but if you resist and rebel,
you will be devoured by the sword."

For the mouth of the LORD has spoken.

See how the faithful city
has become a harlot!
She once was full of justice;
righteousness used to dwell in her—
but now murderers!
Your silver has become dross,
your choice wine is diluted with water.
Your rulers are rebels,
companions of thieves;
they all love bribes
and chase after gifts.
They do not defend the cause of the
    fatherless;
the widow's case does not come before
    them.
Therefore the Lord, the LORD Almighty,
the Mighty One of Israel, declares:
"Ah, I will get relief from my foes
and avenge myself on my enemies.
I will turn my hand against you;
I will thoroughly purge away your dross
and remove all your impurities.
I will restore your judges as in days of
    old,
your counselors as at the beginning.
Afterward you will be called
the City of Righteousness,
the Faithful City."

Zion will be redeemed with justice,
her penitent ones with righteousness.
But rebels and sinners will both be
    broken,
and those who forsake the LORD will
    perish.

"You will be ashamed because of the
    sacred oaks
in which you have delighted;
you will be disgraced because of the
    gardens
that you have chosen.
You will be like an oak with fading
    leaves,
like a garden without water.
The mighty man will become tinder
and his work a spark;
both will burn together,
with no one to quench the fire."

BOX 3.8

Yirmijahu/Jeremiah 4:1-31

"If you will return, O Israel,
return to me,"
declares the LORD.
"If you put your detestable idols out of
    my sight
and no longer go astray,
and if in a truthful, just and righteous way
you swear, 'As surely as the LORD lives,'
then the nations will be blessed by him
and in him they will glory."

This is what the LORD says to the men of
    Judah and to Jerusalem:
"Break up your unplowed ground
and do not sow among thorns.
Circumcise yourselves to the LORD,
circumcise your hearts,
you men of Judah and people of Jeru-
    salem,
or my wrath will break out and burn like
    fire
because of the evil you have done—
burn with no one to quench it.

"Announce in Judah and proclaim in
    Jerusalem and say:
'Sound the trumpet throughout the land!'
Cry aloud and say:
'Gather together!
Let us flee to the fortified cities!'
Raise the signal to go to Zion!
Flee for safety without delay!
For I am bringing disaster from the north,
even terrible destruction."
A lion has come out of his lair;
a destroyer of nations has set out.
He has left his place
to lay waste your land.
Your towns will lie in ruins
without inhabitant.
So put on sackcloth,
lament and wail,
for the fierce anger of the LORD
has not turned away from us.

"In that day," declares the LORD,
"the king and the officials will lose heart,
the priests will be horrified,
and the prophets will be appalled."

Then I said, "Ah, Sovereign LORD, how
completely you have deceived this

people and Jerusalem by saying, 'You will
have peace,' when the sword is at our
throats."

At that time this people and Jerusalem will be told, "A scorching wind from
the barren heights in the desert blows
toward my people, but not to winnow or
cleanse; a wind too strong for that comes
from me. Now I pronounce my judgments
against them."

Look! He advances like the clouds,
his chariots come like a whirlwind,
his horses are swifter than eagles.
Woe to us! We are ruined!
O Jerusalem, wash the evil from your
    heart and be saved.
How long will you harbor wicked
    thoughts?
A voice is announcing from Dan,
proclaiming disaster from the hills of
    Ephraim.
"Tell this to the nations,
proclaim it to Jerusalem:
'A besieging army is coming from a
    distant land,
raising a war cry against the cities of
    Judah.
They surround her like men guarding a
    field,
because she has rebelled against me,' "
declares the LORD.
"Your own conduct and actions
have brought this upon you.
This is your punishment.
How bitter it is!
How it pierces to the heart!"

Oh, my anguish, my anguish!
I writhe in pain.
Oh, the agony of my heart!
My heart pounds within me,
I cannot keep silent.
For I have heard the sound of the
    trumpet;
I have heard the battle cry.
Disaster follows disaster;
the whole land lies in ruins.
In an instant my tents are destroyed,
my shelter in a moment.
How long must I see the battle standard
and hear the sound of the trumpet?

"My people are fools;
they do not know me.
They are senseless children;
they have no understanding.
They are skilled in doing evil;
they know not how to do good."

I looked at the earth,
and it was formless and empty;
and at the heavens,
and their light was gone.
I looked at the mountains,
and they were quaking;
all the hills were swaying.
I looked, and there were no people;
every bird in the sky had flown away.
I looked, and the fruitful land was a
    desert;
all its towns lay in ruins
before the LORD, before his fierce anger.

This is what the LORD says:
"The whole land will be ruined,
    though I will not destroy it com-
    pletely.
Therefore the earth will mourn
and the heavens above grow dark,
because I have spoken and will not relent,
    I have decided and will not turn
    back."

At the sound of horsemen and archers
every town takes to flight.
Some go into the thickets;
some climb up among the rocks.
All the towns are deserted;
no one lives in them.

What are you doing, O devastated one?
Why dress yourself in scarlet
and put on jewels of gold?
Why shade your eyes with paint?
You adorn yourself in vain.
Your lovers despise you;
they seek your life.
I hear a cry as of a woman in labor,
a groan as of one bearing her first child—
the cry of the Daughter of Zion gasping
    for breath,
stretching out her hands and saying,
"Alas! I am fainting;
my life is given over to murderers."

both religious traditions. Others—Joel, Obadiah, Micah, Nahum, Habakkuk, and Zephaniah—are largely unfamiliar to both audiences, if known at all. According to the Judaic religious tradition of the postbiblical rabbis, prophecy in ancient Israel and among the Jewish people came to its end with Haggai, Zechariah, and Malachi, thus confining the status of "prophet" only to those already incorporated into the Torah/Hebrew Bible. For the postbiblical rabbis—and for religiously observant Jews today—it is not that the God of Israel could not elevate others to this high status of primary and universally acknowledged moral critic par excellence, either in the past 2,000 years or the present, it is that, for whatever reasons, the God of Israel has not (or not yet) chosen to do so.

For some scholars of the Torah/Hebrew Bible and others—including religiously devout Jews and Christians and others in the secular academy—two questions regarding these minor prophets have arisen: (1) Whatever became of the "other texts" of these individuals? To be sure, these chapters/sermons simply could not have been their sole prophetic output. Where are their other critical pronouncements regarding the people of Israel? And (2) what were the criteria by which the canonizing rabbis included these texts and not others? Are there unifying themes and ideas that merited their inclusion, and other themes and ideas that caused their exclusion? At this moment in history, the most honest answer to both of these questions is that we simply do not know and, truthfully, cannot even present cogent and plausible responses or explanations to these significant gaps in our knowledge.

However, quite briefly, then, here are the Twelve Minor Prophets of ancient Israel, in the order in which they appear in the Torah/Hebrew Bible.

Hoshea/Hosea's prophecies mirror his own life story. Called by his God during the eighth century B.C.E. to prophesy, he is also called by that same God to marry a prostitute, who betrays him, and whom he takes back into their marriage in love. So too the people of Israel: to dishonor the God of

Israel by engaging in false and idolatrous practices is, from the perspective of both God and Hosea, to "go a-whoring," and while fully worthy of dramatic condemnation, does not ultimately close the door to a loving God for whom the *berith*/covenant with the people Israel remains in effect and, thus, keeps the door open to forgiveness, reconciliation, and recommitment.

Regarding the minor prophet *Yo'el*/Joel, the shaky ground of confirmed knowledge is apparent. Scholars continue to debate when he preached his oratories, with dates ranging between 850 and 500 B.C.E., because of the lack of both biographical and historical details. While condemning Israel for its apostasy (i.e., renunciation of their commitments to their God) and dramatically describing a plague of devouring locusts, he also calls on them to repent with the certainty that their repentance will restore both them and their land.

With the prophet *Amos*/Amos, a contemporary of Hosea, we have what appears to be an interesting paradox: while describing himself as a simple agriculturalist, the language of his sermons indicates one well educated and at ease with a highly stylized use of a beautiful Hebrew. Amos is truly a prophet of outraged conscience, one for whom Israel's moral lapses are a grave offense to Israel's God, and while seemingly equally condemning Israel's neighbors for their own moral iniquities, the *berith*/covenant with God demands a higher standard (see box 3.10).

Only a single chapter/sermon, the prophet **Obadiah** (Hebrew *Ovadyah*, from *Eved-Yah*, "slave" or "servant" of God) is overwhelmingly unknown by the vast majority of Jews and Christians. The focus of his attention was the nation of Edom (i.e., the Edomite people, Esau's descendants), who inhabited the desert areas somewhere between the eleventh and the eighth centuries B.C.E., and who, according to Obadiah, were worthy of destruction because of their corruption. For this writer, to include this text in the Torah/Hebrew Bible illustrates the use of metaphor not only by the original

BOX 3.9

Yehezkel/Ezekiel 1:1-28

In the thirtieth year, in the fourth month on the fifth day, while I was among the exiles by the Kebar River, the heavens were opened and I saw visions of God.

On the fifth of the month—it was the fifth year of the exile of King Jehoiachin—the word of the LORD came to Ezekiel the priest, the son of Buzi, by the Kebar River in the land of the Babylonians. There the hand of the LORD was upon him.

I looked, and I saw a windstorm coming out of the north—an immense cloud with flashing lightning and surrounded by brilliant light. The center of the fire looked like glowing metal, and in the fire was what looked like four living creatures. In appearance their form was that of a man, but each of them had four faces and four wings. Their legs were straight; their feet were like those of a calf and gleamed like burnished bronze. Under their wings on their four sides they had the hands of a man. All four of them had faces and wings, and their wings touched one another. Each one went straight ahead; they did not turn as they moved.

Their faces looked like this: Each of the four had the face of a man, and on the right side each had the face of a lion, and on the left the face of an ox; each also had the face of an eagle. Such were their faces. Their wings were spread out upward; each had two wings, one touching the wing of another creature on either side, and two wings covering its body. Each one went straight ahead. Wherever the spirit would go, they would go, without turning as they went. The appearance of the living creatures was like burning coals of fire or like torches. Fire moved back and forth among the creatures; it was bright, and lightning flashed out of it. The creatures sped back and forth like flashes of lightning.

As I looked at the living creatures, I saw a wheel on the ground beside each creature with its four faces. This was the appearance and structure of the wheels: They sparkled like chrysolite, and all four looked alike. Each appeared to be made like a wheel intersecting a wheel. As they moved, they would go in any one of the four directions the creatures faced; the wheels did not turn about as the creatures went. Their rims were high and awesome, and all four rims were full of eyes all around.

When the living creatures moved, the wheels beside them moved; and when the living creatures rose from the ground, the wheels also rose. Wherever the spirit would go, they would go, and the wheels would rise along with them, because the spirit of the living creatures was in the wheels. When the creatures moved, they also moved; when the creatures stood still, they also stood still; and when the creatures rose from the ground, the wheels rose along with them, because the spirit of the living creatures was in the wheels.

Spread out above the heads of the living creatures was what looked like an expanse, sparkling like ice, and awesome. Under the expanse their wings were stretched out one toward the other, and each had two wings covering its body. When the creatures moved, I heard the sound of their wings, like the roar of rushing waters, like the voice of the Almighty, like the tumult of an army. When they stood still, they lowered their wings.

Then there came a voice from above the expanse over their heads as they stood with lowered wings. Above the expanse over their heads was what looked like a throne of sapphire, and high above on the throne was a figure like that of a man. I saw that from what appeared to be his waist up he looked like glowing metal, as if full of fire, and that from there down he looked like fire; and brilliant light surrounded him. Like the appearance of a rainbow in the clouds on a rainy day, so was the radiance around him. This was the appearance of the likeness of the glory of the LORD. When I saw it, I fell facedown, and I heard the voice of one speaking.

author(s) but by the rabbinic canonizers as well: Why should the Israelite/Jewish people truly concern themselves with the fate of others, no matter the connection? Upon hearing or reading, this text reminds its audience that, just as the God of Israel destroys those others who merit their destruction, so too will that same God destroy his own beloved if they too merit divine wrath.[8]

Beloved by generations of Jews and Christians, from children to adults, the prophet *Yonah*/Jonah's story is that of a reluctant Israelite who simply does not want the job of becoming God's mouthpiece and critic, and who, in his naïveté, attempts to flee from his God by boarding a ship going away from his Babylonian destination of Nineveh, getting himself thrown overboard, and ultimately going to Nineveh and urging them to repent (which they do, further angering him!), and finally end-

ing his journey sitting outside this foreign city and slowly realizing that all is according to God's plan, whether we realize it or not and like it or not. The text itself stops, in the fourth chapter—stops does not end!—with no final thoughts, leading some scholars to suggest, perhaps, an *incomplete* text. Yet the messages themselves are twofold and powerful for its Jewish (and later, to be sure, Christian) audiences: (1) the God of Israel, who commands and demands obedience of his human subjects, is the universal God of all humankind, and (2) only the most naïve among us falsely believe they can flee from the presence of the divine. God chooses those whom God chooses to do his bidding; accept your fate and proceed!

Most well-loved in the story is Jonah's life within the belly of the *dag gadol* (Hebrew, "big fish," and usually mistranslated as "whale"), which,

---

BOX 3.10

Amos/Amos 2:6-16

This is what the LORD says:

"For three sins of Israel,
even for four, I will not turn back [my wrath].
They sell the righteous for silver,
     and the needy for a pair of sandals.
They trample on the heads of the poor
     as upon the dust of the ground
     and deny justice to the oppressed.
Father and son use the same girl
and so profane my holy name.
They lie down beside every altar
on garments taken in pledge.
In the house of their god
they drink wine taken as fines.

"I destroyed the Amorite before them,
though he was tall as the cedars
and strong as the oaks.
I destroyed his fruit above
and his roots below.

"I brought you up out of Egypt,
and I led you forty years in the desert
to give you the land of the Amorites.
I also raised up prophets from among your sons
and Nazirites from among your young men.
Is this not true, people of Israel?"
declares the LORD.
"But you made the Nazirites drink wine
and commanded the prophets not to prophesy.

"Now then, I will crush you
as a cart crushes when loaded with grain.
The swift will not escape,
the strong will not muster their strength,
and the warrior will not save his life.
The archer will not stand his ground,
the fleet-footed soldier will not get away,
and the horseman will not save his life.
Even the bravest warriors
will flee naked on that day,"
declares the LORD.

like the aforementioned ship, casts him out (see box 3.11).

Who knows? Perhaps *Sefer Yonah* / Book of Jonah was the inspiration for Carlo (Lorenzini) Collodi's (1826–1890) universally beloved fairy tale *The Adventures of Pinocchio*, a puppet-child who ultimately becomes human after a series of adventures and misadventures, and who himself briefly lives in and survives inside the belly of a whale.

For the eighth-century prophet *Michah* / Micah, himself believed to have been from a lower socioeconomic circle than those he severely critiques, it is the iniquities, both moral-ethical and ritual-ceremonial, of Jerusalem's leadership that earn his wrath. Like both his predecessors and his successors, it is critique with comfort, condemnation with hope. Indeed, Micah 6:8 is the quintessential statement of both moral and religious responsibility:

He has showed you, O man, what is good.
And what does the LORD require of you?
To act justly and to love mercy
and to walk humbly with your God.

Back, again, to a relatively unknown prophet, *Nahum* / Nahum (from the Hebrew "to comfort," thus "the Comforter"). Addressing the imminent downfall of Nineveh in Babylon, perhaps Nahum should have succeeded Jonah in the ordering of the Minor Prophets in the Torah/Hebrew Bible. Perhaps Nahum, too, is a metaphorical reminder to the Jewish people that the battles against backsliding into iniquity and corruption are not a one-time moment in the past, but an everyday individual and communal struggle and challenge.

Nahum is then succeeded by *Habaqquq* / Habakkuk in the seventh century, whose message is one of absolute trust and faith in the God

BOX 3.11

Yonah/Jonah

But the LORD provided a great fish to swallow Jonah, and Jonah was inside the fish three days and three nights.
From inside the fish Jonah prayed to the LORD his God. He said:

"In my distress I called to the LORD,
and he answered me.
From the depths of the grave I called for help,
and you listened to my cry.
You hurled me into the deep,
into the very heart of the seas,
and the currents swirled about me;
all your waves and breakers
swept over me.
I said, 'I have been banished
from your sight;
yet I will look again
toward your holy temple.'

The engulfing waters threatened me,
the deep surrounded me;
seaweed was wrapped around my head.
To the roots of the mountains I sank down;
the earth beneath barred me in forever.
But you brought my life up from the pit,
O LORD my God.
"When my life was ebbing away,
I remembered you, LORD,
and my prayer rose to you,
to your holy temple.
"Those who cling to worthless idols
forfeit the grace that could be theirs.
But I, with a song of thanksgiving,
will sacrifice to you.
What I have vowed I will make good.
Salvation comes from the LORD."
And the LORD commanded the fish, and it vomited Jonah onto dry land.

of Israel, and the recognition that God uses human agents—in this case the Chaldeans—to accomplish divine purposes. Habakkuk is in turn succeeded by **Zephaniah** (Hebrew, *Tsaphonyah*, "northern prophet," "Yankee!"), who condemns not only Israel but her enemies as well, at the same time holding out the hope that even Israel's enemies will come to recognize the sovereignty of Israel's God. Zephaniah's main concern, however, is that Israel herself will return to the straight and narrow path of ethical and religious righteousness.

The prophet *Haggay*/**Haggai** (Hebrew, "my festival prophet") may be classified as a "prophet of return," after the Babylonian destruction of the First Temple in 586 B.C.E. and the return of those Hebrews/Israelites who chose to do so after Cyrus of Persia's (c. 590–530 B.C.E.) decree permitting them to do so in 538. His critique of his people regards their refusal to immediately rebuild the destroyed temple, preferring instead to address their own (what he regards as selfish) concerns. For him, unless they return to their primary responsibilities, they will fall again.

For the prophet **Zechariah** (Hebrew, *Zacharyah*, "prophet who remembers God"), too, rebuilding the First Temple remains a priority, for only with its rebuilding will God's holy presence return to Jerusalem specifically. For Zechariah and for those who believed with him, such prophetic understandings of God's return and the restrengthening of the *berith*/covenant was a powerful source and message of comfort and hope.

The last of Israel's biblical prophets was *Mal'echi*/**Malachi**, who closes out this section of the Torah/Hebrew Bible (but whose text is the final one in the Christian "Old Testament"). His name is derived from the Hebrew word *mal'ach* ("messenger" or "angel," but in this instance, obviously messenger) with the personal pronominal suffix "my"); thus "my (God's) messenger." This fifth-century prophet, like his predecessors, attempts to get the Hebrew/Israelite people back on the straight and narrow path of both ritual-ceremonial observance and moral-ethical righteousness.[9]

A final note: liturgically, Jewish synagogal worship services, and Sabbath and Festival mornings, are replete with two scriptural readings. The first is *always* from the *Chumash*, the First Five Books of the Torah/Hebrew Bible, in an annualized cycle, and the second, connected by a person, place, event, or idea, is primarily from this second section, the prophets. As the following chart indicates, some prophets are read or chanted (more on this later) numerous times, some less so, and some not at all. Thus, the majority of the world's Jews, unless they choose to read these texts themselves, would have never learned or studied those whose words are not included in the experience of worship. Most significantly, *Sefer Daniyye'l*/ Book of Daniel, important in Christian messianic thinking in later generations, is *not* Judaically understood as a prophet; nor is the text itself included in this section, but, instead, to the third section to which we now turn.

Ketuvim: "The Writings" (The Literary Collection)

As they have come down to us today, the remaining thirteen[10] books of the Torah/Hebrew Bible are themselves true gems of literature and may be further subdivided into Wisdom literature and "non-Wisdom literature" (though there is more than enough wisdom and knowledge to be gleaned from all of them!). The "Wisdom books" are Psalms, Proverbs, Song of Songs, Ruth, Lamentations, Esther, Ecclesiastes, and Job; and the "non-Wisdom books" are Daniel, Ezra, Nehemiah, and 1 and 2 Chronicles.[11] They are collectively presented to us in the following order, with brief comments.

Sefer Tehillim/**Book of Psalms** is perhaps the first liturgical compositions of ancient Israel. It is, in truth, not one book but five *books* of psalms, divided as follows: 1–41, 42–27, 73–89, 90–106, and 107–150. Their primary attributed author is King David[12] (see box 3.12):

Taken together, these 150 poetic compositions of varying length (Psalm 119 being the longest, and an alphabetical acrostic as well) express the longing of the human soul for connection with the divine presence in a wide variety of categories.[13] For Psalms 1 and 150, see box 3.12.

Following these magnificent poetic compositions are epigrammatic *Mishle*/**Proverbs** in a series of chapters, the organization and ordering of which remains complicated and largely hidden to scholars today. What must have made logical sense to the author(s), editor(s), and compiler(s) continues to elude us. However, as a series of teaching texts for

Fig. 3.5 Psalm 79, verse 6 From the Darmstadt Haggadah (c. 1420–1430). The first organized "hymnbook" of the Jewish people, these 150 psalms were liturgical compositions set to a variety of musical settings and remain the heart of Jewish prayer even today. Photo: Bildarchiv Preussischer Kulturbesitz / Art Resource, N.Y.

young men, it uses a contrast between the one who does well and the one who deviates from the proper path and earns the ire of God, parents, and community. Its essential understanding is that found in the twice-repeated statement (1:7 and 9:10): "The fear[14] of the LORD is the beginning of wisdom" (which also appears in Psalm 111:10).

Sefer Iyov/**Book of Job** is, without dissension, the most philosophical and the most problematic text in the whole of the Torah/Hebrew Bible, wisely canonized by the rabbinic authorities, who themselves recognized that all thinking and reflective human beings, Jews and non-Jews alike, quest for an answer to the haunting questions of good and evil, justice and mercy, reward and punishment.

This non-Israelite has it all: family, fortune, and a good name in his community. Unknown to him, forces beyond his human control—God and God's prosecuting angel, *hasatan*, wager a competition that Job's goodness is incontrovertibly linked to his material and personal success. Given a "green light" to contest this reading, *hasatan* is permitted to take Job's family, his fortune, and his good name, and inflict disease on his physical person, all to no avail as Job refuses his wife's suggestion that "he curse God and die" (2:9). Toward the end of the text, while not critiquing his God, he quests for an answer, an understanding, as to the reasons for his fate. Such is not forthcoming, but instead his God offers, in a monologue that is among the most powerful in all biblical literature, a confirmation that the ways of the divine are, ultimately, humanly inscrutable, (Job 38–41). Box 3.13 presents the opening verses of that monologue, its divine rage and sarcasm fully in evidence (Job's response in chapter 42 is the recognition of his own limitations, and he returns to his life, which will be even more fully realized than before).

Drawing an important distinction between eroticism (i.e., the *celebration* of human sexuality) and pornography (i.e., the *denigration* of human sexuality), *Shir Hashirim*/**Canticles/Song of Songs** is a tribute to the former in a series of wonderful (and explicit!) love poems between an engaged

Psalms 1 and 150

Psalm 1	Psalm 150
Blessed is the man	Praise the Lord.
who does not walk in the counsel of the wicked	
or stand in the way of sinners	Praise God in his sanctuary;
or sit in the seat of mockers.	praise him in his mighty heavens.
But his delight is in the law of the Lord,	Praise him for his acts of power;
and on his law he meditates day and night.	praise him for his surpassing greatness.
He is like a tree planted by streams of water,	Praise him with the sounding of the trumpet,
which yields its fruit in season	praise him with the harp and lyre,
and whose leaf does not wither.	praise him with tambourine and dancing,
Whatever he does prospers.	praise him with the strings and flute,
	praise him with the clash of cymbals,
	praise him with resounding cymbals.
Not so the wicked!	Let everything that has breath praise the Lord.
They are like chaff	
that the wind blows away.	
Therefore the wicked will not stand in the judgment,	Praise the Lord.
nor sinners in the assembly of the righteous.	
For the Lord watches over the way of the righteous,	
but the way of the wicked will perish.	

couple (regarded by ancient communal standards as already fully committed) who enjoy each other's physical endowments. While the canonizers themselves may have been comfortable with these texts, the later rabbis (and later Christians) were not, and reinterpreted them metaphorically as that between God (the groom) and the people Israel (the bride) or Christ (the groom) and his church (the bride).

The **Book of Ruth**, which follows, is equally a love story on two levels: that between a Moabite daughter-in-law, Ruth, and her mother-in-law, Naomi, and that between the Israelite husband Boaz and the Moabite wife Ruth. Ruth and Boaz will ultimately loom large for both Jews and Christians as the progenitors of King David, from whose house and loins will come the messiah—for Jews a fully human being but for Christians one who is both fully human and fully divine.[15]

The **Book of Lamentations**, sometimes traditionally attributed to the prophet Jeremiah, is one man's attempt to cope with, make sense of, and find meaning, comfort, and solace in the aftermath of the destruction of the First Temple after 586 B.C.E., and is best expressed in these few verses in chapter 3 (see box 3.14).

Said resolution is not unlike that found in the biblical book *Sefer Qoheleth* / Book of Ecclesiastes, traditionally attributed to King Solomon (which also attributes Song of Songs to him in his youth, and Proverbs in his middle years), as the author quests after the meaning of life, having explored and found wanting both a hedonistic lifestyle and a philosophical resolution as evidenced by the repetitive refrain throughout ("'Meaningless! Meaningless!' says the Teacher. 'Utterly meaningless! Everything is meaningless.'"), he concludes theologically in chapter 12: "Now all has been heard; here is the conclusion of the matter: Fear God and keep his commandments, for this is the whole duty of man. For God will bring every deed into judgment, including every hidden thing, whether it is good or evil."[16]

Symbolic, perhaps, of the whole of the Jewish historical journey, certainly those ongoing attempts to exterminate/annihilate the Jewish people in their totality, the unsuccess and vanquishing of their enemies, and the celebration of Jewish survival is the historically questionable text of the **Book of Esther**, for the major characters—King Ahashuerus, Queen Esther, her cousin Mordecai, and his prede-cessor prime minister and antisemitic archenemy Haman—cannot be confirmed with historical certainty, and the attempted end of the Jewish people of Persia equally cannot be supported. It *is* a victory of the Jews nonetheless, whose celebration, the minor festival of Purim, is discussed in chapter 6.[17]

The **Book of Daniel**, far more important to Christians (possibly the inspirational source for the

---

BOX 3.13

Iyov/Job 38:1-13

Then the LORD answered Job out of the storm.
    He said:

"Who is this that darkens my counsel
with words without knowledge?
Brace yourself like a man;
I will question you,
and you shall answer me.

"Where were you when I laid the earth's
    foundation?
Tell me, if you understand.
Who marked off its dimensions? Surely you
    know!
Who stretched a measuring line across it?
On what were its footings set,
or who laid its cornerstone—

while the morning stars sang together
and all the angels shouted for joy?

"Who shut up the sea behind doors
when it burst forth from the womb,
when I made the clouds its garment
and wrapped it in thick darkness,
when I fixed limits for it
and set its doors and bars in place,
when I said, 'This far you may come and no
    farther;
here is where your proud waves halt'?

"Have you ever given orders to the morning,
or shown the dawn its place,
that it might take the earth by the edges
and shake the wicked out of it?"

BOX 3.14

Aikhah/Lamentations 3:21-26

Yet this I call to mind
and therefore I have hope:

Because of the LORD's great love we are not
    consumed,
for his compassions never fail.
They are new every morning;
great is your faithfulness.

I say to myself, "The LORD is my portion;
therefore I will wait for him."

The LORD is good to those whose hope is in him,
to the one who seeks him;
it is good to wait quietly
for the salvation of the LORD.

New Testament Book of Revelation), is, equally, a story-text that tells of the miraculous survival of Daniel and his friends, and a confirmation that faith in the God of Israel makes all things possible and enables those who are faithful to surmount even the most horrific of obstacles (in this case, placing Daniel within a den of lions, from which he emerges unharmed, and his three friends surviving the fiery furnace). Daniel himself, advisor to King Nebuchadnezzar II of Babylon (who reigned from 605 to 562 B.C.E.), in some ways parallels his predecessor Joseph, of *Bereshith*/Genesis, in that, in addition to serving as a governmental official, he is also an interpreter of royal dreams. (The text also contains the story of refusing to eat certain foods, which would, for later Jewish generations, confirm the importance and value of the Jewish dietary system of "keeping kosher.")

The last four (two) books of the Torah/Hebrew Bible are not truly literary creations, but return the audience to "restoration history" and the glories of ancient Israel, for the book of the priest **Ezra** and the book of the administrator **Nehemiah** tell of the restoration of the religious life of the ancient Israelites, the reorganizing of their community (including the divorcing of their non-Israelite wives), and the refortification of their cities, especially Jerusalem, after exile in Babylonia. The **Books of Chronicles** 1 and 2 retell the stories of the successful reigns of both King Solomon and King David to a community devastated by it own losses under the Romans only two decades previous, sending forth the message that holding to the faith of Israel will again bring about a true renewal of the Jewish people as the God of Israel has so orchestrated in the past.

And with these texts, the Torah/Hebrew Bible ends and the textual foundation for all later Judaic texts is firmly established. Mishnah, Palestinian and Babylonian Talmuds, Midrash, and Codes and *Responsa*—that is, the stories they tell, the poetry they create, the laws they enumerate—will all base themselves on these texts.

Mishnah

The page in figure 3.6 is a representative sample of an actual page of the **Mishnah**, the third-century Palestinian Hebrew codification of the Jewish laws by which the community was governed under the auspices of Rabbi Judah the Leader. It is surrounded by the various authoritative commentaries endorsed over the generations, and is organized as follows: (1) *Zeraim*/Seeds (11 subsections, agriculture and prayer), (2) *Moed*/Festivals (12 subsections, Sabbath and festivals), (3) *Nashim*/Women (7 subsections, marriage and divorce), (4) *Nezikin*/Damages (10 subsections, criminal and civil laws), (5) *Kodashim*/Holy Things (11 subsections, the

Fig. 3.6 The Mishnah The Mishnah or Mishna (Hebrew: הנשמ, "repetition") is the first major written redaction of the Jewish oral traditions called the "Oral Torah" and is the first major work of Rabbinic Judaism. Photo courtesy Creative Commons: http://commons.wikimedia.org/w/index .php?title=File:Mishnah-vilna-moed-A1-shaar.djvu&page=1.

dietary system, sacrifices, temple), and (6) *Tohorot/* Purities (12 subsections, ritual and family purity issues). And while the individual laws themselves do not cite or refer directly to the laws and legal system found in the Torah/Hebrew Bible, there is no question that the *tendenz* or orientation to legal materials and the sanctification of them is reflected in this text also. And while the commentaries are themselves insightful but relatively short, it will fall to both the Talmuds of Palestine and Babylonia to engage in the extended conversations that will mark their texts and provide the solid foundation for the postbiblical Judaism that remains in force today.

Talmuds: Babylonian and Palestinian (Jerusalem)

While originally Palestinian in origin and context, what has come down to us is a smaller Palestinian version and a much longer Babylonian version, the latter achieving its authoritative status as the ground floor for all subsequent Judaic behavior, rit-

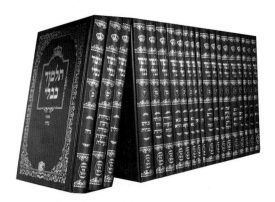

Fig. 3.7 The complete Talmud In contemporary binding, this represents a complete set of the Babylonian Talmud. Photo courtesy Creative Commons: http://commons.wikimedia. org/wiki/File:Talmud_set.JPG

ual-ceremonial and moral-ethical, throughout the world until the birth of Reform/Liberal/Progressive Judaism in the early part of the nineteenth century, whose rejection of the divine transmission of the Jewish legal tradition as reflected both in the Torah/Hebrew Bible and subsequent rabbinic interpretations and iterations of it remains a serious and divisive source of contentiousness to this moment.

The page in figure 2.6 from chapter 2, from the Babylonian Talmud, is like that of the Mishnah: the actual mishnaic text is found in the middle of the page, surrounded by its authoritative commentaries. Its organization and order is exactly the same as the Mishnah of course, but the extended conversations are considerably longer, and, in the process, reveal amazing amounts of insight into the various generations of rabbis who themselves commented on these laws, their communities, their cultural interactions, their religious traditions, their poems, legends, stories, linguistic knowledge, understanding of the Torah/Hebrew Bible, and anything and everything else that is part and parcel of a living Judaic religious tradition.

Box 3.15, a representative example of a highly complex multivolume set of texts, is the opening Mishnah and commentary from the most well known English edition, *The Soncino Babylonian Talmud*, under the editorship of the late Rabbi Dr. Isidore Epstein, originally published in England between 1935 and 1948.

And so it goes, page after page, for more than twenty or more dense volumes. The Talmud remains the primary curriculum for Orthodox Jewish males in their *Yeshivot* (Hebrew, "Houses of Study").

Midrash

The Hebrew word *midrash*, etymologically, is derived from the word *darash*, to "draw out" or "search out," and refers to both an exegetical or hermeneutical process by which texts are explicated or, in the context of this chapter, that vast body of

Judaic literature that purports to "fill in the gaps" in the many stories of the Torah/Hebrew Bible, and while today we would regard such additional stories as the creation of their authors, given their methodologies, the rabbis who created them "saw" them in their texts.

The finest compilation of such midrashic story-texts—bar none—was that published by the late scholar Louis Ginzberg (1873–1953) in a multivolume collection *The Legends of the Jews,* and recently reissued.[18] A comparable collection of such texts, now available also in English, is that edited by the

---

Mishnah and Gemara

Mishnah

From what time may one recite the Shema' in the evening? From the time that the priests enter [their houses] in order to eat their terumah until the end of the first watch. These are the words of R. Eliezer. The sages say: until midnight. R. Gamaliel says: until the dawn comes up. Once it happened that his sons came home [late] from a wedding feast and they said to him: we have not yet recited the [evening] Shema'. He said to them: if the dawn has not yet come up you are still bound to recite. And not in respect to this alone did they so decide, but wherever the sages say "until midnight," the precept may be performed until the dawn comes up. The precept of burning the fat and the [sacrificial] pieces, too, may be performed till the dawn comes up. Similarly, all [the offerings] that are to be eaten within one day may lawfully be consumed till the coming up of the dawn. Why then did the sages say "until midnight"? In order to keep a man far from transgression.

Gemara

On what does the Tanna base himself that he commences: "From what time"? Furthermore, why does he deal first with the evening [Shema']? Let him begin with the morning [Shema']!—The Tanna bases himself on the Scripture, where it is written [And thou shalt recite them] . . . when thou liest down and when thou risest up, and he states [the oral law] thus: When does the time of the recital of the Shema' of lying down begin? When the priests enter to

eat their terumah. And if you like, I can answer: He learns [the precedence of the evening] from the account of the creation of the world, where it is written, "And there was evening and there was morning, one day." Why then does he teach in the sequel: "The morning [Shema'] is preceded by two benedictions and followed by one. The evening [Shema'] is preceded by two benedictions and followed by two"? Let him there, too, mention the evening [Shema'] first?—The Tanna commences with the evening [Shema'], and proceeds then to the morning [Shema']. While dealing with the morning [Shema'], he expounds all the matters relating to it, and then he returns again to the matters relating to the evening [Shema'].

The Master said: "From the time that the priests enter to eat their 'terumah.'" When do the priests eat terumah? From the time of the appearance of the stars. Let him then say: "From the time of the appearance of the stars"?—This very thing he wants to teach us, in passing, that the priests may eat terumah from the time of the appearance of the stars. And he also wants to teach us that the expiatory offering is not indispensable, as it has been taught: And when the sun sets we-taher, the setting of the sun is indispensable [as a condition of his fitness] to eat terumah, but the expiatory offering is not indispensable to enable him to eat terumah. But how do you know that these words "and the sun sets" mean the setting of the sun, and this "we-taher" means that the day clears away?

father of modern Hebrew literature, Hayim Nah-man Bialik (1873–1934) and Yehoshua Ravnitsky, *The Book of Legends* (Hebrew, *Sefer Ha-Aggadah*), and translated by the late William Braude in the United States.[19] While there are available many, many collections of such texts, taken together, these two volumes are a significant introduction to this literature. (For those who are able to read Hebraic texts, the greatest collection is known as *Midrash Rabba* [Hebrew, "The Great Midrash"], and is composed of these separate volumes: *Bereshith*/Genesis, *Shemot*/Exodus, *Vayyikra*/Leviticus, *Bemidbar*/Numbers, *Devarim*/Deuteronomy, *Shir Hashirim*/Song of Songs, *Ruth*/Ruth, and *Eicha*/Lamentations. These were composed between the sixth and twelfth centuries C.E.; the English translations pub-

lished by the Soncino Press are well done but difficult to understand without background.)

Box 3.16 represents one of this author's favorite examples, which attempts to answer the question, "Where was Abraham's wife Sarah when her husband and son were ascending Mount Moriah in response to Abraham's understanding of God's command to offer up this son of his old age?" (The story itself is fanciful and not textually supported, but sadly sweet nonetheless.) The text of *Bereshith*/Genesis would then follow with chapter 23, which begins with the death of Sarah. Thus, this midrashic excursus, however fanciful, "fills in *a*—not the—gap in the story.

Such, then, is an example of midrashic literature. Throughout, many, many of the stories, events,

---

BOX 3.16

Midrash of Genesis 23

While Abraham was engaged in the sacrifice [of Isaac], Satan [the adversarial angel of God] went to Sarah, and appeared to her in the figure of an old man, very humble and meek, and said to her: "Do you know all that Abraham has done to your only son this day? He took Isaac, built an altar, slaughtered him, and offered him up as a sacrifice. Isaac cried and wept before his father, but he did not even look at him, nor had compassion on him." After saying these words to Sarah, Satan went away from her, and she thought him an old man from among the sons of men who had been with her son. Sarah lifted her voice and cried bitterly, saying: "O my son, Isaac, my son, O that I had died this day instead of you! It grieves me for you! After that I have reared you and have brought you up, my joy is turned into mourning over you. In my longing for a child, I cried and prayed till I bore you at ninety. Now have you served this day for the knife and fire [of sacrifice]. But I console myself, it being the word of God, and you did perform

the word of our God, in whose hands is the soul of every living creature! You are just, O Lord our God, for all Your works are good and righteous, for I also rejoice with the word which You did command, and while my eyes weep bitterly, my heart rejoices." And Sarah laid her head upon the bosom of one of her handmaids, and she became still as stone.

She rose up afterward and went about making inquiries concerning her son, till she came to Hebron, and no one would tell her what had happened to her son. Her servants went to seek him in the [study] house of Shem and Eber [Abraham's family], and they could not find him, and they sought throughout the land, and he was not there. And, behold, Satan came to Sarah in the shape of an old man, and said unto her," I spoke falsely to you, for Abraham did not kill his son, and he is not dead," and when she heard the word, her joy was so exceedingly violent that her soul went out through joy [and she died].

and persons of the Torah/Hebrew Bible were recipients of this creative endeavor, and we thus benefit still today from an even larger literature than that originally comprising the Torah/Hebrew Bible.

them. As the Judaic tradition is itself dynamic, growing, and changing, so too are both the literatures of Judaism and the ideas of Judaism to which we now turn.

Zohar

While difficult in its own right, and certainly not for either the uninitiated or the unschooled in the ways of Judaic texts, Jewish mystical literature is itself a commentary on the Torah/Hebrew Bible, but one specifically designed to bring its reader into even closer contact with God than might be solely the case with either prayer or worship. At the heart of this literature stands the *Sefer Zohar* (Hebrew, "Book of Splendor"), which made it appearance in Spain in the thirteenth century, when it was published by Moses de Leon (1250–1305), who claimed its author was none other than the second-century luminary Rabbi Shimon bar [Simon son of] Yochai. Contained within the *Zohar* are discussions about God, the universe, souls, good and evil, redemption, and many, many other topics, all written in an Aramaicized Hebrew, replete with Spanish idioms and colloquialisms of a later era. Like the Midrash Rabba, even in translation, the *Zohar* is a difficult and complicated text.

The text begins with a prologue, which sets the stage for introducing the reader to the rabbis of the second century who surrounded Rabbi Shimon and engaged in conversation with him (see box 3.17).

And, thus, even with this final complicated example from the Judaic literary tradition, the case is made: the philosophies of Judaism addressed in chapter 4 and the theologies of Judaism addressed in chapter 5 have their ultimate origins in the literary traditions and literature of the Jewish people exemplified here: Torah/Hebrew Bible, Mishnah, Talmuds Palestinian and Baylonian, Midrash, and *Zohar* and the ancillary literatures that surround

Two Other Judaic Literatures: Codes and *Responsa*

With the final compilation of the Babylonia Talmud more than 1,300 years ago, rabbinic authorities developed a "commentary tradition" further elaborating on its contents and reflecting the realities, in some cases, in their own communities. However, for laypersons bereft of the luxury of such intensive study, if Jewish life was to survive, endure, and prosper, what was needed was a distillation of the "bottom line" practicalities of Jewish life, ritually-ceremonially, morally-ethically, and communally. Hence, there arose the compilation of collections of so-called Codes of Jewish Law, abstracting from the ever-increasing written expansion of Talmudic materials only the laws themselves, a true "handbook approach" to Jewish life. (Interestingly enough, even the great Judaic rabbi and philosopher Moses Maimonides [1135–1204] saw the need for such an abstracted compilation; his Mishneh Torah ["Second Torah"] was just such a text. Somewhat ironically, however, it too brought forth not only debate and controversy but commentary as well.)

The most well-known of these compilations, in use today and also available in English translation, is titled the *Shulchan Aruch* (Hebrew, "Set" or "Prepared Table"), and is the work of sixteenth-century Spanish rabbi Yosef (Joseph) Karo (1488–1575), an abridgement of his own earlier work *Bet Yosef* (Hebrew, "House of Joseph"), a commentary initially on the work of one of his predecessors, grammarian and scholar Jacob ben Asher (1270–1340) of Toledo, Spain.

BOX 3.17

Zohar

Rabbi Hizkiah opened his discourse with the text, "As a lily among thorns" [*Shir Hashirim/* Song of Songs 2:2]. "What," he said, "does the lily symbolize? It symbolizes the community of Israel. As the lily among thorns is tinged with red and white, so the community of Israel is visited now with justice and now with mercy; as the lily possesses thirteen leaves, so the community of Israel is vouchsafed thirteen categories of mercy which surround it on every side. For this reason, the term *Elohim* [God] mentioned here [in the first verse of *Bereshith/*Genesis, to wit, *Bereshith bara Elohim* . . .] is separated by thirteen words from the next mention of *Elohim*, symbolizing the thirteen categories of mercy which surround the community of Israel to protect it. The second mention of *Elohim* is separated from the third by five words, representing the five strong leaves that surround the lily, symbolic of the five ways of salvation which are the "five gates." This is alluded to in the verse "I will lift up the cup of salvation" [*Tehillim/*Psalms 116:13]. This is the "cup of benediction," which has to be raised by five fingers and no more, after the model of the lily, which rests on five strong leaves in the shape of five fingers. Thus the lily is a symbol of the cup of benediction. Immediately after the third mention of *Elohim* appears the light which, as soon as created, was treasured up and enclosed in that *berith/*covenant which entered the lily and fertilized it, and this is what is called "tree-bearing fruit wherein is the seed thereof." This seed is preserved in the very sign of the covenant. And as the ideal covenant was formed, so the engraven ineffable name [of God] is formed of the forty-two letters of the work of creation.

In the beginning [the very first word of the Torah/Hebrew Bible, *Bereshith*]: Rabbi Shimon opened his discourse with the text, "The blossoms appeared on the earth" [*Shir Hashirim/* Song of Songs 2:12]. "The blossoms" he said, "refer to the work of creation." "Appeared on the earth"—when? On the third day [of creation], as it is written, "And the earth brought forth," thus they appeared on the earth. "The time of pruning is come" alludes to the fourth day [of creation] in which "the pruning of the overbearing" [*Yesha'iyahu/*Isaiah 25:5] took place. "And the voice of the turtle" alludes to the fifth day [of creation], as it is written, "Let the waters swarm, etc. to produce living creatures." "Is heard" points to the sixth day, as it is said, "Let us make man" (namely him who was destined to say first "we will do" and then "we will hear," for the expression in our text, *na'aseh*, "Let us make man," finds its echo in the expression *na'aseh* (we will do) and hear" [*Shemot/*Exodus 24:7]; "in our land" implies the day of the Sabbath, which is a copy of the "land of the living" (the world to come, the world of souls, the world of consolations).

Karo produced his work in Tsefat (modern Safed) in Palestine, and divided it into four parts: (1) laws pertaining to the Sabbath, holidays, prayer, and synagogue life; (2) laws pertaining to the dietary system, ritual slaughtering and food preparation, and conversion; (3) laws pertaining to marriage, divorce, and family matters; and (4) financial affairs (e.g., damages) and legal matters (e.g., the work of the court, the responsibility of witnesses). Once completed, it proved a popular text with a wide Sephardic audience. At the same time, it engendered severe critique from Ashkenazic Rabbi Moses Isserles (1530–1572) of Krakow, Poland, whose differences with Karo reflect differing communal legal resolutions as well. Classical publications of the

Shulchan Aruch today include both Karo's and Isserles's texts.

Comprehensive in scope, here are two examples of its summary materials. The first (box 3.18) is taken from chapter 5 of the first section and concerns the Shema of *Devarim*/Deuteronomy 6:4 ("Listen Israel! Adonai is our God; Adonai Alone"), regarded by many—Jews and non-Jews alike—as the closest Judaic approximation to a creedal affirmation of Judaic faith.

The second example (box 3.19), taken from chapter 6 of the second section, contains the well-known prohibition of mixing milk food with meat foods and thus violating one of the primary tenets of the Jewish dietary system.

Even so, the dynamic nature of both the Judaic religion and the tradition of Judaic texts did not end with the *Shulchan Aruch*. Throughout postbiblical rabbinic Judaism, certain learned rabbis were always looked to for guidance in the most practical of manners as well as philosophical and theological understandings. Limited at times by geographic boundaries, such rabbis received and answered letters of inquiry from distant communities during the course of more than 1,700 years. Such a tradition, known technically as *She'elot u-T'shu'vot* (Hebrew, "Questions and Anwers") and more popularly as *Responsa* literature, continues today but has broadened in two significant ways: First, with the rise of Jewish denominationalism, the various

---

BOX 3.18

Shulchan Aruch (1)[22]

SHEMA (Deut. 6:4-9; Deut. 11:13-23; Num. 15:37-41) must be recited with great concentration and intent (61:1), particularly the first verse; see 60:5; 63:4, 6. It is customary to recite the first verse out loud and to cover the eyes while doing so (61:4-5, 16; 62:5), and to silently say "Blessed be the Name . . ." after the first verse (61:13). On the appropriate intentions at specific parts of SHEMA see 61:2-3, 6-8, 14-15. The TEFILLIN (phylacteries) and TZITZIS (fringes) should be touched when the verses in which they are mentioned are recited (61:25). SHEMA should be recited audibly if possible (see 61:26; 62:3-4), and should be pronounced very carefully (62:1), even when reciting it in a language other than Hebrew (62:2). On specific details about the pronunciation see 61:16-21, 23-24. [Similar care with pronunciation should be taken in reciting other prayers and in reading from Biblical books (61:22).]

BOX 3.19

Shulchan Aruch (2)

The Torah repeats three times that it is forbidden to cook a kid in its mother's milk (Ex. 23:19, 34:26; Deut. 13:21). The repetition tells us that not only is the cooking forbidden, but so is eating or deriving benefit from the cooked mixture (87:1). These Biblical prohibitions apply to the meat or milk of any kosher BEHEMAH (animal) (87:2-3). The sages prohibited eating mixtures of the meat and milk of any kosher animal, or of meat and human milk, or of milk and the flesh of kosher birds, but mixtures of milk with kosher fish or locusts are permitted (87:3-4). Cooking any type of meat in any type of milk is forbidden for appearance's sake (see 87:4).

BOX 3.20

Responsa

Conservative *Responsum*

Question: May women read from the Torah or have an *Aliyah* (honored role in the worship service, in this case offering the before and after blessings) when the Torah is read in public?

Answer: Therefore it is halakhically permitted for women to read from the Torah or to have Aliyot (pl.) when the Torah is read in public.

Reform *Responsum*

Question: Shall women be ordained as rabbis?

Answer: In view of these [aforementioned] teachings and in keeping with the spirit of our age and the traditions of our conference [i.e., Central Conference of American Rabbis], we declare that women cannot justly be denied the privilege of ordination.

Judaic religious movements (Orthodox, Conservative, Reform, Reconstructionist) have followed a more modern convention of enlisting their own luminaries to serve on committees, thus allowing their decisions to be representative of their own sub-communities (though individual "giants" continue to receive direct inquiries). Second, Bar-Ilan University in Israel has made available online, with continuing editions and updates, vast quantities of such rabbinic response in Hebrew only, and has also

made certain selections available on CD-ROM. (Indexes of Orthodox, Conservative, and Reform *Responsa* are also available online.[24])

Two examples can be seen in box 3.20. The first is a summary of a Conservative Jewish answer to the question of women's participation in worship. Contained within the lengthier answer is the use of literary sources, an essential part of the process. The second is a Reform *Responsum* (sing.) to the question of the ordination of women.

IN REVIEW

We have now looked at the major literatures of Judaism, beginning with the Torah/Hebrew Bible and concluding with examples of contemporary *Responsa*. Along the way, we have read examples of the various kinds of literatures that comprise this corpus of material, central to the life of contemporary Jews and their religious traditions. At best, this is only an hors d'oeuvre: books about the Jews and Judaism continue to be published by scholars and popular authors at an astounding rate, covering all manner of subjects. On your next visit to your local bookstore, why not check out the section on Judaism? You will not regret it!

KEY TERMS

Apocrypha

apostasy

Aron Kodesh/Holy Ark

Aseret Hadibrot/Ten Commandments

continues on following page

Atzai Hayyim/Trees of Life	*Nevi'im*/Prophets
Babylonian Talmud	Old Testament
Bemidbar/Numbers	Palestinian Talmud
Bereshith/Genesis	Promised Land
Berith/Covenant	*qiddusha*/holiness
Bible	*Responsum/Responsa*
Chumash	*She'elot u-T'shuvot*
cities of refuge	*Shemot*/Exodus
Deutero-Isaiah	*Shirat Hayam*
Devarim/Deuteronomy	*Shirat Moshe*
First Isaiah	*Shofetim*/Judges
Gemara	*Shulchan Aruch*
Holiness Code	sofer(im)/scribe(s)
Ketuvim/Writings	Torah/Hebrew Bible
Levitical cities	Trito-Isaiah
Merkava/chariot mysticism	*Vayyikra*/Leviticus
midrash	Wisdom literature
Midrash Rabba	Yavneh
Mishnah	*Zohar*
Mishneh Torah	

Questions for Review, Study, and Discussion

1. The "creation story" of Genesis 1, followed by a second story in Genesis 2, has generated an enormous amount of controversy, most particularly with regard to the theory of evolution. After consulting several of the Jewish commentaries noted below, try writing you own commentary reconciling the two stories.

2. Take a look at the various contemporary translations of *any* story in the Torah/Hebrew Bible that you particularly like. Two excellent places to start are www.biblegateway.com and www.oxfordbiblicalstudies.com. How do you assess these different translations? Which do you prefer? Why?

3. Take a careful and close look at the two versions of the Ten Commandments found in the Torah/Hebrew Bible, that of Exodus and Deuteronomy. Can you spot the language differences? Why do you think they are different?

4. Pick another story from the Torah/Hebrew Bible that you like. Consult both Ginzberg's *Legends of the Jews* and Bialik and Ravnisky's *Book of Legends* about your story. How do these *midrashim* (literary expansions) add to your own understanding and appreciation of the story? What lesson do you think the author is trying to impart by elaborating on the biblical text? Has he succeeded?

5. After consulting the three online collections of *Responsa* (note 24), find an issue the three Jewish denominational communities (Orthodox,

Conservative, Reform) address. Are their resolutions the same? Different? Based on what you have learned about them from chapter 2, why do think this is the case?

Suggested Readings

Adler, Morris. *The World of the Talmud*. New York: Schocken Books, 1970.

Berlin, Adele, and Marc Zvi Brettler, eds. *The Jewish Study Bible*. New York: Oxford University Press, 2004.

Bialik, Hayim Nahman, and Yehoshua Ravnitsky. *The Book of Legends*. New York: Schocken Books, 1992.

Brettler, Marc Zvi. *How to Read the Bible*. Philadelphia: Jewish Publication Society, 2005.

Cohen, Abraham. *Everyman's Talmud: The Major Teachings of the Rabbinic Sages*. New York: Schocken Books, 1995.

Ginzberg, Louis. *The Legends of the Jews*. Philadelphia: Jewish Publication Society of America, 2003.

Hertz, Joseph H. *The Pentateuch and Haftorahs with Hebrew Text, English Translation and Commentary*. New York: Soncino Press, 1958.

Holz, Barry W., ed. *Back to the Sources: Reading the Classic Jewish Texts*. New York: Simon and Schuster, 1986.

Kugel, James L. *How to Read the Bible: A Guide to Scripture, Then and Now*. New York: Free Press, 2007.

Lieber, David L. *Etz Hayim: Torah and Commentary*. Philadelphia: Jewish Publication Society of America, 2002.

Plaut, W. Gunther. *The Torah: A Modern Commentary*. New York: Union of American Hebrew Congregations, 1974.

Sarna, Nahum M., and Chaim Potok, eds. *JPS Torah Commentary*. Philadelphia: Jewish Publication Society of America, 1996.

Steinsaltz, Adin. *The Essential Talmud*. New York: Basic Books, 2006.

CHAPTER 4

Cycles *of* THOUGHT

Judaic Philosophy

OVERVIEW

In this chapter, we will introduce ourselves, albeit briefly, to the major philosophers of the always-evolving Jewish intellectual tradition and their thinking. (It is by no means an all-inclusive or exhaustive list!) In so doing, we are also drawing a somewhat questionable distinction between those Jewish thinkers who do "philosophy" and those who do "theology." The latter group we will meet in chapter 5.

Introduction

At the outset, the reader of this text needs to keep one salient fact in mind: that the distinction used in this text between "philosophy" (chapter 4) and "theology" (chapter 5) is a Western way of thinking, unknown in Judaism prior to the so-called modern era, perhaps beginning with Spinoza (1632–1677).

Prior to that time, especially in the lands in which Jews primarily lived—Israel and Babylonia—those who *thought* about that which they believed central to their identity (Israelite cultic religion and its later iteration into Judaism), whether priests or prophets, Pharisees or rabbis, drew no such distinctions. For them collectively, concerns with God, God's relationship to his special covenanted people, and even the more humanly universal concerns of life and death, good and evil, were part and parcel of the working out of what it meant to be who they were in the world. For us, as Western readers, however, with the Protestant Reformation (sixteenth century) and then the Enlightenment (eighteenth century), the sundering of political power between the Roman Catholic Church and the now secularized nation-states of Europe also carried with it intellectual divisions of thought, particularly between philosophy independent of religion and theology. For Jews, however, still largely confined behind high ghetto walls, this evolution of thinking was largely foreign to what went on in communal and synagogal life. Thus, the story of Judaic thought begins in community.

The Earliest Periods of Judaic Thought

The collected texts that ultimately come together in the Torah/Hebrew Bible reflect the intellectual concerns of both their authors and their editors,

though we are on far less sure footing regarding the latter than the former. Divided into three parts—*Chumash*/Five Books of Moses, *Nevi'im*/Prophets, and *Ketuvim*/Writings—each section separately and all three collectively may be viewed as addressing ideas with which the communities of its readers were preoccupied: the Five Books of Moses with God, creation of both world and people, and the special covenant relationship between that God and this people, Israel; the Prophets with ethical mandates and lapses, rewards and punishments, which flow directly out of that covenantal relationship with God; and the Writings with a whole host of ideas (e.g., human sexuality in *Shir Hashirim*/Song of Songs, reward and punishment and good and evil in *Iyov*/Job, the meaning of life in *Qoheleth*/Ecclesiastes). We find no distinction between philosophy and theology here, but all such discussions were filtered through the lens of historical reality. What was happening to the Jews was understood to be the *direct* result of the involvement of their God with them and their involvement with him. (Issues of divine gender would have to await the postbiblical period; the worlds of the Middle East were male dominated and male oriented, and such conversa-

BOX 4.1

What Is Jewish Philosophy? Two Perspectives

1

It is the Jewish context which determines what is uniquely Jewish about Jewish philosophy—a context of encounter between philosophy and Judaism, dealing with Jewish and philosophic sources which together formed the existing Jewish tradition. Such encounters continually formed a new Jewish synthesis, which in turn became Jewish tradition for later generations, who themselves then had to deal with the renewed encounters of their Judaism with philosophy.

Raphael Jospe, *What is Jewish Philosophy?*
(Ranaana, Israel: The Open University of Israel, 1990), 75.

2

Jewish philosophy, or rather the philosophy of Judaism, is the thinking and rethinking of the fundamental ideas involved in Judaism and the attempt to see them fundamentally, that is, in coherent relation one with another so that they form one intelligent whole.

Leon Roth, *Is There a Jewish Philosophy? Rethinking the Fundamentals*
(Oxford: The Littman Library of Jewish Civilization, 1999), 8.

tions would have been seen as most peculiar and even irrelevant.)

With the fixity of the Torah/Hebrew Bible in the year 90 C.E., under the guidance of Rabbi Yochanan ben Zakkai in Yavneh, and even including the codification of Mishnaic law by Rabbi Judah the Leader in the third century in Roman-controlled Palestine, truly reflective intellectualizing regarding the *meaning* of the biblical text would find its true beginnings in the Alexandrian Egypt of Philo (20 B.C.E.–50 C.E.).

Philo of Alexandria

Little biographical detail is known about Philo's life, other than rather brief comments in his text *Legatio ad Caium* ("Embassy to Gaius"), and an even briefer comment about him in the first-century Jewish historian Josephus's (37–100 C.E.) *Jewish Antiquities*. Philo seems to have been a member of a wealthy and respected Jewish family in Alexandria, well-versed in Greek philosophy, knowledgeable about the Torah/Hebrew Bible (though his knowledge of the text in Hebrew rather than its translation into Greek—known as the Septuagint—has been much debated), and is believed to have visited the temple in Jerusalem at least once. In the years 39–40 C.E. he was chosen, along with his brother

and nephew, by Alexandrian Jewry to journey to Rome and request a meeting with the Emperor Gaius Caligula (12–41 C.E.) in an unsuccessful attempt to resolve the hostilities that had broken out between the largest Jewish community outside of Palestine and Egypt's Greek populace. He apparently then returned to Alexandria and resumed his scholarly activities.

What Philo does not tell us, though he does describe Alexandrian Jewry somewhat in his work *Flaccus*, is how he acquired his knowledge of Greek philosophy. We must assume, therefore, that his family's socioeconomic standing enabled him to acquire both a Judaic education and a Hellenistic one, for in all likelihood, his first language was Greek (and some Latin as well), as would have been the case with Jews of his standing.

His essays, preserved by the fathers of the church rather than the Jewish community, were largely commentaries on the *Pentateuch* (Five Books of Moses), and reflected his energetic attempts to harmonize Judaic and Greek thought, using the allegorical method perfected by the Greek philosophers known to us as Stoics, and giving sophisticated understandings of the work of Aristotle (384–322 B.C.E.), Plato (428/427–348/347 B.C.E.), and the Pythagoreans as well. That he would have read and understood the Torah/Hebrew Bible in

BOX 4.2

Philo, *On the Creation* (De opificio mundi)

Of other lawgivers, some have set forth what they considered to be just and reasonable, in a naked and unadorned manner, while others, investing their ideas with an abundance of amplification, have sought to bewilder the people, by burying the truth under a heap of fabulous inventions. But Moses, rejecting both of these methods, the one as inconsiderable, careless, and unphilosophical, and the other as mendacious and full of trickery, made the beginning of his laws entirely beautiful, and in all respects admirable, neither at once declaring what ought to be done or the contrary, nor (since it was necessary to mould beforehand the dispositions of those who were to use his laws) inventing fables himself or adopting those which had been invented by others.

this way already marks a true departure from an orthodox or literalist reading of those same texts. His surviving writings include *On Abraham, On the Decalogue, On Joseph, On the Life of Moses, On the Creation of the World, On Rewards and Punishments, On the Unchangeableness of God*, and *Questions and Answers on Genesis,* and *Questions and Answers on Exodus.* His more philosophical and apologetic works include *On the Eternity of the World, On the Contemplative Life*, and *Hypothetica* or *Apologia Pro Judaeos* ("Apology/Defense of/for Judaism").

Among the concerns reflected in his writings are the following: intellectual contemplation and reflection, ethics, God, creation, eternality, miracles, the physical universe, and angels. According to *The Internet Encyclopedia of Philosophy*, "he laid the foundations for the development of Christianity in the West and in the East, as we know it today,"[1] which may very well explain the preservation of his texts by Christians rather than Jews. Judaically, however, we may very well attribute to Philo the earliest beginnings of the "midrashic method," that is, searching out the many and varied ways of reading the biblical text both to explicate its meaning, revealing its many layers and levels of sophistication, and to see in it the intellectual equivalent of whatever modes of thought were and are current at any given historical moment.[2]

The Talmudic Commentaries

Subsequent to Philo, the Jewish historical journey is defined by the Roman destruction of the Second Temple (70 C.E.) in Palestine, the last outbreak of hostilities against Rome (135 C.E.), attempts to create a viable religious life both in Palestine and Babylonia, and coming to grips with the emergence of a fast-growing, newer interpretation of a messianist Judaism that will evolve into Christianity and part company with its parent by the fourth century. After the creation of the Mishnah in third-century Palestine, the constructions of its own set of "midrashim," or Talmudic commentaries (Gemara),

will now preoccupy Jewish intellectual leadership over the next several centuries.

Both the Talmuds of Palestine and Babylonia reveal generations of Judaic thinkers and intellectuals concerned not only with their own thoughts but with the pragmatic survivals of their own communities as well. Contained within these encyclopedic texts are explications of laws and the technical processes of doing so, stories, poems, popular myths and legends, biblical commentaries, philosophical and theological musings and contemplations, extensive narratives reflecting the realities of their own communities, insights into the larger communities where they have now come to minority status, and not surprisingly, a somewhat more limited knowledge of that which was intellectually current in the general population. The work of Talmudic compilation, spanning several centuries by the greatest Jewish minds in each generation, would sustain both the thinkers and their communities, and foundationally, set the stage for all subsequent Jewish life.

The structure of both Talmuds is essentially the same: The "heart" of these two Talmuds is the Mishnaic compilation of laws. However, the word *mishnah* in the Hebrew may also mean an individual law, as it does in this particular case (just as the Hebrew word *torah* refers to the entire corpus writ large [Torah] but also to an individual law, writ small as well).[3] Thus, each commentary, which in truth is a rather freewheeling attempt to record the conversations—Gemara—that are understood to have taken place in both the Palestinian and Babylonian rabbinical academies has as its center a given Mishnah. What follows, then, are the comments of several generations of rabbinic thinkers, each building on the previous generations of thinkers, and according their predecessors higher authoritative status. Somewhat unique, however, is the inclusion of both majority *and* minority views, especially if the resolution of a given legal position is that of the majority—but not always.

As one would expect, two main "schools" of thought are evidenced: a more liberal view, usually associated with that of Rabbi Hillel (110 B.C.E.–10 C.E.), and a more conservative view, usually associated with that of Rabbi Shammai (50 B.C.E.–30 C.E.), both towering first-century figures. Those who would follow them would also appear to represent either the liberal or conservative camps, though there is no historical data that would lead us to conclude that such views required, either initially or later, formal identification.

As noted in the previous chapter, the Talmud of Palestine is smaller, its commentaries addressing fewer of the laws contained in the Mishnah than its Babylonian counterpart, and the latter becoming the central organizing text of Jewish life up to and including our own day. This difference in size may in fact be a reflection, though not usually discussed, of the relative unease within Roman Palestine versus the relative calm and tranquility of the Jewish community of Babylonia.[4]

Thus, realistically, from the time of Philo in the first century until approximately the eighth century, with Muslim hegemony in Spain, Jewish intellectual ferment will reside within As Western Christianity comes to dominate its world, Jews will find themselves socially, politically, religiously, and economically seriously disadvantaged, and the quest for safety, security, and survival will become paramount.

The Ninth to the Fourteenth Centuries

To be honest, however, the ghettoized life of Jews was not all dark and foreboding, for even as the Roman Catholic Church flexed its religio-political muscles, church fathers themselves studied Torah/Hebrew Bible, albeit with the aim of proving the "truths" of Christianity, condemning the Jews as a deicide people, and affirming the "falsity" of Judaism. Accounts are found of priests, bishops, arch-bishops, and even cardinals—the "princes" of the Church—studying Hebraic texts and commentaries, Talmudic texts included, with rabbis as they sought to understand their world and God's relationship to it through their Christ.

But it is with the Muslim takeover of Spain in the tenth century that we find Jews seriously engaged in intellectual and philosophical discourse with their Muslim contemporaries, as Islamic thinkers, mathematicians, and astronomers welcome the conversations, and Jewish thinkers expose themselves to an additional world of thought.

While some critics have argued that, during this period and the subsequent *Reconquista* (Spanish, "Reconquest") by the Spaniards in the fifteenth century, Jews served as little more than conduits, conveying the Hebraic texts to Muslims and Hebraic and Muslim texts to Christians, such a historical reading is far too limited in outlook. For Judaic thinkers to have developed the high standards of literacy and knowledge needed to understand Islamic philosophy, translate such texts into Hebrew for their own readerships, and then to present such texts to a reenergized Christian Spain (as well as France, Italy, and Germany) would have required more than one generation of careful and patient interaction and study, and attracting only the finest minds within the Jewish communities of the day. The story of the ibn Tibbon family, fathers and sons, of Provence, France, in the twelfth and thirteenth centuries is the prime example of sophisticated translators whose own knowledge of the materials at hand is reflected in the very lucidity of their translations.

Then, too, during approximately this same period, we find the flowering of the Judaic mystical tradition known as the *Kabbalah* (Hebrew "received tradition"). Though self-perceived and presented as having originated in the second century in Palestine, its expositors never saw either its texts or its commentaries as something divorced from other arenas of Judaic thought. It too, therefore, may be correctly included within the Judaic philosophical/theological tradition.

Representative, but by no means exhaustive, of this period are three seminal thinkers: the poet and philosopher Yehuda Ha-Levi (1075–1141), the grammarian and philosopher Dunash ben Labrat (920–990), and the physician and philosopher Moses ben Maimon, or Maimonides (1135–1204).

Yehuda Ha-Levi

Ha-Levi (Hebrew "the Levite," i.e., tracing his own lineage according to family tradition to the original biblical tribe of Levi), born in Tudela, Spain, was born to a wealthy Jewish family and enjoyed the fruits of his father's success. Educated as a physician, he developed a love for Hebrew poetry and was well acquainted with the poetry of both Muslim and Christian poets but also studied both Greek and Muslim philosophy. As he enmeshed himself more and more in Hebraic learning, however, he also developed a passion to move to the Holy Land of Israel. Legend has it that, after first arriving in Egypt, he rejected offers to remain but went on to Jerusalem, where he was supposedly murdered by a marauding Arab horseman (though there is no evidence to back this up).

His philosophical thought and writing is contained in his best-known work, *Al Kuzari* (Arabic, "Concerning the Khazar [King]"), and reportedly tells of a series of dialogues between the ruler of the Khazars of Central Asia and a philosopher, a Christian, a Muslim, and a Jew as to which was the "true faith," and which he and his people should therefore adopt. (Because both the Christian and the Muslim understand Judaism as their progenitor, the king rejects them and thus accords the Jew the opportunity to share his knowledge in competition with the philosopher.) In the first dialogue, the Jew tells the king that the God of Israel needs no proof of his existence, but that his existence is in fact demonstrated by the miraculous interventions done by him on behalf of the Israelites/Jews (e.g., their very survival both in Egypt and the wilderness, and their reception of divine law

in the wilderness of Sinai). He then goes on to affirm the development of an ethical system, the goal of religious learning, and also that the God of Israel created the world out of nothing (Latin, *creatio ex nihilo*), a truth confirmed by the sacred text of the Jews, the Torah/Hebrew Bible, but not even suggested by the great Greek philosophers. He concludes by addressing such key concepts as immortality, resurrection, and most especially, reward and punishment, all of which are already found in the Torah/Hebrew Bible and which cannot be fully understood apart from God and the people Israel's understanding of him.

In his second dialogue, the Jew draws important distinctions between the categories of divine attributes, though he (and, of course, Ha-Levi) rejects any differentiation between so-called essential attributes of God and other (nonessential) attributes, all being one and the same. (Here Ha-Levi rejects ideas already propounded and given currency by such Jewish thinkers as Sa'adia Gaon [882/892–942 C.E.] and Bachya ibn Pakuda [c. 1250–1340 C.E.].) For Ha-Levi, God's attributes can be classified as *active, relative*, or *negative* as they are evidenced in God's interaction with humanity, especially the Jewish people, and again, demonstrated in the Torah/Hebrew Bible and subsequent Jewish writings. Other topics addressed, all of which were part of Jewish (and Islamic) philosophic discourse in Spain, included the Land of Palestine, prophecy, the sacrificial system, the ancient tabernacle, Israel's spiritual superiority and its rejection of asceticism, and the beauty of the Hebrew language compared to other languages.

In his third dialogue with the king, the Jew refutes the teachings of Karaism (an antirabbinic and more conservative literalist movement of the time) and shows him why the oral tradition (Hebrew, *Torah she-b'al peh*, "Torah which is upon the mouth," that is, the teachings of Judaism as they were first transmitted, in addition to the Torah/Hebrew Bible, and only later written down as concern for their preservation demanded because of historical exigencies) is superior and the very foundation upon which the Talmud is based.

In his fourth dialogue, the Jew (Ha-Levi) explicates the various names of God, understanding them—with the exception of the most holy four-lettered name, or Tetragrammaton (Hebrew, *Yod-Heh-Vav-Heh*)—as indicative of God's *active* attributes, and proceeds to a discussion of the prophets of ancient Israel as possessors of the purest forms of divine knowledge as their prophetic words were, in fact, divine words rendered in human speech. He then demonstrates that both medical and astronomical knowledge as then understood were already contained within the Torah/Hebrew Bible.

His fifth and final dialogue with the king is a thorough refutation of the various philosophical schools then in vogue, rejecting the Greek thought of Aristotle and Plato as inferior to that of the Torah/Hebrew Bible. In so doing, he argues against their understandings of cosmology (the study of the entire universe and humanity's place in it), and their views of the souls of human beings. (Here he opts for free will as opposed to any deterministic perspective and sees no contradictions between that position and God's omniscience and providence.) He does, however, embrace the understanding that every being is composed of both matter and form, and that the human person, possessed of superior intellect over that of the animal, is therefore possessed of a *rational* soul, a spiritual entity that is immortal.

Reading somewhat between the lines of this classic, though ahistorical text of Judaic philosophy, it is not hard to discern Ha-Levi's agenda: a thorough refutation of those philosophical schools of thought that had begun to attract the Jews of Spain, who had less and less knowledge of their own texts (Torah/Hebrew Bible and Babylonian Talmud), religious traditions, and history. In this venture, he allied himself, consciously or not, with Philo: there is no reason whatsoever to go outside Judaism; whatever intellectual streams seem initially attrac-

tive are far inferior to that which is already in one's possession.

Dunash ibn Labrat

Dunash ibn Labrat (920–990), born in Morocco, though far less known today than either Ha-Levi or Maimonides, was an important figure nonetheless. Though remembered primarily as both an outstanding poet of the Hebrew language who introduced Arabic poetic meter into his poems and as a foremost grammarian of the language itself who resolved many of its internal linguistic anomalies, his philosophical work, *Teshuvot al Rav Sa'adiah* (Hebrew, "Responses concerning Rabbi Sa'adiah"), was a serious critique of his own teacher, Sa'adia Gaon (882–942), leading to controversy both during his lifetime and after his death. The philosophical issues that he raised have yet to be resolved. During his stay in Córdoba, Spain, he also attacked Menachem Jacob ibn Saruq, the tenth-century lexicographer and secretary to physician and diplomat Hasdai ibn Shaprut (915–970/990), arguing that ibn Sarug's *Makhberet* (Hebrew, "Notebook") had more than 150 errors, which would cause others to violate both halakha (Hebrew, "Jewish law") and belief. The work of ibn Labrat and the controversies surrounding him are evidence of the Judaic intellectual vigor of the time, where agreement and disagreement, argument and counterargument in the intellectual arena was the order of the day.

Maimonides

No figure, however, is more central to the "Muslim–Spanish period" than the physician, rabbi and communal leader, and philosopher Moses ben Maimon, better known as Maimonides (1135–1204), whose Hebrew acronym "RaMbaM" is universally recognized among religiously devout and textually literate Jews. Born in Córdoba, Spain, he was only ten years old when his family resettled in Fez, Morocco, where he acquired most of his education and later also wrote his highly acclaimed commentary on the Mishnah of Rabbi Judah, the *Perush Ha-Mishnayot*. From there, he lived briefly in the Land of Israel, ultimately settling in Fostat, Egypt, and becoming royal physician to the sultan Saladin (c. 1138–1993). Other legal texts of Maimonides included his *Sefer Hamitzvot* ("Book of the Commandments"), addressing all 613 responsibilities, both positive and negative, as culled from the Torah/Hebrew Bible by the rabbis; and Mishneh Torah ("Second Torah"), also known as the *Sefer Yad Ha-Chazaka* ("Book of the Strong Hand"), a recodification of the laws of the original Mishnah and rivaling it in the brilliance of its organizational

Fig. 4.1 Moses Maimonides (1135–1205 C.E.) Eighteenth-century mezzotint, from an engraving by Marieuay. Maimonides was the preeminent medieval Jewish philosopher and is responsible for the widely acclaimed commentary on the *Mishnah*, the *Mishneh Torah*, and *Guide for the Perplexed*. Photo: © Bettmann/CORBIS

structure and completeness as well as his own comments. In addition, as rabbinic communal leader, he wrote many *Responsa* (letters addressed to both individuals and communities seeking religious guidance); as a physician, he also wrote numerous medical treatises, particularly in the area of pharmacology and the use of medicinal herbs.

Rabbinically, in his Mishnaic commentary, he summarized the essential understandings of Jewish faith in his "thirteen principles," which today remain included in traditional *siddurim* (Hebrew, Jewish Sabbath and festival prayer books) and remain a source of study. Each begins with the phrase "I believe with perfect faith . . ." (see box 4.3).

It is, however, his philosophical masterwork, *Moreh Nevuchim* (Hebrew, "Guide for the [intellectually sophisticated and knowledgeable but] Perplexed") that has endeared him to subsequent generations of philosophers, and whose seminal ideas have found themselves reflected in the works of such Christian thinkers as Albertus Magnus (1193–1280), Thomas Aquinas (1125-1274), and Duns Scotus (1266-1308).

If truth be told, Maimonides was something of a "closet elitist." For him, and others equally learned, the Torah/Hebrew Bible was to be understood on two levels: the first level of its own transparency by which it could be understood by the masses, and the second level of it "truer" meaning, understood by those already learned in philosophy. Since Maimonides was both a neo-Artistotelian and Neoplatonist, but not without disagreement, his *Guide* was an elaborate commentary, explicating and elucidating the biblical text and harmonizing it with the great intellectual ideas of his day. (In this, he too follows the work of Philo.)

At the heart of this reconciliation/harmonization is the central idea that the revealed truths of God are not in conflict with those perceived by the human mind, an idea already propagated by Christian scholastics. In this elaborate and difficult text, he addresses such problems as (1) the limits of linguistically describing God's attributes (to say that God is *good* is to limit our understanding of goodness in relation to God. Better to say that God is "not good" or "beyond good," thus freeing our minds from such limited thinking.), (2) intellectual perfection as coming directly from God and most manifest in his direct recipients, the prophets of the Torah/Hebrew Bible, (3) evil as the absence of the very presence of God (following Aristotle), (4) drawing a critical distinction between true beliefs, which lead ultimately to knowledge of God and the perfect intellect, and "necessary beliefs," which are required for the maintenance of the social order, and (5) the soul's immortality rather than the body's literal physical resurrection and a highly spiritualized afterlife. It was this latter position that led to bitter conflicts during his lifetime (and after, even as late as the sixteenth century), to the point of intellectual attacks on his person by other Jewish thinkers of his day—Abraham ben David (1125–1198) of Posquieres, France; Meir Abulafia (1170–1244); and Moses ben Nachman, Nachmanides (1194–1270) of Catalonia, Spain, among others[5]—and the actual burning of his texts by Dominican friars in the year 1232 (a sad instance of internal Jewish controversy being used and abused by the dominant power structure to instigate an antisemitic behavior in the false guise of "keeping peace and harmony" within a subjugated minority community). He remains to this day, however, one of the major figures if not *the* major figure in Jewish philosophy.

BOX 4.3

The RAMBAM's Thirteen Principles of Jewish Faith

1. I believe with perfect faith that G-d is the Creator and Ruler of all things. He alone has made, does make, and will make all things.
2. I believe with perfect faith that G-d is One. There is no unity that is in any way like His. He alone is our G-d. He was, He is, and He will be.
3. I believe with perfect faith that G-d does not have a body. Physical concepts do not apply to Him. There is nothing whatsoever that resembles Him at all.
4. I believe with perfect faith that G-d is first and last.
5. I believe with perfect faith that it is only proper to pray to G-d. One may not pray to anyone or anything else.
6. I believe with perfect faith that all the words of the prophets are true.
7. I believe with perfect faith that the prophecy of Moses is absolutely true. He was the chief of all prophets, both before and after Him.
8. I believe with perfect faith that the entire Torah that we now have is that which was given to Moses.
9. I believe with perfect faith that this Torah will not be changed, and that there will never be another given by G-d.
10. I believe with perfect faith that G-d knows all of man's deeds and thoughts. It is thus written (Psalm 33:15), "He has molded every heart together, He understands what each one does."
11. I believe with perfect faith that G-d rewards those who keep His commandments, and punishes those who transgress Him.
12. I believe with perfect faith in the coming of the Messiah. How long it takes, I will await His coming every day.
13. I believe with perfect faith that the dead will be brought back to life when G-d wills it to happen.

Union of Orthodox Jewish Congregations,
www.ou.org

The Fourteenth to the Seventeenth Centuries

By the end of the fifteenth century, Jewish intellectual life shifts away from Spain, largely as a result of the exile of Spanish Jewry in 1492. Those who will continue their quest, both within and outside of the Jewish communities of their day, will find more hospitable and conducive environments in Italy and the Netherlands. Figures such as Judah Abravanel (1465–1523), Menassah ben Israel (1603–1657), Uriel de Costa (1585–1640), and, yes, even the controversial and perceived heretical Baruch Spinoza (1632–1677), among numerous and countless others, will advance the cause of Judaic learning and philosophy through their interactions and intersections with their non-Jewish counterparts as Western Europe itself grapples with the search for truth and meaning both inside and outside the Catholic Church–nation-state nexus and its lessening influence as a result of the Protestant Reformation in the sixteenth century.

Abravanel

Born in Lisbon, Portugal, during the time of turmoil in Spain, Abravanel's family was attempting to relocate to Naples, Italy, prior to his birth, but was initially prevented from doing so by order of King Ferdinand (1452–1516) and Queen Isabella (1451–1504) because of their recognized prominence and economic and social standing, a continuing source of bitterness to Abravanel all his life. In 1494, the family again fled, the result of the French invasion of Naples; Abravanel, already a grown man, moved instead to Genoa, Italy. Returning again to Naples in 1501, he remained there until the Spanish takeover in 1506, and then moved to Venice, Italy, where he died in 1523.

Abravanel's most well-known philosophical text is his *Dialoghi d'amore* (Italian, "Dialogues of Love"), and well reflects one of the predominant intellectual interests of his day in the larger circles in which he traveled, but one of far less interest within his own Jewish community. While the text itself is strongly humanistic in outlook and reflects the work of both Aristotle and Plato, the writings of earlier Jewish thinkers such as Solomon ibn Gabirol (1021–1058) and Moses Maimonides (1135–1204) are also in evidence. The text itself, originally supposedly written and published in Italian (though some scholars have argued for a Ladino original in the popular mixed language of the Jewish community of his day, a language somewhat akin to the popular and later Yiddish used by Germanic Jewish communities), and later translated into French, Latin, and Hebrew.

The three "dialogues" that constitute the *Dialoghi* are conversations between the characters Philo, representing appetite, and Sophia, representing wisdom. The resolution of their conversations results in a philosophical understanding of love itself. In the first, Philo and Sophia discuss the distinction between love and desire, Sophia arguing that they are separate and distinct and Philo arguing that they are best understood when they are positively merged together. Sophia then asks if this same argument would hold where God was concerned. Philo responds that love of God, the reason and end of good in the world, is never complete because human beings are limited and incapable of such completeness. From there, the conversation turns to happiness, and both agree that true happiness resides in wisdom (the work of the mind), coming as it does from and through one's love of God himself.

In the second dialogue, both agree that love itself and its quest is the dominant motivation in all life and because of this is universal in conception. In the third and final dialogue, Philo and Sophia address God's love for his creation, drawing a further distinction between the pure intellect and limited soul.

While both philosophical and metaphorical, in concert with other such texts of the time, it may also be possible to "read" *Dialoghi d'amore* perhaps in a more political way: In a world not yet perfected, but capable of so much more, the sad and tragic journey of the Jews of Spain, indeed Abravanel's own life and that of his family, is the very antithesis of love of non-Jew for Jew; reversed, it would usher in a more harmonious and tranquil world where the intellect, common to all humanity, Jew and non-Jew alike, could aspire to its true achievement and unite with God.

Manasseh ben Israel

Much different from Abravanel was Menassah ben Israel (1604–1657). Born in Madeira, Spain, his family moved to the Netherlands when he was six years old. There he acquired much success as a rabbinic leader, author, and printer at a time of great Jewish–non-Jewish interaction. Among his earliest published works was one titled *El Concliator* (Spanish, "Reconciliation"), which was a popular attempt to harmonize the apparent discrepancies of the Torah/Hebrew Bible.

In 1650, an English translation of his text *Hope of Israel* made its way to Oliver Cromwell (1599–1658) in an England already in the grip of a certain messianic fervor. Both politically and economically astute, Cromwell saw in the Jews' return to England, from which they had been expelled in 1290, yet another way to develop British commercial ventures and toward that end invited successful Jewish merchants from Amsterdam and other places to settle there. In 1655, ben Israel accepted Cromwell's invitation and arrived in London that same year. Though not without objection, by the end of that same year Jews were readmitted, and the next year ben Israel published his important text *Vindiciae judaeorum* (Latin, "Vindication of Judaism"). Significantly, it was during his absence from the Netherlands that the Jewish community there excommunicated his student Baruch Spinoza; in all probability an event that never would have taken place had he remained there.

Uriel da Costa

A quite tragic case within that same Jewish community was that of Uriel da Costa (1586–1640). Born in Portugal into a family of *conversos* (Spanish, "secret Jews"), he became a student of Catholic canon law and began to study the "Old Testament," already with the knowledge of his family's Jewish history. In 1617, together with his family, he fled Portugal. He arrived in the Netherlands as a young man and continued his studies. However, he became increasingly disenchanted with both postbiblical Rabbinic Judaism and the leadership of the community. In 1624, he published the book that led to his undoing, *An Examination of the Traditions of the Pharisees*. It became so controversial that he was fined heavily, excommunicated, and his book was publicly burned. Fleeing to an unwelcoming Jewish community in Germany, he returned to Amsterdam in 1633 and sought a rapprochement with the community, and was preliminarily successful. His mind, however, gave him no rest, and he found himself excommunicated a second time, but this time accompanying the public reading of the *cherem* (Hebrew, "ban") was the administering of thirty-nine lashes as prescribed by halakha (Hebrew, "rabbinic law"). His deepening depression led him in 1640 to write and publish *Exemplar Humanae Vitae* (Latin, "Example of a Human Life") and, ultimately, to kill himself with a pistol.

His brief and tragic life has since led to a variety of responses to his role in the development of Jewish thought: as a forerunner to modern biblical criticism; as a proponent of free religious thought divorced from the entanglements of organized communal authority (in his case Jewish); as a heretic dangerous to the Jewish people; as one initially estranged from organized Jewish life who, in his desire to return, sees most sharply the discrepancies between an idealized Judaism and a realized Judaism; and, most obviously, as a precursor to Baruch Spinoza.

Baruch de Spinoza

No figure in all of Judaic thought has been more controversial than Baruch de Spinoza (Latin, Benedictus de Spinoza). Heretic and Pre-Modernist, rationalist and pantheist, Spinoza's role in the development of Western Enlightenment and post-Enlightenment thought cannot be underestimated. Within the Jewish community, as an excommunicant, his influence may be misperceived as negligible. However, with the rise of modernist Judaisms (Reform, Conservative to a lesser degree, Recon-

Fig. 4.2 Baruch de Spinoza (1632–1677 c.e.) Spinoza was a Jewish philosopher whose *Theologico-Political Treatise* defended freedom of thought and tolerance. Statue by Frederic Hexamer (1833–1909). Photo courtesy Creative Commons: http://commons.wikimedia.org/wiki/File:Denhaag_kunstwerk_baruch_de_spinoza.jpg

structionist, and Humanist, both secular and religious), whose appreciation of modern scientific biblical criticism sets them apart from both Hasidic and non-Hasidic Orthodoxy, Spinoza's views continue to occupy an important and slowly recognized place.

Like da Costa, Spinoza was born into the immigrant Portuguese Jewish community of Amsterdam and acquired a thorough Judaic education. Turning to the field of optics and lens grinding to support himself after his father's death, his increasingly rationalistic outlook and conflicts with the organized Jewish communal leadership over the nature of both the Torah/Hebrew Bible and the Talmud and halakha left them with no choice but to excommunicate him in 1656.

It would be, however, far too easy to rend a thoroughly negative critique of the leaders of Amsterdam Jewry in the cases of both da Costa and Spinoza. Having suffered grievously under the Spaniards at the end of the fifteenth century, prior to their relocation to a more hospitable and tolerant Netherlands, this damaged community was still in the midst of its own reconstruction and saw in such thinkers that which would lead their people away from both communal commitment and religious practice and belief. And while there is little to no evidence that such was on the agenda of either thinker, a religious world without constraint, where any and all ideas (no matter how much they depart from time-honored and traditional understandings) was still perceived, even in such a welcoming environment, as antithetical to the very structures that had literally saved Jews during their long and tortuous two-thousand-year migration westward. Safety and security within a ghettoized community—ghettoized in both thought and deed—versus temptations from and increasing exposure to larger worlds of thoughts and ideas remains an unresolved tension among Jews even today.

Such concerns, however, were not part of Spinoza's thinking. As a philosopher, his fame rests on two primary works: his *Theologico-Political Treatise* and his *Ethics*. For Spinoza, everything that exists is of one substance or reality, and is thus governed by one set of principles or rules, the primary one of which is necessity. "God" and "Nature" are merely synonyms for the same infinite reality, and can-

not deviate from these operating principles (i.e., Pantheism). Here, already, one realizes a direct conflict with the Judaic notion of God as Creator and person as presented in the Book of *Bereshith*/Genesis.

BOX 4.4

Spinoza's *Theologico-Political Treatise* from Chapter One

(1:1) Prophecy, or revelation is sure knowledge revealed by God to man. (2) A prophet is one who interprets the revelations of God to those who are unable to attain to sure knowledge of the matters revealed, and therefore can only apprehend them by simple faith.

(1:3) The Hebrew word for prophet is "nawvee'", i.e. speaker or interpreter, but in Scripture its meaning is restricted to interpreter of God, as we may learn from Exodus vii:1, where God says to Moses, "See, I have made thee a god to Pharaoh, and Aaron thy brother shall be thy prophet"; implying that, since in interpreting Moses' words to Pharaoh, Aaron acted the part of a prophet, Moses would be to Pharaoh as a god, or in the attitude of a god.

(1:4) Prophets I will treat of in the next chapter, and at present consider prophecy.

(1:5) Now it is evident, from the definition above given, that prophecy really includes ordinary knowledge; for the knowledge which we acquire by our natural faculties depends on knowledge of God and His eternal laws; but ordinary knowledge is common to all men as men, and rests on foundations which all share, whereas the multitude always strains after rarities and exceptions, and thinks little of the gifts of nature; so that, when prophecy is talked of, ordinary knowledge is not supposed to be included.

(1:6) Nevertheless it has as much right as any other to be called Divine, for God's nature, in so far as we share therein, and God's laws, dictate it to us; nor does it suffer from that to which we give the preeminence, except in so far as the

latter transcends its limits and cannot be accounted for by natural laws taken in themselves. (7) In respect to the certainty it involves, and the source from which it is derived, i.e. God, ordinary knowledge is no whit inferior to prophetic, unless indeed we believe, or rather dream, that the prophets had human bodies but superhuman minds, and therefore that their sensations and consciousness were entirely different from our own.

(1:8) But, although ordinary knowledge is Divine, its professors cannot be called prophets, for they teach what the rest of mankind could perceive and apprehend, not merely by simple faith, but as surely and honourably as themselves.

(1:9) Seeing then that our mind subjectively contains in itself and partakes of the nature of God, and solely from this cause is enabled to form notions explaining natural phenomena and inculcating morality, it follows that we may rightly assert the nature of the human mind (in so far as it is thus conceived) to be a primary cause of Divine revelation.

(1:10) All that we clearly and distinctly understand is dictated to us, as I have just pointed out, by the idea and nature of God; not indeed through words, but in a way far more excellent and agreeing perfectly with the nature of the mind, as all who have enjoyed intellectual certainty will doubtless attest. (11) Here, however, my chief purpose is to speak of matters having reference to Scripture, so these few words on the light of reason will suffice.

His ethical stance, however, was even more radical. "Good" and "evil" are not objectively so, but rather subjectively so according to the dictates of the individual. Here too, ethical behaviors are governed by necessity. This understanding, too, while the very epitome of a strident rationalism, would find itself at odds with normative Judaic thought, which regards the foundation of ethics as coming directly from [the mind and will of] God, not always humanly discernible, but the goal of which is right person, right family, right society in imitation and appreciation of divine behavior.

Thus, one finds in Spinoza, the Jew, one who struggled with the perceived narrowness of the normative thought of his community, his own rationalism, and the larger world of philosophic thought. While yet to be fully reclaimed and reembraced by the Jewish communities and religiously denominational movements that define contemporary Judaic life, as a Pre-Modernist, Spinoza's commitment to the free exercise of one's thinking set the standard not only for modernity as a whole but for Jewish modernity as well.

The Eighteenth and Nineteenth Centuries

The worlds of the eighteenth and nineteenth centuries were heady ones indeed for Enlightenment and post-Enlightenment Western Europe. The marriage between the Roman Catholic Church and the governments that controlled the various nation-states of Europe had been dissolved, and the various Protestantisms that now dotted the landscape had not—and would not—acquire the political power of their predecessor and parent.

For Jews, too, it was a time of cautious optimism and exhilaration. By the end of the seventeenth century, the ghetto doors were opening, Jews were being admitted to universities and professions,

with some rushing headlong into assimilation. The communities themselves, benefiting from this "new Europe," continued to struggle with an internal dilemma born of historical circumstance: Would interaction with the large world sound the death knell of organized Jewish religious life by weakening the bonds of successive generations, or would the structures already in place need to be strengthened by further rigidity in halakha (Jewish law) and with it a concomitant strongly voiced rejection to life outside?

Moses Mendelssohn

Into this world of seemingly polar opposites was born Moses Mendelssohn (1729–1786). The son of a poor *sofer* (a writer of Jewish texts) in the city of Dessau, Germany, his early biblical and Talmudic education was at the hands of the local rabbi, David Fränkel (1704–1762), who introduced his young protégé to Maimonides, kindling within him an intellectual hunger, and when appointed as Chief Rabbi of Berlin, Fränkel took his young student with him. In Berlin, Mendelssohn mastered Latin, French, and English, became tutor and eventual business partner to a wealthy Jewish merchant, and there met the leading German luminary of the day, Gotthold Lessing (1729–1781), with whom he developed a lifelong friendship, which would serve as the inspiration for Lessing's play *Nathan der Weise* (German, "Nathan the Wise"). In 1762, Mendelssohn won an important prize offered by the Berlin Academy, for his work on the relationship between mathematics and metaphysics. That same year, the king granted him status as a *Shutz-Jude* (German, "Protected Jew"), thus permitting him permanent residence in Berlin.

Both philosophically inclined and devoutly religious, Mendelssohn saw no conflict between the two, living as he himself did in the two worlds of the larger society and the Jewish religious community. (Sadly, his own children did not follow in his footsteps: only one remained loyal to Judaism;

identity and adherence to Judaism. (Such debates still go on within organized Jewish life today, not only in Europe but in the United States *and* Israel as well.)

Hermann Cohen

For the next century, Germany itself was the true center of European intellectual life, and Jews fared reasonably well, with appointments to university faculties and serious philosophical works that could only have resulted from serious study of the works of those who dominated the scene, particularly Immanuel Kant (1724–1804). This last giant of the Enlightenment addressed not only issues of moral philosophy but also of religious and political philosophy, and remains to this day one of the seminal thinkers in all of Western philosophy.

Among Kant's leading interpreters and disciples, born four decades after his death, was Hermann Cohen (1842–1918) in Dessau, Germany. Educated at the Jewish Theological Seminary in Breslau, as well as its university, Cohen would later occupy a professorship in philosophy at the prestigious University of Marburg. According to the Jewish Virtual Library, Cohen was "probably the most important Jewish philosopher of the nineteenth century."[6]

As a Kantian, Cohen argued that what truly matters is our understanding of how we view the world and our place in it, whether or not such is truly in accord with the world as it really is. Our behavior, therefore, reflects our understanding of the world, and we human beings, being fundamentally rational and reasonable, must behave accordingly, governed as we must be by a set of universal ethical principles, applicable to all. Ethics, for Cohen, as for Kant, realizes its ideals in the work of social justice for all citizens. What distinguishes us from the animal kingdom, our minds, is our ability to voluntarily *choose* the ethical, framed by our *idea* of God.

The "source" for these ideas, according to Cohen, is Judaism itself, an inherently rational

Fig. 4.3 Moses Mendelssohn (1729–1786) This pioneering Jewish thinker and philosopher argued that one could be a Jew at home and a valued member of the larger society as a whole. Etching by Ludwig Bechstein (1801–1860). Photo courtesy Creative Commons: http://commons.wikimedia .org/wiki/File:Moses_mendelssohn.jpg

the rest converted to Christianity.) In 1767, he published his *Phädon or about the soul's immortality*, and in 1783 published an elegant German translation of *Sefer Shemot*/Book of Exodus, replete with rabbinic as well as his own commentary. That same year he published his most important text, *Jerusalem*, and argued that the nation-state does not have the intellectual right to interfere with the religion of its citizenry, but rather, given the variety of persons and communities, there are many valid expressions of religious truth, the primary evaluation of which must be individual and collective behavior. For his supporters and defenders, Mendelssohn epitomized the "newly modern" Jew, successfully living in two worlds. For his critics and attackers, his was the road to assimilation and the loss of meaningful Jewish religious system wherein religio-ceremonial behavior is interwoven with moral-ethical behavior. Anything religio-ceremonial that advances the drive toward universal social justice in the Judaic religious system is thus to be valued; anything that appears to be in conflict with such noble goals is to be discarded.

Cohen's ideas found a readily welcoming audience in nineteenth-century German Jews, paralleling the equally important world of German Reform Judaism, which saw no discordancy, and which, like Cohen, shared a commitment to an "ethical monotheism" superior to a preoccupation with ritual and ceremonial behaviors it associated with its more traditional (read "Orthodox") brethren, and accepting of Jews into the larger society. In 1919, his wife published his *The Religion of Reason Out of the Sources of Judaism,* his clearest expression of his views but which ultimately contradicted his earlier thinking.

During his later years, an ugly antisemitic wave was beginning to sweep across both Germany and France. Antisemitic orators and politicians had already been elected to the *Reichstag*, Germany's Parliament, before 1900; in France, the trial of French army captain Alfred Dreyfus (1859–1935) called seriously into question the successful integration of Jews into modern Europe. Most dramatically and importantly for Cohen, God was no longer the "idea," which he espoused during his Marburg years, but the purest of beings, whose significance is validated by his relationship with humanity and humanity's quest for holiness, which is its attempt to imitate God. Because Judaism understands humanity as copartner with God in the ongoing work of creation—an unfinished product of God—its superiority to other religious expressions is self-evident. The goal of such work is to bring out the universal messianic kingdom, after first having achieved internal peace and harmony with community. The religious rituals and traditions of Judaism, coupled with the *mitzvot* (Hebrew, "religious and moral obligations"), are thus aids in that objective.

As before, it is the Jew's *choice* to obligate himself or herself to the performance of such responsibilities.

The Twentieth and Twenty-first Centuries

Paralleling the cleavage between those who study and *do* philosophy and those who study and *do* theology, Jewish thinkers more and more turned to secularized and universalized thought, as they increasingly found themselves more and more integrated into western Europe and the United States at the start of the twentieth century. Except for the continental disruptions occasioned by the First World War and the horrific destruction occasioned by the Second World War and the Holocaust/Shoah, this trend continues at this dawn of the twenty-first century. While any listing of such thinkers would by definition be incomplete, the names in table 4.1 (suggested by the [1972] *Encyclopedia Judaica* article on "Philosophy") certainly opens the doors to further investigation[7].

Representative of these "modernists," whose biographies and work can only be described ever so briefly, are the following philosophers, all of whom are still widely read today and have achieved a measure of continuing prominence within contemporary Jewish intellectual circles.

Born in Kassel, Germany, Franz Rosenzweig (1886–1929) rejected the idealism of his dissertation study of philosopher Georg Wilhelm Friedrich Hegel (1770–1831) in favor of a more existential-phenomenological approach and came under the influence of Hermann Cohen. Rosenzweig is best remembered today for his monumental attempt to connect God, humanity, and the world itself with creation, revelation, and redemption in his masterwork *Der Stern der Erlosung* (German, "The Star of Redemption"), the two triangles intersecting to form the Judaic *magen david*, or "star of David."

TABLE 4.1

Notable Twentieth-Century Jewish Philosophers

Adler, Mortimer (1907–2001)	American Aristotelian/Thomistic philosopher
Alexander, Samuel (1859–1938)	British metaphysical philosopher
Arendt, Hannah (1906–1975)	German-American political theorist
Baumgardt, David (1907–1971)	German-American historian of philosophy
Benda, Julien (1867–1956)	French philosopher of rationalist/scientific inquiry
Benjamin, Walter (1895–1942)	German Marxist philosopher
Bergman, Samuel H. (1883–1975)	German-Israeli philosopher of science
Bergson, Henri (1859–1941)	French philosopher of language and mathematics
Black, Max (1909–1988)	British-American analytic philosopher
Bloch, Ernst (1885–1977)	German Marxist philosopher
Boas, George (1891–1980)	American historian of philosophy
Brunschvicg, Léon (1869–1944)	French idealist philosopher
Buber, Martin (1878–1965)	Austrian-Israeli existentialist philosopher
Cassirer, Ernst (1874–1945)	German idealist philosopher
Cohen, Morris R. (1880–1947)	American logical positivist philosopher
Fackenheim, Emil (1916–2003)	German-Canadian philosopher of the Holocaust
Feigl, Herbert (1902–1988)	Austrian-American empirical philosopher
Frank, Semyon (1877–1950)	Russian philosopher of metaphysics
Frank, Philipp (1884–1966)	Austrian-American logical-positivist philosopher
Geiger, Moritz (1880–1937)	German phenomenological philosopher
Goodman, Nelson (1906–1998)	American philosopher of language and aesthetics
Gurwitsch, Aron (1901–1973)	American philosopher of phenomenology
Halevy, Elie (1870–1937)	French philosopher of history
Heinemann, Fritz (1889–1970)	German philosopher of logic
Hook, Sidney (1902–1989)	American philosopher of pragmatism
Husserl, Edmund (1859–1938)	Austrian philosopher of phenomenology
Jankélévitch, Vladimir (1903–1985)	French moral philosopher
Jerusalem, Wilhelm (1854–1923)	Austrian philosopher of education
Joel, Karl (1864–1934)	German philosopher of history and nature
Jonas, Hans (1903–1993)	German-American philosopher religion and history

continues on following page

TABLE 4.1 (CONT.)

Kallen, Horace (1882–1974)	American political philosopher
Klibansky, Raymond (1905–2005)	German-Canadian philosopher of history
Kojéve, Alexander (1902–1968)	Russian-French political philosopher
Koyré, Alexander (1892–1964)	Russian-French philosopher of history and science
Lask, Emil (1875–1915)	German neo-Kantian philosopher
Lévinas, Emmanuel (1906–1995)	French existential and ethical philosopher
Lukacs, Gyorgy (1885–1971)	Hungarian Marxist philosopher
Marcuse, Herbert (1898–1979)	German-American Marxist philosopher
Mauthner, Fritz (1849–1923)	German philosopher of language
Meyerson, Emile (1859–1933)	Polish-French philosopher of science
Nelson, Leonard (1882–1927)	American philosopher of mathematics
Pap, Arthur (1921–1959)	Swiss-American analytic philosopher
Perelman, Chaim (1912–1984)	Polish-Belgian philosopher of law
Pines, Shlomo (1908–1990)	French-Israeli philosopher of Judaism and Islam
Popkin, Robert Henry (1923–2005)	American historian of philosophy
Popper, Karl (1902–1994)	Austrian-British philosopher of science
Reinach, Adolf (1883–1917)	German philosopher of phenomenology and law
Reines, Alvin (1958–2004)	American philosopher of Judaism
Richter, Raoul (1871–1912)	German philosopher of pragmatism and law
Rosenzweig, Franz (1887–1929)	German philosopher of religion and Judaism
Rotenstreich, Nathan (1914–1993)	Israeli philosopher of Judaism
Roth, Leon (1896–1963)	British-Israeli philosopher of Judaism
Scheler, Max (1874–1928)	German philosopher of phenomenology and ethics
Shestov, Lev (1896–1938)	Russian-French philosopher of irrationalism
Simmel, Georg (1858–1918)	German philosopher of sociology
Stein, Edith (1891–1952)	German metaphysical philosopher
Wahl, Jean (1888–1974)	French philosopher of innovation
Waltzer, Richard (1906–1975)	German-British philosopher of Greek philosophy
Weil, Simone (1909–1943)	French philosopher of metaphysics and religion
Weiss, Paul (1901–2002)	American philosopher of metaphysics
White, Morton (b. 1917)	American philosopher of history of ideas
Wittgenstein, Ludwig (1889–1951)	Austrian-British philosopher of language and logic
Wolfson, Harry A. (1887–1974)	American philosopher of Judaism and Jewish thought

His other important and significant contribution was his collaboration with fellow philosopher Martin Buber (1878–1965), whose translation of the Torah/Hebrew Bible into a more musical, cadenced, melodic German—in this case the First Five Books of Moses—was an attempt to allow the reader to "hear" the Hebrew and come closer to the original when he or she could not read the original.

Buber himself was born in Vienna, Austria, into an intensely committed Jewish family, unlike his more assimilated colleague. Though his own philosophic journey ultimately led him to reject the religious practices of his youth, his examinations of religious consciousness, dialogical relationships, and communal responsibilities never severed his connec-

Fig. 4.4 Martin Buber (1878–1965) Known as the "philosopher of dialogue," Buber remains known not only for his studies and popularizations of Hasidic literature and stories, but finding God where human beings truly meet and exist in relationship to each other. Photo: Jewish Chronicle Archive/HIP/Art Resource, N.Y.

tions to Judaism. A lifelong Zionist, he left Germany in 1938, the year before the outbreak of the Second World War, and accepted a professorship at the Hebrew University in Jerusalem. An early advocate of binationalism with the resident Arab population, Buber was vilified by some and revered by others. Best known is his slender volume *Ich und Du* (German, "I and Thou"), in which he posits three significant existential relationships: the "I–It" relationship one has with the inanimate; the "I–thou" relationship one has with one's fellow human beings; and the "I–Thou" relationship one has with God. He also invested much of his energy into retelling the folktales of his Hasidic predecessors and the wonder-working rabbis of Hasidic Judaism in his (1948) two-volume set, *Tales of the Hasidim: I The Early Masters* and *II The Later Masters*. His (1957) volume *Eclipse of God: Studies in the Relation between Religion and Philosophy* was his philosophic response to the tragedy of the Holocaust/Shoah without graphically addressing its horrors, but understanding the events as evidence of God "turning His face away" from humanity for one awful moment.

Born in Breslau, then Germany now Poland, Edith Stein (1891–1942) came from a devout Orthodox Jewish family but later converted to Roman Catholicism and entered the Carmelite Order, taking the name Sister Teresa Benedicta of the Cross. Escaping to the Netherlands in 1942, she was arrested by the Nazis and shipped to Auschwitz-Birkenau death camp, where she, along with her sister, perished. As a philosopher, she was a student of Edmund Husserl (1859–1938), who himself converted to Christianity. After receiving her doctorate, Stein became a member of the philosophy faculty at the University of Freiburg, from which she resigned in 1922 to pursue her Catholicism. As a philosopher, Stein's work addressed phenomenology, empathy, and metaphysics. Two of her more important works were *Knowledge and Faith* and *Finite and Eternal Being: An Attempt to an Ascent to the Meaning of Being.*

Controversy continues to surround Stein even to this day, and has been something of a divisive issue between Jews and Catholics, who do not agree on the reasons for her murder at the hands of the Nazis: as a Jew, regardless of conversion, or as a Catholic in opposition to Nazi tyranny. Her canonization as a saint of the church in 1998 and an attempt by her Carmelite Order to erect a chapel at Auschwitz-Birkenau have only furthered the divide.[8]

Also a victim of the Nazis, though indirectly, was the French philosopher Simone Weil (1909–1943), born in Paris, who taught philosophy at a secondary school for girls. A bit of a recluse and eccentric, this brilliant thinker mastered Greek by age twelve, later learning Sanskrit as well. Her interests ranged from the metaphysical and spiritual to the secular, reading the texts of Judaism, Christianity, Hinduism, and political philosophy as well. In her writings, most of which were published posthumously, she addresses such issues as secularity, obligations and rights, oppression and liberty, human equality, and truth and freedom of thought. In translation, her works include *Gravity and Grace* (1947), *The Need for Roots: Prelude to a Declaration of Duties Toward Mankind* (1949), *Waiting for God* (1950), and *Oppression and Liberty* (1955).

Other Jewish philosophers who suffered under Nazi tyranny to varying degrees were Walter Benjamin (1892–1940), whose work encompassed both literary and cultural critique but who approached his subjects from a Marxist perspective, addressing the relationship between materialism and aesthetics; Herbert Marcuse (1898–1979), who left Germany in 1933 and later taught both philosophy and politics at Columbia University, Harvard and Brandeis Universities, and the University of California, San Diego, whose left-wing Marxist critiques of capitalism garnered him the title "father of new left," a sobriquet he himself rejected; political philosopher Hannah Arendt (1906–1975), student (and lover) of Martin Heidegger (1889–1976), whose own work *Being and Time* remains one of the most important works in modern philosophy, but who never formally renounced his association with the Nazis or condemned their actions.

Arendt, who taught at the University of California, Berkeley, Princeton University, Columbia University, Northwestern University, and the University of Chicago, is best remembered for her controversial coverage and reporting of the Eichmann Trial in Jerusalem in 1962 for the *New Yorker*, and later published in book form in 1963 as *Eichmann in Jerusalem: A Report on the Banality of Evil*, in which she also negatively critiques the Jews of Germany and elsewhere for their failure and for what she regarded as their own complicity in their destruction. Her philosophical oeuvre includes *The Origins of Totalitarianism* (1951), examining Stalinism, Nazism, antisemitism, and imperialism; *The*

Fig. 4.5 Hannah Arendt (1909–1967) Rejecting the label of philosopher, Arendt preferred the sobriquet "political theorist" and is best remembered for her controversial (1964) book *Eichmann in Jerusalem: A Report on the Banality of Evil.* Photo: © Bettmann/CORBIS

BOX 4.5

Hannah Arendt, *Eichmann in Jerusalem*
Postscript

I also can well imagine that an authentic controversy might have arisen over the subtitle of the book; for when I speak of the banality of evil, I do so only on the strictly factual level, pointing to a phenomenon which stared one in the face at the trial. . . . He merely, to put the matter colloquially, never realized what he was doing. It was precisely this lack of imagination which enabled him to sit for months on end facing a German Jew who was conducting the police interrogation, pouring out his heart to the man and explaining again and again how it was that

he reached only the rank of lieutenant colonel in the S.S. and that it had not been his fault that he was not promoted. . . . He was not stupid. It was sheer thoughtlessness—something by no means identical with stupidity—that predisposed him to become one of the greatest criminals of that period.

Hannah Arendt, *Eichmann in Jerusalem: A Report on the Banality of Evil*, rev. and enlarged ed. (New York: Penguin, 1964), 278.

Human Condition (1958); *Between Past and Future* (1961); *On Revolution* (1963); *The Jew as Pariah: Jewish Identity and Politics in the Modern Age*; and *Life of the Mind* (1978).

Philosopher Emmanuel Levinas (1906–1995) was born in Kaunas, Lithuania, and became a citizen of the French Republic in 1930. Captured along with his military unit in 1940, he survived the war in a prisoner-of-war camp in Germany, returning to France at war's end and resuming his teaching career. Primarily a moral philosopher and ethicist, his point of reference and departure was the person of "the Other," who presents himself or herself to you, and who, in so doing, cannot be claimed by you as an object, but as someone who demands responsibility from you by being part of the world that the two of you cohabit. Among his influential works are *Time and the Other* (1948), *Totality and Infinity* (1961), and *Difficult Freedom: Essays on Judaism* (1963 and 1976).

Finally, Emil Fackenheim (1916–2003), born in Halle, Germany, ordained rabbi in Germany, sent to Canada in 1940, and who received his Ph.D. from the University of Toronto, where he later taught philosophy until his retirement, returns

us full circle to one who was both philosopher and theologian and whose work, originally addressing the philosophy of G. W. F. Hegel, came more and more to occupy itself with Jewish concerns. Fackenheim was briefly interned at Sachenhausen concentration camp in Germany (1938–1939), the experience of which deeply embedded itself into his consciousness, especially as the revelations of the Holocaust/Shoah became more and more public. Best known for giving his voice to the "614th Commandment,"[9] not granting Adolf Hitler (1889–1945) and the Nazis any posthumous victories by rejecting one's Judaism, the implications of this "categorical imperative" has—and had for Fackenheim himself—far-reaching implications. A Zionist who later moved to Israel, where he died in 2003, for Fackenheim, the primary obligation of the State of Israel was the safety, security, and survival of the Jewish people, thus muting, in the eyes of many, his own criticisms of its military and governmental policies. He also saw antisemitism and aggressive missionizing and proselytizing toward the Jewish people as attacks against the Jewish people, even more so after the Second World War. Internally, some who supported this position viewed intermarriage itself as akin to antisemitism. More importantly, voices within the Jewish community found little within this position on which to build a *positive* foundation for post-Holocaust/Shoah Jewish survival, and even less to repair, rebuild, or construct a relationship with larger non-Jewish communities to now address Jewish concerns. For those who read his many works (e.g., *God's Presence in History* [1970], *The Jewish Return into History* [1978], *To Mend the World* [1982], *What is Judaism?* [1988], and *The Jewish Bible After the Holocaust* [1991]) and ponder his thoughts, Emil Fackenheim continues to be one of the most important thinkers at the end of the twentieth century and the beginning of the twenty-first century.

Conclusion

Thus, while originally fully ensconced within the world of the Jewish religious tradition and thought, more and more, Jewish philosophy has become the purview of the academy, its thinkers benefiting from the overall secularization of Western thought in general, but more and more removed from the expressed concerns and perceived daily and ongoing struggles of the Jewish people. The same cannot be said of "Jewish theology," to which we turn in the next chapter.

IN REVIEW

We have now introduced ourselves, or been introduced to, more than twenty-five significant Jewish intellectual figures in the world of Jewish philosophy (whew!). Each in his or her own way has made an important contribution to the evolving nature of the world of both Jewish thought and the Jewish religious tradition. As should be obvious, to an important degree, Judaism itself is continually defined and redefined by its "idea content."

KEY TERMS

Al Kuzari	Mishnah
cosmology	Mishneh Torah
covenant	Mitzvah/mitzvot
Dialoghi d'amore	*Moreh Nevuchim*
Enlightenment	oral tradition
Exemplar Humanae Vitae	pantheism
G–d	Protestant Reformation
Gemara	Pythagoreans
Hope of Israel	Stoics
Ich und Du	Talmud
Kabbalah	Tetragrammaton
Karaism	*Theologico-Political Treatise*
midrash	Thirteen Principles
midrashic method	*Vindiciae judaeorum*

Questions for Review, Study, and Discussion

1. Pick one philosopher from each of the five periods noted in this chapter. Read not only his or her biography but a sample of his or her writings as well. Now compare and contrast these thinkers. In what ways are they different? Similar? Do you see an evolution in their thinking? What conclusions do you draw about them and the ideas with which they were concerned?

Suggested Readings

Edmonds, David, and John Eidinow. *Wittgenstein's Poker: The Story of a Ten-Minute Argument Between Two Great Philosophers*. New York: HarperCollins, 2001.

Frank, Daniel. *History of Jewish Philosophy*. New York: Routledge, 1997.

Guttman, Julius. *Philosophies of Judaism: The History of Jewish Philosophy from Biblical Times to Franz Rosenzweig*. New York: Holt, Rinehart and Winston, 1964.

Kraemer, Joel L. *Maimonides: The Life and World of One of Civilization's Greatest Minds*. New York: Doubleday, 2008.

Nadler, Steven. *Spinoza: A Life*. New York: Cambridge University Press, 1999.

Roth, Leon. *Is There a Jewish Philosophy? Rethinking Fundamentals*. Oxford: Littman Library of Jewish Civilization, 1999.

Seidler, Victor J. *Jewish Philosophy and Western Culture: A Modern Introduction*. New York: I. B. Tauris, 2007.

Steward, Matthew. *The Courtier and the Heretic: Leibniz, Spinoza, and the Fate of God in the Modern World*. New York: W. W. Norton, 2006.

CHAPTER 5

Cycles *of* BELIEF

OVERVIEW

As with the previous chapter, we will introduce ourselves to some of the leading intellectual luminaries of the Jewish religious tradition, this time "theologians" instead of philosophers. While the distinction is problematic as far as Jews are concerned both historically and contemporarily, for our introductory purposes, it does make sense as we continue to journey forward in discovering these important foundations of Judaism and the Jewish people.

Introduction

The caveat of chapter 4 remains: up until the so-called modern era, those Judaic thinkers who addressed themselves to Jewish concerns did not draw a distinction between Judaic philosophy and Judaic theology; indeed, they did not view themselves as either philosophers *or* theologians but rather as Jews concerned about their Judaism and their people, how best to communicate the idea-content of that which they regarded as central to their own existence and identity, and where appropriate, how best to incorporate into their Judaism the ideas of the larger society with which they increasingly found themselves interacting. As regards the latter, addressing larger issues through the prism of a Judaic lens takes us all the way back to Philo of Alexandria (Philo Judeaus, 20 B.C.E.– 50 C.E.), and expresses a similar concern: that the ways and the ideas of the outside world may prove more seductively appealing—the ongoing tension between assimilation (inside out) and incorporation (outside in)—leading to a diminishing of numbers of Jews and thereby a weakening of Judaism itself.

With the broadest of brushstrokes, therefore, this chapter is divided into four theological epochs: (1) biblical, (2) rabbinic, (3) medieval, and (4) modern. While scholars may continue to debate whether or not the persons involved were philosophers or theologians, and whether the ideas themselves better fit the category of philosophy or theology, this simple division allows us to revisit some of the material of chapter 4, introduce additional material, and refocus our lens on Judaism itself, thereby expanding our understanding of its vitality and complexity.

Biblical Theology

The Torah/Hebrew Bible is *not* a book of theology as such, concerned with such classically identified Christian theological conundrums as the nature and essence of God, proofs for divine existence, and the like. Indeed, the very word *theology* is a Greek construct of two words, *theos* ("God") and *logos* ("word" or "doctrine"), and therefore equates to knowledge of the divine. Its Hebrew equivalent, *da'at Elohim* ("knowledge of God") is a modern invention, enabling Hebraically knowledgeable Jews and Hebraically knowledgeable Christians to enter into sustained dialogue as they examine the classic texts of Judaism (Torah/Hebrew Bible, Mishnah, Talmuds, Midrash, Kabbalah, Codes, *Responsa*, the foci of chapter 3), either together or separately.

Because the Torah/Hebrew Bible is not a book of theology as the term is both historically and pres-

ently understood, though "the God of Israel" (and all humankind) is very much the central actor in the drama, we suggest, therefore, an affirmation that precedes the text and that has been the very cement that has held the Jews together since their earliest beginnings up to and including the present moment: *Berishona Elohim* (changing the first word and including the third word with which *Bereshith*/ Genesis begins): "In the beginning God." Period. From this acknowledgment, ultimately, flows all of the understandings of God as the Torah/Hebrew Bible portrays him (not her!), and includes his relationship with all humankind, but most especially with the Hebrews/Israelites/Jews, as represented by the Sinaitic *berith*/covenant.

And yet, if indeed this God is the center of this book—which Jews have long understood to be *his* book—then it *is* a theological tract that redefines our Western notions and refocuses our energies not on God but on our relationship with God as the proper arena for thought and discussion, after first gleaning from the text itself its own understandings of the Incomparable One, who cannot be limited by human language or discernment.

At the outset, it should be noted that for an accurate assessment of biblical humanity's understanding, it remains appropriate contextually to use the masculine to describe God and his attributes. Modern readings and the use of gender-neutral language, the stirrings of which already appear in the rabbinic era, while appropriate for us today, tend to distort the past, leading to a false perception of liberalism among the ancients, even while acknowledging that such historic male language may have had a more inclusive meaning than heretofore realized.

The Biblical God

What then do we know about this God? Initially, the ancient Hebrews/Israelites perceived him as the Supreme One among others who existed (e.g., *Shemot*/Exodus 15: "Who is like You *among the gods*, Adonai?"), but over time, came to the realization that, in truth, he was the Only One, and the perceptions of those ancient peoples with whom ancient Israel came into contact were not only false, but that those who espoused such ideas were worthy of their enmity and worse.

Then too, his very singularity (i.e., his "oneness") could not be divorced from his creativity. He created this world we inhabit, and while reference is made periodically throughout the Torah/Hebrew Bible to the *Adonai tsava'ot* (Hebrew, "heavenly hosts," the "divine courtiers"), who may have been consulted, the initial acts of creation were his alone. In his genius, however, he created an unfinished or incomplete product, and graciously permitted humanity to copartner (with a decidedly small *p*) in such important work. (Indeed, Adam and Eve's role in *Gan Eden*/the Garden of Eden in *Bereshith*/Genesis, including their expulsion—and subse-

quent generations as well, according to the rabbis—remains testimony to that unequal partnership.)

This *berith*/covenant with the Hebrews/Israelites is, therefore, a *second* attempt to address and reflect yet an additional attribute of this God: his predominant concern with morals and ethics. The failure of humanity to do so in the story of Noah (*Bereshith*/Genesis 5–9) seemingly necessitates, on his part, trying again to create humanity, but also entering into a contractual relationship with a people willing to accept the offer, wavering between fulfilling its demands and abusing them, but continuing to see history as the unfolding of a divine plan in which they themselves play a central role.

A Chosen People

Having *chosen* the Hebrews/Israelites as his own people, this God now demands of them an inner

Fig. 5.1 The Gathering of Manna Moses instructs the Israelites to take only what can be consumed that day. Peter Paul Rubens (1577–1640). Photo: Réunion des Musées Nationaux/Art Resource, N.Y.

and an outer responsibility, neither of which can be separated from the other. Indeed, the Hebrew word *qiddusha,* rendered customarily into English as "holiness," is better translated as "separated" or "set apart," aspects of which, in later rabbinic tradition, will understandably be translated as "holy," with, however, one important insight.

Vayyikra/Leviticus 19:2 reads in the Hebrew *qedoshim tihyu ki qadosh ani Adonai Elohechem,* and is usually translated as "You *shall* be holy for I, the Lord your God, am Holy." A better translation of this foundational verse for the entire Judaic ethical system would be "You *must* be holy, for I, the Lord your God am Holy!" As holiness is defined not only in this nineteenth chapter but also in the ones preceding and succeeding it, holiness is ethical holiness, mandated in community, and the Hebrews/Israelites have no "wiggle room" whatsoever to escape from this commitment. To be God's own is to be ethically separate (and, yes, at times read "superior") from the surrounding nations. Because the God to whom the Hebrews/Israelites now commit themselves demands such high ethical strivings, the children of Israel must function always with that goal in mind. Hence, its inner responsibility is to be, in terms of a recent recruitment slogan for the United States military, "all you can be."

By extension, externally, the Hebrews/Israelites are to serve as a "light to the nations" (*Yesha'yahu*/ Isaiah 51:4), giving concrete evidence of the reality of the one God of Israel to those with whom the Hebrews/Israelites come into contact, and by their ethical and ritual practice, inviting others into the community of the "separated ones."

This notion of being *chosen* by God to be his own carries with it heavy responsibilities, and while there always remains the possibility of misreading its stated purpose and elevating either individual or collective self-importance, there is little if any biblical textual evidence that such misguided arrogance was part of the pronouncement. Tragically, however, throughout the Jews' historic journey, their enemies have, on numerous occasions, thrown back into the face of the Jewish people the false charge that being the "chosen people" made them see themselves as arrogantly superior to all others, and thus fully worthy of whatever condemnations, up to and including physical violence, were to come their way.

A more modern reading of "chosen people," all the more so in the aftermath of the Holocaust/ Shoah, but one equally consistent with its ancient meanings, would be that today the Jewish people are the "*choosing* people of God," affirming anew, in the aftermath of the greatest tragedy it has ever experienced, its commitment to its God, its ritual-ceremonial and moral-ethical value systems, and the larger world of which it is increasingly a part. All this despite all the nihilistic reasons for rejecting its God, no longer participating in its historical religious behaviors, surrendering its identity, behaving as badly as many societies and nation-states do today, and merging into these larger populations.

An Eternal God

Continuing commitment to God, however, will not allow the Jewish people to surrender, but to persevere despite the odds, and continue to make its contributions to the civilizing and betterment of humanity. And there is yet another foundational aspect of this biblical theological *weltanschauung* (world-perspective).

The God to whom the Jews have remained committed since their founding is, definitively, an eternal God, having neither birth/beginning nor death/ending. Therefore, to be in covenant with this God is to share, in some small part, in that eternality, not as individuals or as generations, but as a people destined to endure as long as planet earth itself endures. Such is the true essence of Judaic faith: An eternal God covenants with a finite community and in so doing shares something of his eternality with them, despite all the vagaries of history and a journey filled with tragedy. As God has endured, so too will this people endure, not always in the same places, not always in the same numbers, but it will endure forever.

A Transcendent and Immanent God

Last, the God of the Torah/Hebrew Bible is both transcendent (in the "highest of heavens") and immanent (in close enough contact to hear the groanings and moanings of an enslaved people in Egypt who prays for succor and release). Indeed, a midrashic text once suggested that when the children of Israel went into slavery, the God of Israel *went* with them, but that when the children of Israel came out of slavery, that same God *led* them. The God of the Torah/Hebrew Bible has been described by the rabbis, based on their readings of many texts, as a *Shomea tefilla*/a hearer of prayer.

Thus, these theological ideas about God and Israel, as reflected and refracted through the texts of the Torah/Hebrew Bible become, in the aftermath of the Roman destruction of the Second Temple in the year 70 C.E., the foundation on which the rabbis will build their system of Judaic religion in the generations to come.

Rabbinic Theology

The "Pharisaic revolution," which preceded the rabbinic period, was in truth a *democratization* of the process of Judaic religion and an early precursor of rabbinic Judaism in that prayer, textual study, and ethical behavior were the province of anyone of sufficient intellectual caliber and ethical integrity, who could then be welcomed into its ranks. It did not see itself as antithetical to the priestly system of the Temple but an expansion of its mission; it did, however, understand itself in opposition to the conservative Sadducees, whose resistance to change and expansion from the priestly traditions of the Temple was their own attempt to preserve an hereditary

leadership and none other. With the destruction of the temple, however, the surviving Sadducees and the priests were displaced and unemployed (as they had initially been with the destruction of the First Temple by the Babylonians in the year 586 B.C.E.). To their credit, the Pharisees and their rabbinic successors must merit the reward of "saviors," not only of Judaism but of the Jewish people as well.[1]

Not having a temple, the rabbis replaced their center with that of intense study of the Torah/Hebrew Bible as the means by which connection to God was best achieved, equating its study with prayer, and mining its riches in the construction of their ritual-ceremonial and moral-ethical value systems. The God of the ancients remained their God;

Fig. 5.2 A Rabbi After the demise of the priesthood with the destruction of the Temple by the Romans in 70 C.E., rabbis came to the fore as the religious leadership of the Jewish people and remain so even today as both deciders and authors of religious decisions. Rembrandt Harmensz van Rijn (1606–1669). Photo: Erich Lessing / Art Resource, N.Y.

and the theological understandings of the ancients remained their understandings as well. The one God of Israel is a Creator God who *chose* Israel as his own by entering into the *berith*/covenant with them, demanding of them the highest ethical behavior, and remains a God who is both near and far, transcendent and immanent, but who is ultimately continuously active in the affairs of his creation.

Concerned as the rabbis were with such central ideas and their elaboration, pragmatic concerns were the order of the day. As postbiblical Judaism develops in Roman Palestine and in Babylonia, and the westward migration of Jews begins in earnest, the development of a religio-ethical system becomes vitally necessary to the very physical, moral, and spiritual survival of the people. Thus, if one were to follow a more Christianized approach to Judaic theological thought, and look for—and hope for—a more systematic exposition of its ideas, one would come up short. Throughout postbiblical Judaic literature, primarily the two Talmuds of Palestine and Babylonia, and the corollary midrashic literature, ideas such as the nature and essence of God, reward and punishment, good and evil, miracles, sin and repentance, immortality and eternality, God's interactivity, and angels *are* discussed, but not in any systematic way whatsoever. And while individual rabbis themselves may have addressed many of these topics, their expositions cannot be culled out of these larger texts as stand-alone representatives of either rabbinic or Judaic thought, but must be viewed as part and parcel of a more freewheeling conversation of ideas embedded within a mind-set directed toward Jewish doing and not just Jewish thinking. [2]

Medieval Theology

Bridging the gap somewhat, as the rabbis summarize the past theologically and expanding on it, they find themselves being attracted to and interacting

with both philosophical and theological currents in larger society (e.g., Aristotelianism and neo-Aristotelianism; Platonism and Neoplatonism). Along these lines, the justly famous "Thirteen Principles of Faith" of Maimonides (1135–1204) remains the fullest expression of Judaic theological thinking to date. It should be noted, however, that he was not alone in his conceptualizations of what was, essentially, a Judaic theological enterprise, and we are on relatively safe grounds to regard this period as the finest flowering of Judaic theological and philosophical thought.

Starting with the Torah/Hebrew Bible itself, however, the *Aseret Hadibrot* ("Ten Essences" or "Ten Commandments") of both *Shemot*/Exodus (see Box 3.4, page 57) and *Devarim*/Deuteronomy are, in their own way, a theological summary of the essence of Hebraic/Israelite religious thought, thus enabling later thinkers to expand on them. Theologically, we may therefore say the following of these texts: God is (1) interactive, (2) exclusive, (3) incorporeal, (4) jealous, (5) punishing, (6) loving, (7) moral and ethical, and (8) creative. Yet, while seemingly enumerating these attributes of God, the *Aseret Hadibrot* says nothing of God's essence or nature, but says everything about how Hebrews/ Israelites are to respond to God in their relationship with him based on these attributes, with the added responsibility of Sabbath observance (and that, perhaps, symbolic of the whole holiday/holy day/festival/fast day tradition as it will evolve).

Philo himself was perhaps the first to fully articulate the essential theological attributes of Judaism based on his (Greek) reading of the Torah/Hebrew Bible. For him, (1) God is and rules, (2) God is one, (3) the world was created, (4) creation is one, and (5) God's providence rules creation.

Several centuries later, Sa'adiah Gaon (882–942) in Babylonia will expand them to eight: (1) The world is created, (2) God is one and incorporeal, (3) belief in revelation, (4) man is called to righteousness, (5) belief in reward and punishment, (6) the soul is pure, (7) belief in the resurrection of the dead, and (8) the messiah will come; reward, punishment, and the final judgment will take place.

Spanish rabbi Abraham ibn Daud (1110–1180) then reduced them to six: (1) the existence of God, (2) God's unity, (3) God's spirituality (incorporeality), (4) God's other attributes, (5) God's power, and (6) God's providence. Tunisian rabbi Hananel ben Hushiel (990–1053) will reduce them, again, this time to four: (1) belief in God, (2) belief in prophecy, (3) belief in a future, and (4) belief in the coming of the (very human, charismatic, and devout) messiah. But it will be Maimonides' declaration of the *Shelosha-Asar Ikarim* (Hebrew, "Thirteen Fundamental Principles") in his commentary on the Mishnah, based on the 613 *mitzvot*/commandments as the rabbis found them in the Torah/Hebrew Bible which holds the place of honor in the Judaic religious tradition and is continuously reprinted in its *siddurim* (Hebrew, Jewish Sabbath and festival prayer books), and each of which begins with the religious affirmation "I believe with perfect faith . . ." (see Box 4.3, page 91).

Other Judaic theological thinkers who flourished during this same period include such figures as the ethicist Bahya ben Joseph Pakuda (eleventh century), Judah Halevi (1175–1141), Levi ben Gershom (Gersonides, 1288–1344), Hasdai Crescas (1340–1411), Joseph Albo (1380–1444), Isaac ben Moses Arama (1420–1494), Isaac Abravanel (1437–1508), Joseph ben Hayyim Jabez (fifteenth–sixteenth centuries), and Moses ben Joseph di Tani (1505–1585). During this same rabbinic/medieval period, Judaic kabbalistic mystical literature flourished as well and was seen and understood as part and parcel of the entire intellectual enterprise of Jewry.

Modern Theology

As has already been suggested, the so-called modern period in Jewish history begins only in 1791, as the Jews of France become the first community on the European continent to be granted the right to vote, in the context of the French Revolution (1789–1799). Additionally, Jews will benefit as well from the growing secularization achieved by the eighteenth-century Enlightenment. As ghetto walls come tumbling down, Jews are admitted to universities and increasingly enter more fully into both commercial and political life within their host countries.

At the outset, this period could also be characterized as the "age of Jewish denominationalism." As Jews struggle to a greater or lesser degree with their newfound freedoms, four so-called movements arise (the term *denominations*, however, reflects more a Christian than a Jewish perspective): (1) Orthodoxy, (2) Hasidism, (3) Reform Judaism, and (4) Conservative Judaism.

Orthodoxy

Modern Orthodox Judaism, the most fundamentalist of these various movements, strives mightily to preserve the ways of the past and understands the Torah/Hebrew Bible as the text of God transmitted at Sinai. Legal materials dominate, and rabbinic Talmudic interpreters (rather than innovators or creators) function as authoritative spokes*men*, whose own predecessors are accorded higher status. This movement begins, in truth, with the codification of Judaic legal materials abstracted from the Talmud by Rabbi Joseph Karo (1488–1575) in the sixteenth century.[3] Prior to his work, we could best characterize the Judaisms practiced in various locales as "traditional," rather than fully Orthodox. That is to say, while the outlines of Jewish life were amazingly similar in both the practice of holidays, holy days, festivals, fast days, and life-cycle celebrations (e.g., birth, coming of age, engagement/marriage/divorce, and death), there remained wide latitudes of difference based on geographical, cultural, and historical circumstances. Such variation is perhaps best reflected in the various prayer rites of Sabbath worship, the outline or order of worship already standardized for the most part. Such examples include *Minhag* (Hebrew, "custom" or "rite") *Polin* (Poland), *Minhag Russit* (Russia), *Minhag Ashkenaz* (Ashkenazic), and *Minhag Sepharad* (Sephardic).

Hasidism

Traditional religious Judaism, quite obviously, has had the longest history associated with it. However, over time, others saw those in positions of religious authority and the Judaisms they espoused as increasingly sterile, devoid of emotional connection, intellectually too rarified for those whose concerns with daily existence did not allow sustained periods of intense study, and "out of touch" with the newest realities of European Jewish life. Two of the three Jewish movements—Hasidism and Reform Judaism—arose as responses to these per-

ceived critiques of traditional Judaism. Conservative Judaism, or Positive-Historical Judaism, as it labeled itself, arose in response to the perceived excesses of Reform Judaism by those who rethought their own traditional Judaism but were unwilling to align themselves with what they saw as a radicalization of traditional Judaism.

Conservative Judaism

Commensurate with the rise of the liberalizing and radicalizing Reform Judaism in Germany in the early nineteenth century, opposition arose. Its chief spokesman, Rabbi Samuel Raphael Hirsch (1808–1888), articulated what would later become known as "neo-Orthodoxy," also called *Torah im Derekh Eretz* (Hebrew, "Torah with civil discourse"). Hirsch saw no conflict between a strict adherence to

BOX 5.1

Samuel Raphael Hirsch, "Religion Allied to Progress"

"Religion allied to progress": [the leaders of Reform have] with undaunted courage embroidered [this slogan] in scintillating colours on to the banner of our present-day religious struggles, that the educated "progressive" sons and daughters of the new age might rally to this new flag of the prophet and advance with it unhindered. How leaderless was this new congregation of prophets before this new messenger with this new message of salvation appeared among them! Since the beginning of the century the ancient religion had been to them—ancient; it no longer fitted into the society of the sons and daughters of the new age with their frock coats and evening dresses. In club and fraternity, at the ball and supper party, at concerts and in salons—everywhere the old Judaism was in the way and seemed so completely out of place. And even in the counting-house and in the office, in the courtroom and at the easel, on board ship and in the train—throughout the stream-driven

lightning activity of the new age the old Judaism acted as a brake on the hurrying mark of progress. Above all it seemed to be the only obstacle in the race for emancipation. No wonder then that without hesitation they shook off the old obstructive religion and hurried into the arms of "progress." And in the political market-place where emancipation was to be purchased, the modern sons of Judah could be seen in every corner offering to exchange the old Judaism for something else, since in any case it had lost all its value for their own use. For many a decade modern Jewry thus soared aloft like dust on the wigs of a butterfly and tasted freedom in the unwonted airy heights; and yet they felt a pain in their hearts where the absence of religion left a void, and at the end they were ashamed while enjoying the brilliance of modern life to be walking the earth without religion; they felt restless and miserable.

the Jewish religious tradition through halakha (Jewish law) and interacting with larger societal issues, but always opted for "the Jewish way" to resolve any conflicts or difficulties. Together with Rabbi Israel Azriel (or Ezriel) Hildesheimer (1820–1899), also of Germany, and the father of so-called modern orthodoxy, these giants of Judaism stood in dramatic opposition to the liberalizations of Reform Judaism but did not cut themselves off from their own larger society. Even today, interestingly enough, their combined legacies remain much debated and discussed within Orthodox Jewish circles, but far less so within other Judaic movements.

Reform Judaism

Reform or Liberal Judaism (or Progressive Judaism, as it is known on the European continent), also a modernist German Judaic religious movement, had its earliest beginnings in 1810 in Sesson on the grounds of a school for Jewish and Christian children built by the Jewish philanthropist and layperson Israel Jacobson (1768–1828). There, he built a beautiful synagogue building, adding organ music (admittedly a Reformist orientation since no instrumental music had been associated with Jewish worship since the destruction of the Second Temple in 70 c.e.), and singing hymns and praying in both German and Hebrew.

Leading Modern Jewish Intellectuals in the Pre-Holocaust Period

As Jews began combining their opportunities for university education with Jewish education, men of intellect were attracted to both, figures such as Abraham Geiger (1810–1874), and the more extreme Samuel Holdheim (1806–1860), among others. Their own modernist views were further helped by the pioneering work of Leopold Zunz

Fig. 5.3 Service at Reform synagogue This shows a service at a Reform (liberal, progressive) synagogue. Note especially the wearing of both tallit (prayer shawl) and kippah (head covering), not historically associated with this liberal Jewish religious movement. Photo courtesy Creative Commons: http://commons. wikimedia.org/wiki/ File:ReformJewish Service.jpg

(1794–1886), the father of academic critical study of Judaic literature (German, *Wissenschaft des Judentums*). With such thinking came a reforming of the lengthier traditional Jewish worship services, especially on the Sabbaths and holy days, including, again, the use of instrumental music, movement away from the desire to return to the homeland (i.e., Zionism), and a perception of Jews as a religious community rather than a nation-state in exile. Other reforms included rejection of a sought-for messiah, limited commitment to, rather than a full rejection of, the dietary system, and a reconceptualization of the "oral tradition" (as manifested in Talmudic/rabbinic Judaism) as a humanly crafted and evolving product rather than a further embodiment of divine instructions. By the middle of the nineteenth century, Reform congregations could be found in the major cities of Germany, though Reform Judaism would have to await Bohemian rabbi Isaac Mayer Wise's (1819–1900) journey to the United States to achieve its fullest flowering.

Its rapid growth, even among those with a more liberal rather than "orthodox" orientation, did not sit well with all. In the 1840s and 1850s, a backlash against such Reformist tendencies was already being articulated in the work of Rabbi Zecharias Frankel (1801–1875), head of the Jewish Theological Seminary of Breslau. A proponent of solid intellectual research, Frankel saw both halakha (Jewish law) and Judaism itself as dynamic changeable entities in response to changing circumstances, but always thoroughly grounded in the past and in the *legal* approach to change (itself by definition "conservative"). It was Frankel who termed his approach to Judaism "Positive-Historical," though like Reform Judaism, it would have to await the arrival in America of British Cambridge University scholar and rabbi Solomon Schechter (1847–1915)—who would take over the Jewish Theological Seminary of America in New York (established in 1886 by rabbis Sabato Morais [1823–1897] and Henry Pereira Mendes [1852–1937]) after its break with American Orthodox Judaism—for it to achieve its fullest potential.

A quite different route, however, was that taken in eastern Europe by what has come to be called *Hasidic* Judaism (from the Hebrew term *hasid*, "pietist," etymologically derived from the word *chesed*, or "loving-kindness"). More than any other single figure, its founder was Polish/Russian/Galician/Ukrainian Rabbi Israel ben Eliezer (1698–1760), known to his followers and later generations as the *Ba'al Shem Tov* (Hebrew, either "master of the good name" [of God], or "good master of the name" [of God]).[4]

The *Besht*'s (the acronym derived from *Ba'al Shem Tov*) orthodoxy was not at issue. His concern was what he perceived to be the "joylessness" of traditional Jewish observance and practice, and that the primary emphasis on Talmudic study had replaced spiritual concerns and a focus on God himself. His love for God and the people themselves, his love for vocal music, often without words, as a worshipful expression of both his love for God and the Jewish people, his use of stories (i.e., parables) and sayings open to multiple interpretations even by the unlettered, and a decidedly kabbalistic or mystical component to his understanding attracted others to his banner. From there, like-minded communities (Hasidic "courts" led by Hasidic *rebbes* [Yiddish for "rabbis"]) were established throughout much of eastern Europe, much to the chagrin and displeasure of other Orthodox non-Hasidic rabbis, the so-called *Misnagdim* (Hebrew, "opponents"), chief among whom was the leader of Lithuanian Jews, the *Vilna Gaon*, Rabbi Elijah ben Solomon Zalman (1720–1797). In 1777, as leader of his and surrounding communities, and with the support of the overwhelming majority of Polish rabbis, the Vilna Gaon published a *cherem* (Hebrew "ban of excommunication") against the *Hasidim* (Hebrew plural, "followers of Hasidism"), accusing them of heresy. He was to follow this up four years later, in 1781, by excommunicating its acknowledged leader, Rabbi Shneur Zalman (no relation) of Liadi, Poland (1745–1812), and founder of *Chabad* Hasidism (Hebrew, ChaBaD = *chochma* ["wisdom"], *bina*

BOX 5.2

From "Thirty-six Aphorisms" of the Baal Shem Tov

1. Everything is by Divine Providence. If a leaf is turned over by a breeze, it is only because this has been specifically ordained by G-d to serve a particular function within the purpose of creation.

2. Every single thing that a person sees or hears is an instruction to him in his conduct in the service of G-d.

3. "Love your fellow as yourself" (Lev. 19:18) is an interpretation of and commentary on "Love the L-rd, your G-d" (Deut. 6:5). He who loves a fellow Jew loves G-d because the Jew has within himself a "part of G-d Above" (Job 31:2). When one loves a fellow Jew, he loves the Jew's inner essence, and thereby loves G-d.

4. To love a fellow Jew is to love G-d. For it is written, "you are the children of G-d" (Deut. 14:1); when one loves the father, one loves the children.

5. G-d's love of each and every Jew is infinitely greater than the love of elderly parents to their only child born to them in their later years.

6. A sign emitted because of a fellow's pain breaks all the impenetrable barriers of the heavenly "accusers." And when a person rejoices in the joy of his fellow and blesses him, it is as dear to G-d and accepted by Him as the prayers of Rabbi Yishmael the High Priest in the Holy of Holies.

7. The love of G-d for every Jew extended not only to the Jew's soul but also to his body. G-d loves all Jews without distinction; the greatest Torah genius and scholar and the most simple Jew are loved equally by G-d.

from www.chabad.org

(N.B.: The use of hyphenation "G-d" and "L-rd" is the devout Jewish person's way of signifying that the holiness of the divine presence of God is far beyond written expression which is, ultimately, limiting.)

["understanding"], *da'at* ["knowledge']). Ultimately, however, the Vilna Gaon and other opponents of Hasidism were unable to stop either the spread and the splintering of this form of Orthodox Judaism, which continues to enjoy success today in the United States, Israel, Europe, the former Soviet Union, Australia, and South America.[5]

Jewish Philosophy and Theology in the Post-Holocaust Period

As the secularization of western Europe continued, and with it the United States, Judaic thought developed its own cleavage as well: philosophy, including Judaic philosophy, became more and more relegated to the academy, and theology became more and more the province of the synagogue and religious education. Additionally, increasing interaction with the larger—in this case Christian—community caused Jewish religionists to again take seriously such theological issues as the existence and essence of God; good and evil; reward and punishment; sin, forgiveness, and redemption; and similar issues but, more and more this time, in conversation with their Christian counterparts.

The horrors of the Holocaust/Shoah of 1933–1945 and the birth of the Third Jewish Commonwealth, the State of Israel, on May 14, 1948, quickened anew the work of theology as Jewish thinkers found themselves grappling most profoundly with theological issues and resolutions in attempting to come to grips with events of such enormous historical importance. With regard to the former, questions such as the relationship of God (activity, inactivity, silence, indifference) to the murderous destruction of almost six million Jewish men, women, and children; the meaning of the *berith*/covenant with God in its aftermath; how to reconstruct post-Holocaust/Shoah religious life in terms of its celebratory aspects; understandings of what it means to be human; Christianity's role in providing foundational thought undergirding National Socialism; and the role of Jews and Judaism in the post-1945 world now became the province of Judaic (and Christian) theological thought. With regard to the latter, a wide variety of theologians from all the Judaic theological traditions have addressed questions such as the role and responsibility of the reborn *Medinat Yisrael* (Hebrew, "State of Israel") in religious Judaism; the meaning, or lack thereof, of Zionism as a religious or non-religious, or secular or political movement; Israel as a home for all manner of Jewish religious interpretations or only Orthodox Judaism (a continuing source of at times bitter tensions and rancorous debate among Jews); Israel's deviance from or commitment to Jewish law; and the claims of Jewish ethical traditions in competition with the demands of the modern nation-state. Thinkers such as Leo Baeck (1873–1956), Martin Buber (1878–1965), Milton Steinberg (1903–1950), Abraham Joshua Heschel (1907–1972), Joseph B. Soloveitchik (1903–1993), Mordecai Kaplan (1881–1983), Richard L. Rubenstein (b. 1924), and Emil L. Fackenheim (1916–2003), among many others, have all written on one of more of these issues, and have made distinctive and important contributions to advancing Judaic theological thought. (Martin Buber and Emil Fackenheim have already been discussed in chapter 4, "Cycles of Thought: Judaic Philosophy," and will not be repeated here.)

German liberal rabbi Leo Baeck, survivor of Theresienstadt concentration camp (and former World War I army chaplain), was already a leader of German Jewry when he published his seminal work *The Essence of Judaism* in 1905, in response to Adolf von Harnack's (1851–1930) *What is Christiantiy?* published in 1900. In it, Baeck defended Judaism without apologetics, in language reminiscent of both neo-Kantian and contemporary existential thought. At war's end, he first settled in England, and later came to the United States, where he taught at the Hebrew Union College-Jewish Institute of Religion, in Cincinnati, Ohio. During this period (1964), he published his second great masterwork, *This People Israel*, which he actually began during his years of confinement. Baeck's status not only as a thinker but as the epitome of moral courage in times of adversity has resulted in numerous institu-

Fig. 5.4 Leo Baeck (1873–1956) This image of Baeck was designed for a German postage stamp, honoring the first anniversary of Baeck's death in 1956. Photo: Courtesy of Creative Commons, http://commons.wikimedia.org/wiki/File:DBP_278_Leo_Baeck_20_Pf_1957.jpg

tions named for him in New York, Great Britain, and Israel.

Fellow Holocaust/Shoah survivor Abraham Joshua Heschel was also first brought to the United States by the Hebrew Union College-Jewish Institute of Religion, but he later moved to New York and taught at the (Conservative) Jewish Theological Seminary of America, beginning in 1946, as Professor of Jewish Ethics and Mysticism. His concerns with spirituality and ethical activism, derived from his study of the prophets of the Torah/Hebrew Bible, led to his active involvement in both the American civil rights struggles and the anti–Vietnam War movement in the 1960s. (Among the most famous pictures of him is of his marching with the late Rev. Dr. Martin Luther King Jr. [1929–1968], in opposition to the same war.) Among his seminal works are *The Prophets* (1962); *The Sabbath: Its Meaning for Modern Man* (1951), which draws a distinction between Judaism as a "religion of time" and other

faiths as "religions of space"; *Man Is Not Alone: A Philosophy of Religion* (1951), which asserts that it is indeed possible for human beings to apprehend God; *God in Search of Man: A Philosophy of Judaism* (1955), which assesses specifically how Jews may best respond to the various philosophical and theological ideas enumerated in *Man Is Not Alone*; and *Torah from Heaven* (1962), which many regard as his most important writing, a three-volume summary of rabbinic theology as reflected in the non-halakhic or aggadic literature.

Among Heschel's colleagues at the Jewish Theological Seminary of America was Lithuanian-born Mordecai Menachem Kaplan (1881–1983). Ordained by the same institution in 1902, he began his career in an Orthodox synagogue but returned seven years later to teach generations of rabbinical and Jewish educational students. More and more, his ideas, both theologically and pragmatically, broke with his initially Orthodox orienta-

BOX 5.3

Quotations Taken from Heschel's Writings

"Racism is man's gravest threat to man—the maximum hatred for a minimum reason."

"All it takes is one person . . . and another . . . and another . . . and another . . . to start a movement."

"Wonder rather than doubt is the root of all knowledge."

"A religious man is a person who holds God and man in one thought at one time, at all times, who suffers harm done to others, whose greatest passion is compassion, whose greatest strength is love and defiance of despair."

"God is either of no importance or of supreme importance."

"Just to be is a blessing. Just to live is holy."

"Self-respect is the fruit of discipline, the sense of dignity grows with the ability to say no to oneself."

"Life without commitment is not worth living."

"Above all, the prophet reminds us of the moral state of a people: Few are guilty but all are responsible."

"When I was young, I admired clever people. Now that I am old, I admire kind people."

"The course of life is unpredictable . . . no one can write his autobiography in advance."

tion as he came to see Judaism as embodied in his concept of a "religious civilization," and the God of Israel in naturalistic terms. He is credited with founding the fourth, though still small, Jewish religious movement, Reconstructionist Judaism, which is more liberal than Conservative Judaism but less so historically than Reform Judaism, though this distinction no longer holds, as Reform Judaism itself has reembraced much of the Judaic religious traditions it had previously abandoned. He is also credited with developing the concept of the all-encompassing Jewish community center where all manner of activities, from Judaic learning to crafts-making to physical activities, take place. In 1922, he celebrated with his daughter, Judith, the first *Bat Mitzvah*, coming-of-age ceremony, on the Friday evening of the Sabbath (and thus avoiding the question of a female reading from a sacred Torah scroll). His two most important texts are *Judaism as a Civilization: Towards a Reconstruction of American Jewish Life* (1981) and *The Meaning of God in Modern Jewish Religion* (1994), the latter a posthumous collection of his shorter theological writings.

At the other end of the spectrum was Rabbi Joseph Soloveitchik (1903–1993), the leading Orthodox thinker who, following the likes of S. R. Hirsch and others, saw no conflict with the Judaism of halakha (Jewish law) and Orthodoxy, and the larger currents of ideas. Succeeding his late father as dean of the Orthodox seminary affiliated with Yeshiva University in New York City, he later moved to Boston, where he remained until his death. His status as a rabbi and philosophic/theological thinker, reflected in his two most best-known and popularized works, *The Lonely Man of Faith* (1992) and *Halakhic Man* (1983), saw him achieve a pre-eminent status across the Orthodox Jewish world and the title "Ha-Rav" (Hebrew, "*The* Rabbi" [par excellence]), by which he was known to many.

In *The Lonely Man of Faith*, Soloveitchik saw a human being as composed of two essential halves: the creative, who nourishes his own creativity to attempt to achieve mastery over his environment,

and the submissive, who desires little more than to submit to the will of God. The true "man of faith," then, is the one who is best able to integrate these two halves into himself and best serve God in the process.

In *Halakhic Man*, Soloveitchik provides a theological and philosophical foundation for halakha and grounds his understanding of it in the pragmatic world of reality and the here and now. For him, and those who follow and agree with him, the true and uniquely Jewish path to God is through Jewish doing as it manifests itself in halakhic practice, not in an ongoing concern with either the life of the spirit or the hereafter. Because of his many years as seminary dean in ordaining literally thousands of Orthodox rabbis and influencing the curriculum of their studies, Soloveitchik's world perspective on such issues as Torah study (positive), university education coupled with Jewish education (positive), Reform and Conservative Judaisms (negative), Reform and Conservative rabbis (negative), and engagement in Jewish–Christian theological encounters (negative) remain very much a part of the modern Orthodox Jewish world today.

Again, in the aftermath of the horrors and revelations of the Holocaust/Shoah of the Second World War (1933–1945), theological confrontations not only for Jewish leaders but Jews at every level came more and more into the public arena, most especially among the non-Orthodox. Many within the Orthodox world incorporated this tragedy into an already existent *weltanschauung* (world perspective) as yet the latest tragedy afflicting God's covenanted community, the result, perhaps, of violations of the *berith*/covenant, the "sins" of assimilation, secular Zionism, or other understanding, and went on with the business of rebuilding Jewish life.

One who best represents these "post-Auschwitz theologians," as they have come to be called, is Richard L. Rubenstein, formerly professor of religion at Florida State University in Tallahassee, Florida, and last, President of the University of Bridgeport, in Connecticut.[6]

Rubenstein is perhaps best known for his 1966 collection of essays *After Auschwitz: Radical Theology and Contemporary Judaism,* wherein he argues that the traditional Judaic notions of God and covenant with that God have "died" (and thus forever linking him with the American radical Protestant death of God movement and its leading thinkers such as Thomas J. J. Altizer [b. 1927]). Exploring what kind of Judaism could then be created in response, he opts for a "holy paganism," by which he means that the search for religious meaning must now be earthbound. In his later years, he has turned his thoughts to the larger category of genocide as well as what he regards as the "holy war clashes" between Islam and the West.

Like much of Jewish philosophy, Jewish theology continues to be primarily the work of academics associated with either religiously identified or secular institutions of higher learning. However, unlike the former, so-called working rabbis actively engaged in Jewish synagogal and communal life have also published important works, and thus have enabled their concerns to reach a broader arena of Jews, and possibly Christians as well. One such example is the 1998 book *Arguing with God: A Jewish Tradition*, written by Rabbi Anson Laytner, who presently serves as the Executive Director of the Seattle, Washington, chapter of the American Jewish Committee. In his text, he concretely shows that addressing God directly, challenging and arguing with God, over the presence of evil in the world, and attempts to respond to it, are part and parcel of an authentic Judaic religious tradition.

Conclusion

From these brief surveys as adumbrated in this chapter and in the chapter previous, we must conclude that Judaic thought is alive and well, and that those who espouse such a diversity of views are equally healthy. Be they Judaic philosophers in the academy or Jewish theologians in the larger Jewish community, especially those working in congregational and organizational settings, the intellectual lore of the Jewish religious tradition, both historically and contemporarily, continues to exercise a profound impact on many Jews. There is every indication that it will continue to do so far into the future.

IN REVIEW

As before, we have now had the opportunity to meet some of the outstanding Jewish theologians, both past and present. Taken together with those we met in chapter 4, we can only conclude that, part and parcel with the religious texts of Judaism, there exists a strong intellectual tradition of both thinking and writing that continues today and remains one of the ways into an understanding not only of what Judaism is but who the Jews are.

KEY TERMS

Aseret Hadibrot	*Cherem*
assimilation	chosenness
Berith/Covenant	Conservative Judaism
Chabad Hasidism	*Da'at Elohim*

continues on following page

Hasidic Judaism

immanent

incorporation

Medinat Yisrael

Misnagdim

Mitzvot/commandments

neo-Orthodoxy

oral tradition

Orthodox Judaism

qiddusha/holiness

Reconstructionist Judaism

Reform Judaism

Shelosha-Asar Ikarim

theology

transcendent

Wissenschaft des Judentums

Zionism

Questions for Review, Study, and Discussion

1. Pick one theologian from each of the four periods noted in this chapter. Read not only his or her biography, but a sample of his or her writings as well. Now compare and contrast these thinkers. In what way are they different? Similar? Do you see an evolution in their thinking? What conclusions do you draw about them and the ideas with which they were concerned?

2. Now compare those you have chosen in this chapter with those you chose in the previous chapter. In what ways are they different? Similar? What issues/concerns do you see as points of divergence among them? What does this tell you about the richness of the Jewish intellectual tradition?

Suggested Readings

Dorff, Elliot N., ed. *Contemporary Jewish Theology: A Reader*. New York: Oxford University Press, 1998.

Gilman, Neil. *Doing Jewish Theology: God, Torah & Israel in Modern Judaism*. Woodstock, Vt.: Jewish Lights, 2008.

Heschel, Abraham Joshua. *Heavenly Torah: As Refracted Through the Generations*. New York: Continuum, 2006.

Jacobs, Louis. *A Jewish Theology*. Chappaqua, N.Y.: Behrman House, 1973.

Montefiore, Claude Joseph Goldsmid, and Herbert Martin James Loewe, eds. *A Rabbinic Anthology*. New York: Schocken Books, 1974.

CHAPTER 6

Cycles *of* TIME

The Judaic Calendar

OVERVIEW

In this chapter, we will introduce ourselves to *all* of the Jewish festivals, holidays, holy days, and fast days of the Jewish calendar, noting their richness and diversity and realizing that the process that the various Jewish denominational movements vary in their own observances of them. Have fun!

Introduction

If one truly wants to discover who the people known as "the Jews" really are and what the thing they themselves call "Judaism" really is, the best ways for doing so is what the anthropologists call an *ethnographic* study: that is, visiting the communities in their synagogues during the various holy days, holidays, festivals, and fast days; observing the behaviors of those in attendance; and asking intelligent questions of the participants (after first having done a good bit of preliminary background reading of texts such as this one). What one will discover is the following: that the texts themselves, at best, only provide portraits painted with the broadest of brushstrokes, that individual synagogal communities are enriched by incredible diversity in practice, though largely uniform in outline (reflecting denominational or movement understandings), and perhaps most importantly, the various adumbrations of the Judaic religious traditions are alive and well at any given moment in history. What follows, then, in that broadest and barest of outlines, are all-too-brief discussions of those celebratory events that mark the Judaic calendar and the most universally held observances of them. What is not addressed, however, is how each holy day is celebrated in Orthodox Hasidic, Orthodox non-Hasidic, Conservative, Reform, and/or Reconstructionist communities, for such in-depth discussions could easily fill several volumes and move the reader away from the overview provided by this text. For such closer examinations, it is therefore advisable to consult directly the various *official* publications of the movements themselves. Each has a variety of published materials designed with a pragmatic focus, and enabling its own adherents to best observe "the Jewish way" as it understands it. Equally, all tend to provide historical contexts and the *abcs* of contemporary observance.

Last, as part of one's own ethnographic adventure, one needs to visit synagogues representative of each of the movements presented in this text to appreciate the full flavor of the diversity of the Judaic experience. Visiting only one distorts the understanding and too narrowly focuses the learning.

Calendar

Having absorbed the above perspective, let us revisit chapter 2, "Cycles of History," where we noted that the Judaic calendar is lunar based (according to the cycles of the moon) rather than solar based (according to the cycles of the sun), which is common to Western tradition. (This difference of calendar explains why Jewish holidays "change" as they are recorded in Western calendars—usually within a two-month time frame—though, of course, they always remain the same according to the Hebraic calendar!) Furthermore, it is a complicated mathematical instrument, fully worked out by the rabbis early on in the history of Judaism (specifically Rabbi Hillel II in the fourth century), containing, for example, seven leap years in every nineteen-year cycle (years 3, 6, 8, 11, 14, 17, 19). Its months average 29 or 30 days; its year 354 days, necessitating an additional month (*Adar* I or *Adar Rishon*/First *Adar*; *Adar Sheni* or Second *Adar*, the "regular" Adar of the Hebrew calendar) to balance the annual cycle and "bring it into line," so to speak, with the solar calendar. Complicating the system even more, as it has evolved, the Judaic calendar of holy days begins in the fall, with Rosh Hashanah (the Jewish New Year), actually the *seventh* month of the calendar year, a far more introspective event of new beginnings than the raucous celebrations associated with December 31 (and the morning after).

Additionally, *all* Jewish holy days begin the evening before the day, following a rabbinical reading/interpretation/understanding of the creation story associated with the following verses of the first chapter of *Bereshith*/Genesis:

And there was evening and there was morning—
    the first day (v. 5)
    the second day (v. 8)
    the third day (v. 13)
    the fourth day (v. 19)
    the fifth day (v. 23)
    the sixth day (v. 31)

(Discussion of the Sabbath will be reserved for later in this chapter.)

Also, the holidays themselves vary in length, from one day's duration to eight days' duration, depending on both historical circumstances and textual readings, with an additional proviso that certain holy days will not fall on certain days of the week.

Adding to this already heady mixture, the designation of the year number itself was the result of an early rabbinic attempt to calculate the origin of the world according to the chronology of the reigns of the kings of Judah and Israel referenced in the Torah/Hebrew Bible and working backward. While today we certainly would not credit this attempt with scientific validity—understanding planet Earth to be far older—this powerful Judaic religious tradition remains accepted by all Judaic religious movements. Thus, the year 2006–2007 (Western solar) equates to the Jewish religious year 5768, 2007–2008 (Western solar) equates to the Jewish religious year 5769, and so on. Table 6.1 summarizes both Judaic calendar months and Jewish holy days.

What follows next, then, are descriptions of the various Jewish holidays, holy days, festivals, and fast days according to their calendared order, beginning with Rosh Hashanah in the month of Tishrei and concluding with Tisha B'Av the following summer.

TABLE 6.1

	Month	Length	Equivalent	Holiday(s)
1	Nisan	30 Days	March-April	Passover
				Yom Ha-Shoah
				Fast of the First Born
2	Iyar	29 Days	April-May	Lag B'Omer
				Yom Ha-Atzmaut
				Yom Ha-Zikkaron
				Yom Yerushalayim
3	Sivan	30 Days	May-June	Shavuot
4	Tammuz	29 Days	June-July	Fast of Tammuz
5	Av	30 Days	July-August	Tisha B'Av
6	Elul	29 Days	August-September	
7	Tishrei	30 Days	September-October	Rosh Ha-Shanah,
				Tzom Gedaliah
				Yom Kippur
				Sukkot, Hoshannah
				Rabba, Shemini
				Atzeret, Simchat
				Torah
8	Heshvan	29/30 Days	October-November	
9	Kislev	30/29 Days	November-December	Hanukkah
10	Tevet	29 Days	December-January	Fast of Tevet
11	Shevat	30 Days	January-February	Tu B'Shevat
12	Adar I (Leap Year)	30 Days	February March	
12/13	Adar II (Leap Year)	29 Days	February-March	Purim
				Feast of Esther

One final note, however: The holy days themselves can be clustered together according to their origin and emphasis: (1) *major holidays* (those which derive their origin from the First Five Books of the Torah/Hebrew Bible): Rosh Hashanah, Yom Kippur, Sukkot, Shemini Atzeret, Passover, Shavuot; (2) *minor holidays* (those derived from the remainder of the Torah/Hebrew Bible or other Jewish texts): Purim, Hanukkah; (3) *rabbinic holidays* (those created after the destruction of the temple in the year 70 c.e.): Lag B'Omer, Tisha B'Av, Tu B'Shevat; (4) *modern holidays*: Yom Hashoah, Yom Ha'atzmaut. (There are, in addition, what we could label "minor, minor holidays," that is, events observed by some rather than all of the various Judaic movements, usually the more Orthodox, for example, *Tzom G'dalia*, a fast day commemorating the murder of G'dalia, governor of Jerusalem during the reign of Nebuchadnezzar (reigned 605–562 b.c.e.); the Fast of Tevet, marking the siege of ancient Jerusalem; the Fast of Esther, commemorating Esther's own fast prior to her entrance into the her husband's court as referenced in the Book of Esther; the Fast of the Firstborn, prior to the celebration of Passover in commemoration of those Israelites saved from the deaths of the firstborn Egyptians. Two others—Yom Hazikkaron/Israeli Memorial Day and Yom Yerushalayim/Jerusalem Reunification Day—are, in truth, nation-state days, and, while important to Jews, are little observed outside the modern State of Israel.)

Shabbat

Falling completely outside the annualized calendar of Judaic celebrations, the holy Sabbath, or Shabbat as it is familiarly known from the Hebrew, is celebrated fifty-two times a year by religious Jews the world over. It is, realistically, the supreme expression of Judaic religiosity, and may (along with the *Aseret Hadibrot*/Ten Commandments) be among the most significant contributions of Jews and Judaism to humanity.

Its "event" is initially derived from the creative activities of God himself, as recorded in the second chapter of *Bereshith*/Genesis:

Thus the heavens and the earth were completed in all their vast array.

By the seventh day God had finished the work he had been doing; so on the seventh day he *rested* from all his work. And God blessed the seventh day and made it holy, because on it he *rested* from all the work of creating that he had done. (Gen 2:1-3)

The Hebrew of God's resting—*wayyishbot*—is the word from which the day is named (the *only* day so named in the creative process) and the one from which our word *Sabbath*, or Hebrew *Shabbat*, is derived.

Its import is further legitimated by its two appearances, first in *Shemot*/Exodus, and second in *Devarim*/Deuteronomy among the aforementioned *Aseret Hadibrot*, where an accompanying explanation spells out the restrictions by which it is to be observed. (The *only* one of the ten with such commentary.) First from *Shemot*/Exodus 20:8-11:

Remember the Sabbath day by keeping it holy. Six days you shall labor and do all your work, but the seventh day is a Sabbath to the Lord your God. On it you shall not do any work, neither you, nor your son or daughter, nor your manservant or maidservant, nor your animals, nor the alien within your gates. For in six days the Lord made the heavens and the earth, the sea, and all that is in them, but he rested on the seventh day. Therefore the Lord blessed the Sabbath day and made it holy.

And second from *Devarim*/Deuteronomy 5:12-15:

Fig. 6.1
A Jewish family celebrating the Shabbat Every week Jews throughout the world welcome the Shabbat (Sabbath) which, according to the Jewish religious tradition, is a foretaste of what the future messianic kingdom will be like. Photo: Bill O'Connell/ Workbook Stock/Getty Images

Observe the Sabbath day by keeping it holy, as the LORD your God has commanded you. Six days you shall labor and do all your work, but the seventh day is a Sabbath to the LORD your God. On it you shall not do any work, neither you, nor your son or daughter, nor your manservant or maidservant, nor your ox, your donkey or any of your animals, nor the alien within your gates, so that your manservant and maidservant may rest, as you do. Remember that you were slaves in Egypt and that the LORD your God brought you out of there with a mighty hand and an outstretched arm. Therefore the LORD your God has commanded you to observe the Sabbath day.

Significantly, both versions reaffirm that this day, in emulation of divine rest, is to be followed by all living creatures in the community, Israelites and non-Israelites, and animals as well. The Deuteronomic version, however, adds the divine imprimatur that observance is also at the command of the one who brought the Israelites out of their Egyptian enslavement.[1]

The concept of "work" that frames this celebration has become an internally divisive issue within the various streams of religious Judaism, with the Orthodox communities far stricter in their understandings and the less traditional communities less so. Early rabbinic tradition in the Mishnah, specifically *Tractate Shabbat* 7:2, for example, spells out thirty-nine categories of forbidden activities, including the following: activities associated with agricultural responsibilities (sowing, plowing, reaping), activities associated with food preparation (grinding, sifting, kneading, baking), activities associated with clothing manufacture (dyeing, spinning, weaving), activities associated with animal maintenance (trapping, slaughtering, curing), activities associated with building (building, tearing down), and lighting or extinguishing fires. Traditionally observant Jews tend to expand their interpretations of these categories to include not turning on any electric appliances whatsoever (radio, television, computer); not driving cars; preparing all food prior to the onset of the Shabbat itself; celebrating its holiness by relatively brief Friday evening worship services succeeded by a meal replete with special tablecloths, utensils, foods, and the like; lengthier Saturday morning services; midday meals, afternoon naps, or family walks; a bit of holy text study in the later afternoon; and returning to the synagogue for final worship and the ceremony of *Havdalah* (Hebrew "division"), officially marking the end of the Shabbat and a return to the ordinary days of the work week. More liberally observant Jews tend to also associate their celebration of Shabbat with worship both Friday evenings and Saturday mornings, special meals included, but allow for the accoutrements of modern life and pleasurable

activities that might require automobile driving and payment options (visiting the zoo, theater, movie). All movements, however, affirm their commitment to the sanctity of refraining from work (now defined more broadly as that activity from which one derives one's income), but the more liberal communities continue to recognize that, sometimes, the exigencies of modern life require Shabbat violation.[2]

For Jews who take seriously the religious understanding of the Sabbath as refraining from all manner of work, the challenge remains to contemporize these historical categories into modern parlance, especially for those whose residence is urban rather than pastoral/agricultural. What constitutes work?

The Shabbat evening meal is, like other festive occasions, framed by devotional blessings: over the candles, over sacramental wine (Hebrew *Kiddush*, "sanctification"), over food (Hebrew, *Motzi*, from the phrase "the one who brings forth food [literally, "bread"] from the earth"). The choice of foods—meats, fish, chicken, and side dishes—are as likely to reflect regional, geographic and subcultural variations as not.

Thematically interwoven themes makes this premier holy day a true symbol of the Judaic religious tradition: First, it is that reminder of *imitatio*

BOX 6.1

What Constitutes "Work"?

According to the Mishnah Shabbat 7:2, the following are the thirty-nine categories of work:

Sowing, plowing, reaping, binding sheaves, threshing, winnowing, selecting, grinding, sifting, kneading, baking, shearing wool, washing wool, beating wool, dyeing wool, spinning, weaving, making two loops, weaving two threads, tying, untying, sewing two

stitches, tearing, slaughtering, flaying, salting meat, curing hide, writing two letters, erasing two letters, building, tearing a building down, extinguishing a fire, kindling a fire, hitting with a hammer, and taking an object from the private domain to the public domain or transporting an object in the public domain.

Dei, imitation of God, resting from work as God rested from work. Second, it is appreciation of the descendants for the liberation from Egyptian slavery by God. And, third, it is understood by many to be a foretaste of what life will be like when, at long last, the long-sought-for *mashiach*/messiah of the Jews makes his appearance. (Worship traditions, music, and prayer refer to the Shabbat either as *kalah* ["bride"] or *malkah* ["queen"].)

Rosh Hashanah

The Jewish year begins, as noted, at the start of the seventh calendar month, Tishrei, with Rosh Hashanah (literally "head" or "beginning" of the year), and has long been Judaically identified as the "birthday of the world." All during the preceding month of Elul, there is the excitement of anticipation of yet another new beginning, another recognition of having come full circle—in joy and in sorrow, in life and in death—and of having survived to this point. Rabbinically, the tradition arose of a special pre–Rosh Hashanah worship experience over midnight the Saturday evening before. (If, however, Rosh Hashanah were to occur on the next day, Sunday, then this service would be pushed back to the previous weekend.) Known as *Selichot* (Hebrew, "forgivenesses"), it takes its name from a series of penitential psalms and other prayers all designed to help prepare the worshiper for the awesome days to come, and it sets its time based on Psalm 119:62 ("At midnight I rise to give praise to You"). A modernist accretion to this service in some congregations has been the formal changing of the covers of

Fig. 6.2 Rosh Hashanah Rosh Hashanah inaugurates the beginning of the annual Jewish religious year on the first day of the month of Tishri with special services, music, and prayer. This festival is also symbolized by the blowing of the shofar (ram's horn) and apples dipped in honey to reflect the hope for a sweet year-to-come. Photo: Jack Guez/AFP/Getty Images

the Torah scrolls themselves from their "ordinary" colors to white.

The name itself—Rosh Hashanah—does not appear in the Torah/Hebrew Bible as such. In *Vayyikra*/Leviticus 23, it is called both *Yom Hazikkaron* ("Remembrance Day," distinct, however, from Israeli Memorial Day of the same name) and *Yom Hateruah* ("Sounding Day," reference to the shofar or ram's horn, calling the ancients to both prayer and introspection.) It is a *major* holy day—work is not permitted—with lengthy worship services in both the evening and the morning. While biblically observed for one day only, traditional Jews observe it for two, the result of calendaring difficulties many hundreds of years ago.

Among its more popular traditions are the eating of apples and honey (for a sweet new year), a round braided loaf of bread, *challah* (reminder of the full circle of life), the sending of Rosh Hashanah/New Year greeting cards (a particularly Western innovation), a festive dinner meal with attendant blessings (as is the case with *all* festival occasions), and the greeting of one's friends and family, *L'shanah tovah tikatevu*, "May you be inscribed in the Book of Life [for another year]." (Ten days following, at the close of Yom Kippur, the Day of Atonement, the greeting is modified to *L'shanah tovah tichatemu*, "May you be engraved/sealed in the Book of Life [for another year].") Upon leaving the synagogue worship service, it is also appropriate to say *L'shanah tovah u'm'tukah*, "[Best wishes] for a good and sweet [new] year."

Rosh Hashanah also introduces what is known as the *Yamim Nora'im*/Ten Days of Awe (also called the *Aseret Y'emi T'shuvah*/Ten Days of Repentance/Penitence), which conclude with Yom Kippur. During the interregnum, the Shabbat between is known as *Shabbat Shuvah*, the Sabbath of Penitence/Repentance/Turning, taking its name from the additional scriptural reading for the morning worship, Hosea 14:1 ("Return O Israel to the LORD your God; your sins have been your downfall").

Many congregations and communities also

hold special memorial services at their cemeteries during this time to pay respect to loved ones who have died. Additionally, there is the ceremony of *Tashlich* ("Casting," from Micah 7:18, where God will cast the sins of Israel into the depths), practiced near a stream of flowing water. Historically, at least beginning in the fourteenth century, Jews wrote their "sins" on slips of paper and literally cast them into the water. Some ecologically minded modernists have used pieces of bread while reflecting on their "sins" to do the same.

Most identified, however, with the holiday itself is the sounding of the ram's horn, shofar, in the synagogue itself (except if Rosh Hashanah itself falls on Shabbat). Three distinctive sounds make up its "calls"—*Tekiah*, or long note, *Shevarim*, or broken notes, and *T'ruah*, or staccato notes—succeeded in each series by a *Tekiah G'dolah* or long *Tekia*.

As noted, while extremely celebratory among religious Jews, Rosh Hashanah also has its serious side as it calls the worshiper to begin to reflect back on past successes and failures, as well as those who matter most—family and friends—who have both died during the past twelve months and/or those in dire circumstances. By extension, it also causes the worshiper to reflect on the fate of the Jewish people itself, how far it has come on its journey, its current responsibilities in the world, and in the present moment, concerns with the State of Israel and its ongoing crises.

For the next ten days, traditionally observant Jews who attend daily worship notice a modification of the liturgy as certain prayers are omitted and others added, all in preparation for Yom Kippur.

Yom Kippur

Considered by many Jews the world over to be the holiest day of the year, Yom Kippur, the Day of Atonement, a twenty-four-hour fast day, is also known as the "Great Sabbath" or the "Sabbath of Sabbaths." Its authenticity is derived from the passage in *Vayyikra*/Leviticus 16:29-30:

Fig. 6.3 Orthodox Jews atone before Yom Kippur begins For the majority of the world's religious Jews, Yom Kippur (Day of Atonement) is the holiest day of the year, a twenty-four-hour fast day devoted to prayer and penance. Photo: David Silverman/Getty News Images/ Getty Images

This is to be a lasting ordinance for you: On the tenth day of the seventh month you must deny yourselves and not do any work—whether native-born or an alien living among you—because on this day atonement will be made for you, to cleanse you. Then, before the LORD, you will be clean from all your sins.

This was also the one day in ancient Jerusalem when the *Kohan Gadol*/High Priest entered the *Qodesh Qodashim*/Holy of Holies in the Holy Temple and uttered the unpronounceable name of God (the four-lettered Tetragrammaton), taking upon him-

self the sins of his people and pleading to God on their behalf.

Culminating the *Yamim Nora'im*/Ten Days of Awe, this *major* holy day is also a no-work day, when one finds oneself in the synagogue for all-day prayer: evening service, morning service, afternoon service, memorial service, and concluding service.

The evening service is identified with the mournful chanting of the *Kol Nidre* ("all vows") by the Cantor (worship leader), which pleads with God to disavow any unfulfilled promises made to God during the past year. It says nothing whatsoever about promises made to one's fellow human beings, this being clearly understood by the worshiper, though over the generations, anti-semites have attacked this prayer as evidence of Jewish perfidy, and over the years some rabbis have unsuccessfully even called for its removal from the liturgy.

> All personal vows we are likely to make, all personal oaths and pledges we are likely to take between this Yom Kippur and the next Yom Kippur, we publicly renounce. Let them all be relinquished and abandoned, null and void, neither firm nor established. Let our personal vows, pledges and oaths be considered neither vows nor pledges nor oaths.[3]

Traditionally observant Jews will make it a point to dress in all white, including footwear, prior to entering the synagogue for prayer. Fasting during this one day for those able to do so (for example, minors are not required to do so, nor are those in ill health who require both medication and food to sustain their lives) is intended to refocus one's energies and mind on matters of serious important (the concerns of the "soul," the plight of the less fortunate, and other spiritual matters).

The *Yizkor*, or Memorial Service, on Yom Kippur afternoon is the opportunity to pray in remembrance for those within the inner circle of family—father, mother, husband, wife, brother, sister, son, or daughter—who have died during the past year. While the tradition arose for those still having living parents to absent themselves from this part of the worship day, modernists have expanded the circle to include *all* family members and friends as well as the entire Jewish people in response to the tragedy of the Holocaust/Shoah and those who have none to mourn their deaths.

The Concluding Service or *N'eilah* is literally wrapped up with the "closing" of the gates of Heaven, which symbolically reinforces the notion that one's destiny during the course of the next twelve months has been written by God in the holy Book of Life. Having fasted all day, many if not most synagogues, regardless of denominational movement, sponsor some sort of "break-fast," from simple bread and juice (prior to returning home to a festive meal) to more elaborate full meals.

For the communities of praying Jews, the positive mood of beginning again is palpable, and the feelings that the year to come will prove better than

BOX 6.2

Tips for Yom Kippur Fasting

For those able to do so, Yom Kippur, the Day of Atonement and holiest day of the Jewish calendar year, is a twenty-four-hour fast from sundown of the previous evening until sundown of the following day, with the entire full day spent in synagogue in prayer. Accordingly, those Jews who are able to do so thus refrain from either eating or drinking during this entire day. According to Tracey Rich at Judaism 101 (www.jewfaq.org), the following are her "tips" for a successful fast:

1. Taper off addictive or habitual substances.
2. Vary your meal schedule.
3. Drink plenty of water.
4. Don't overeat (in preparation for fasting).
5. Eat foods that are easy to digest.
6. Get plenty of protein and complex carbohydrates.
7. Go to synagogue.
8. Don't talk about food or hunger.
9. Take a nap [if possible] in the afternoon.
10. Sniff spices.

the year concluded sets the tone and agenda for the rest of the religious year.

One tradition to get ready for what is to come is to return home and immediately retreat to the backyard and drive into the ground one peg with which one will later construct the temporary booth in celebration of the holiday five days hence of Sukkot.

Sukkot

Still within the realm of *major* holy days, Sukkot ("Booths") is a dual reminder that (1) when ancient Israel fled their Egyptian enslavement and wandered the desert for forty years, they continuously encamped and constructed *temporary* dwellings, and (2) even early on in their resettlement of the Holy Land of Israel, as agriculturalists who lived for safety and security behind fortified walls, both harvesting and planting seasons required them to *temporarily* sojourn in their fields to care for their crops.

The religious mood now changes from the sober fasting of Yom Kippur to the more celebratory mood of Sukkot. The temporary dwelling constructed by the family (*sukkah*, singular) must meet three requirements: (1) it must be temporary ("put-up-able" and "take-down-able"), (2) it must be a three-sided enclosure (though a covering over the fourth—the entrance—is permitted), and (3) one must be able to look up and see the heavens (the roof covering is, thus, assembled from branches somewhat haphazardly).

This major holy day finds its own validation within the third book of the Torah/Hebrew Bible, that of *Vayyikra*/Leviticus 23:

Fig. 6.4 A Painted Sukkah This magnificently painted sukkah (booth) from Fischbach, Germany, and presently in Israel, is striking evidence of Jewish creativity associated with Jewish holiday celebrations. Both home and synagogue sukkot (pl.) may be equally elaborately adorned or simply decorated. Photo: Erich Lessing/Art Resource, N.Y.

The LORD said to Moses, "Say to the Israelites: 'On the fifteenth day of the seventh month the LORD's Feast of Tabernacles begins, and it lasts for seven days. The first day is a sacred assembly; do no regular work. For seven days present offerings made to the LORD by fire, and on the eighth day hold a sacred assembly and present an offering made to the LORD by fire. It is the closing assembly; do no regular work.

("'These are the LORD's appointed feasts, which you are to proclaim as sacred assemblies for bringing offerings made to the LORD by fire—the burnt offerings and grain offerings, sacrifices and drink offerings required for each day. These offerings are in addition to those for the LORD's Sabbaths and in addition to your gifts and whatever you have vowed and all the freewill offerings you give to the LORD.)

"'So beginning with the fifteenth day of the seventh month, after you have gathered the crops of the land, celebrate the festival to the LORD for seven days; the first day is a day of rest, and the eighth day also is a day of rest. On the first day you are to take choice fruit from the trees, and palm fronds, leafy branches and poplars, and rejoice before the LORD your God for seven days. Celebrate this as a festival to the LORD for seven days each year. This is to be a lasting ordinance for the generations to come; celebrate it in the seventh month. Live in booths for seven days: All nativeborn Israelites are to live in booths so your descendants will know that I had the Israelites live in booths when I brought them out of Egypt. I am the LORD your God.'"

In the evolution of postbiblical rabbinic Judaism, two different interpretations of the key word *yashav* ("to dwell," "to sit") associated with the responsibility to build and bless the dwelling have developed: for some observant families, they will not only eat their meals inside the sukkah, but sleep there as well. Others, perhaps a bit more liberal, will take only their meals inside this temporary structure (weather permitting). Young children have also been known to provide wall decorations associated with the holiday in addition to fresh fruits hung with string from its ceiling.

The above passage also notes the gathering of the *arba minin*, four kinds of agriculturally representative fruits: *etrog*, citron or lemon; *lulav*, or palm branch; *aravot*, two willow branches; and three myrtle branches, *hadasim*. Once the sukkah is finished, there is a blessing associated with the waving of these four kinds of fruit, symbolic of ancient Israel's land-based agricultural heritage.[4]

This biblical holy day was to be observed for seven days; traditional Jews, however, observe it for eight days, letting the two days at the end remain separate events, while more liberal Jews tend to combine these two into one and still honor the biblical understanding of seven days of *Sukkot*. Day seven is also known as *Hoshannah Rabbah* ("Great Supplication") and carries its own liturgical and synagogal responsibilities.

As is the case with the intermediate days of Passover, they are known as *hol hamoed*, "ordinary" festival days, in contradistinction to those at the beginning and end of the festival, when no work is permitted.

Shemini Atzeret and Simchat Torah

As noted, in verse 36, Israel is to hold a "sacred assembly" on the "eighth day" (the word *after* understood) at the conclusion of this festival of Sukkot. While Shemini Atzeret may have been observed separately, it has come to be seen as an integral part of the holiday observance (with its own liturgical additions), as has the rabbinic innovation of *Simchat Torah* ("Joy of the Torah"), thus making this a true nine-day event, with "sacred doings" on the first and second and seventh, eighth, and ninth days. (We should also note that all this occurs within this first/seventh month; thus the first twenty-four days of the month of *Tishri* are holiday intensive!)

Having observed both Sukkot and Shemini Atzeret, Jews now escalate their celebration with Simchat Torah, which signals both the completion of the annual cycle of Shabbat scriptural readings (*Devarim*/Deuteronomy 34), and a "new beginning" with *Bereshith*/Genesis 1, and thus beginning the annualized reading cycle all over again. Perhaps the most well-known celebration of Simchat Torah is that portrayed in the media, which shows Hasidic men (and women separately) dancing with scrolls of the Torah in their arms and passing these scrolls to their fellow worshipers as they parade around their sanctuaries seven times. Other denominational movements in recent years have increased their own joyousness in celebration of this event, perhaps influenced somewhat by a Hasidic spillover.

One additionally interesting modernist innovation is the ceremony of *Consecration* practiced by the more liberal movements of Conservative, Reform, and Reconstructionist Judaisms (and further discussed in the next chapter). This new event, without either biblical or rabbinic history attached to it, marks the introduction of the newest children

into the religious education process, and occurs in congregations in the preschool, kindergarten, and/ or first grade years.

After these twenty-four days of intensive religious celebration among the religiously observant of all denominational movements, it is time for a break for approximately one month, allowing the intervening Shabbatot (plural of Shabbat) to work their own magic on the worshipers until the next event: Hanukkah.

Hanukkah

Technically a *minor* holiday according to the Jewish religious tradition (and thus one does not refrain from working), its story of Maccabean victory over the Syrio-Greeks under Antiochus (215–162 B.C.E.) in 162 B.C.E. is told in both the Talmuds and the books of the Maccabees. By virtue of its gift-giving propensities and calendar association with Christmas, falling as it does anywhere between late November through the end of December, other than Passover, it is perhaps the one day most well known by non-Jews and the one where creativity has escalated its status in the pantheon of Judaic holidays, most especially in

Fig. 6.5 Lighting the Hanukkah Menorah Soviet and Ethiopian Jewish immigrant children are shown here lighting a menorah, celebrating Hanukkah. Photo: David Rubinger/ Time Life Pictures/ Getty Images

Western countries (where Jewish–non-Jewish inter-actions have fared best).

The story itself sets the tone for its religious observance. While recognizing but downplaying somewhat the military victory, the emphasis has been and remains on the rededication of the ancient temple in Jerusalem where, according to the tradition, only enough oil was initially discovered to rekindle the *ner tamid* ("eternal flame," symbol of God's holy presence within the sanctuary). The "miracle" associated with the festival is that this small container burned continuously for eight days

BOX 6.3

Recipe for Latkes

Among many Jews, the food most associated with the celebration of Hanukkah is the latke, or potato pancake. (N.B.: The association, however, is not with the potato, but rather that it is fried in oil, thus the connection to the oil of the Hanuk-kah menorah, or oil lamp, in the holy sanctuary of the ancient temple, which burned, according to religious tradition, with a minimal supply of oil until a larger quantity could be found.) Here is a simple recipe for making latkes (makes approxi-mately 12 palm-sized latkes):

    4 medium potatoes
    1 medium onion
    2 eggs
    ½ cup matzah meal (flour or bread crumbs
        can be substituted)
    1 tsp. each salt and black pepper (more or
        less to taste)
    vegetable oil

Shred the potatoes and onion into a large bowl. Press out all excess liquid. (If using a food processor, use the chopping blade for 2 or 3 seconds after pressing out liquid to avoid stringy fly-aways.) Add eggs and mix well. Add matzah meal gradually while mixing until the batter is doughy, not too dry. (You may not need the whole amount, depending on how well you drained the veggies.) Add a few dashes of salt and black pepper. (Don't taste the batter—it's re-ally gross!) Don't worry if the batter turns a little orange; that will go away when it fries.

Heat about one-half inch of oil to medium-high heat. Form the batter into thin patties about the size of your palm. Fry batter in oil. Be patient: this takes time, and too much flipping will burn the outside without cooking the inside. Flip when the bottom is golden brown.

Place finished latkes on paper towels to drain. Eat hot with sour cream or applesauce. They reheat okay in a microwave, but not in an oven unless you cook them just right.

Potato Latkes Photo: © Brand X/SuperStock

and nights until a sufficient quantity of consecrated oil could be found to keep it burning in perpetuity.

Thus, ever since, Jews celebrate Hanukkah (Hebrew for "rededication," though the holiday is also called the "Festival of Lights," for obvious reasons) for eight nights and days and reenact the miracle by kindling a *menorah* (light-containing and highly stylized ritual candle holder), one candle each night until, at the end, all eight are lit. (Ritual states that one places the candles in the menorah right to left, but lights the candles left to right.)

Potato pancakes, called *latkes*, are traditionally eaten (with either sour cream and capers or applesauce) because of their association as food fried in oil. Modern Israelis have added the alternative possibility of *sufganiyot*, or jelly-filled donuts, also initially fried in oil.

Gifts for children are also associated with the observance, and the most common tradition is to reserve one gift for each night, some families starting small and culminating with one "super present" at the end.

Also well known is a spinning-top game with two different names: the Yiddish *dreydel* or Hebrew *s'vivon* is marked by one Hebrew letter on each of its four sides, reminding the player of the first words of the sentence, "A great miracle happened there" (outside the land), or, "A great miracle happened here" (inside the land). The game is played with nuts or matchsticks—but never with money as Jews have historically denigrated gambling as unworthy of "a kingdom of priests and a holy people"—and is directed toward children, and begins with all players putting one item in the "pot." Taking turns, the following begins to apply until a winner is announced. If the uppermost letter is

> *nun* (Yiddish, *nisht*), the player takes nothing from the pot;
> *gadol* (Yiddish, *ganz*), the player takes everything from the pot and the remaining players each put one additional item back into the pot to resume play;

> *heh* (Yiddish, *halbe*), the player takes one-half of the items in the pot;
> *shin* (Yiddish, *shtell*), the player must put one item into the pot.

The winner is declared when only one player has everything, and all the others have nothing.

A particularly enjoyable addition to the celebration is the use of Hanukkah *gelt* (Yiddish, "money") in various sizes and made from chocolate, though originally literally small coins were given to children to increase their interest and attention. The chocolate variety is enjoyed, by the way, by children of all ages!

Tu B'Shevat

Tu B'Shevat (literally the ninth day of the month of Shevat) is a rabbinic innovation, and understood to be the "New Year of the Trees." To be sure, tree planting was a most important part of the agricultural fecundity of ancient Israel upon its return to the Land after its Egyptian experience, and the responsibility to plant trees is already referenced in the Torah/Hebrew Bible in *Vayyikra*/Leviticus 19. For the modern State of Israel and its prestate pioneers, reforestation was and is inseparable from renewing the land itself. Governmental responsibility over such work remains in the hands of the Jewish National Fund (JNF), and has been so for much if not all of the last century. Among the more important forests in Israel itself has been the "Holy Martyrs" Forest of six million trees, as well as those planted in memory and honor of U.S. Presidents Harry S. Truman (1884–1972) and John F. Kennedy (1917–1963), who did much to make the dream of a reborn Israel a reality. In Israel today, and in many religious communities through the world, planting trees remains a tradition, as is the eating of various fruits associated with Israel herself (for example, grapes, figs, pomegranates, olives, and dates). In recent years, any number of communities have celebrated this rabbinic holiday with a "Tu B'Shevat

Seder" (paralleling, but to a lesser degree, that of the Passover), which may already have its own roots in the kabbalistic traditions of the Middle Ages.

Purim

This *minor* Jewish holiday, basing itself on the story and celebration of the Scroll/Book of Esther in the Torah/Hebrew Bible, may in fact be the inspiration for the Roman Catholic celebration of Mardi Gras, with its carnival aspects, the last celebration before the Lenten period in preparation for both Good Friday and Easter.

First of all, there is the unusual retelling of the story itself in the synagogue: Consisting of four primary characters—the heroine Esther (Hebrew name Hadassah), her cousin and hero Mordecai, the villain Haman, and the comic foil and relief King Ahashuerus of Persia (the historical anomalies have already been discussed in chapter 2)—whenever the name of the villain is read, Jews are instructed to drown out his name (symbolic of the ultimate Hebraic curse, "May your name be forever blotted out"—that is, "May you die without heirs," or "May your heirs die without progeny," thus

bring your line to its end)—with the use of a noisemaker, *greggar* in Yiddish or *ra'ashan* in Hebrew, and vocal sounds as well. There is also a costume parade of children, though historically men and women in Jewish communities also dressed up as one of the four characters, and a carnival-like and games-related event within synagogues and/or Jewish communities, has taken place.

The story itself is relatively brief; the entire text is only nine chapters and a three-verse tenth chapter: The king replaces his disobedient queen with a new, younger one—shades of Cinderella, perhaps (modified, of course). His antisemitic Prime Minister, Haman, perceives the Jews as an alien population, persuades the king that their extermination will benefit him economically, and is given the green light to do so. Haman's plans are thwarted by Esther's own machinations after Mordecai's appeal, as well as the king's love for his queen. Haman, his sons, and his army are put to death, and each year, Jews the world over celebrate this victory over genocidal evil (whether or not the story itself is grounded in real history).

There is also the eating tradition of *Hamantaschen*, to remind the eaters of either "Haman's

Fig. 6.6 Enjoying the festival of Purim Here are costumed Jewish children in royal costumes (beard and all!), probably King Ahashuerus and the evil villain, Prime Minister Haman. Note also the *greggar* or noisemaker, which is to be used when the Scroll of Esther is read in the synagogue, to "blot out" the villain's name. Photo: David Silverman/Getty News Images/Getty Images

hat" or "Haman's pocket"—cake-like desserts filled with sweet fruit filling such as poppy seed, apricot, or prune.

Purim is derived from the Hebrew word *pur*, or "lot," referencing the fact Haman casts "lots" (*purim*) to determine the day on which the Jews are to be exterminated.

One particularly meaningful custom associated with Purim is the giving of *mishloach manot* ("sending of portions"), especially foodstuffs but

BOX 6.4

Recipe for Hamentaschen

Normative Jewish religious tradition shares a strong connection with food. Like Rosh Hashanah (apples with honey), Hanukkah (latkes), Purim too has a "traditional" food—hamentaschen. Here is a simple recipe:

⅔ cup butter or margarine
½ cup sugar
1 egg
¼ cup orange juice (without pulp)
1 cup white flour
1 cup wheat flour (DO NOT substitute white flour! The wheat flour is necessary to achieve the right texture!)
2 tsp. baking powder
1 tsp. cinnamon
Various preserves, fruit butters, and/or pie fillings.

Blend butter and sugar thoroughly. Add the egg and blend thoroughly. Add orange juice and blend thoroughly. Add flour, ½ cup at a time, alternating white and wheat, blending thoroughly between each. Add the baking powder and cinnamon with the last half cup of flour. Refrigerate batter overnight or at least a few hours. Roll as thin as you can without getting holes in the batter. (Roll it between two sheets of wax paper lightly dusted with flour for best results.) Cut out 3 or 4 inch circles.

Put a dollop of filling in the middle of each circle. Fold up the sides to make a triangle, folding the last corner under the starting point, so that each side has corner that folds over and a corner that folds under (see picture at right). Folding in this "pinwheel" style will reduce the

likelihood that the last side will fall open while cooking, spilling out the filling. It also tends to make a better triangle shape.

Bake at 350 degrees for about 15–20 minutes, until golden brown but before the filling boils over!

Traditional fillings are poppy seed and prune, but apricot is my favorite. Apple butter, pineapple preserves, and cherry pie filling all work quite well. I usually use Pathmark grocery store-brand fruit preserves, and of course the traditional Simon Fischer brand prune lekvar. I have also made some with Nutella (chocolate-hazelnut spread); I find it a bit dry that way, but some people like it.

The number of cookies this recipe makes depends on the size of your cutting tool and the thickness you roll. I use a 4 ¼ inch cutting tool and roll to a medium thickness, and I get 20–24 cookies out of this recipe.

Hamentaschen for Purim
Photo: © Sterling Photo / iStock

also possibly charitable donations, the former to family and friends and the latter to those in need. The custom of the Fast of Esther, while a three-day fast during its creation in the Middle Ages, has been shortened to one day among traditional Jews in honor of Esther's own fast prior to her entering the royal court without permission, and is commemorated on the day before Purim unless that day is Shabbat, when it is pushed back to Thursday (Shabbat's own preparations taking priority).

Passover (Pesach)

Two weeks into the start of the actual calendar year, in the first month of Nisan, Jews observe the quintessential Judaic holy day after the Shabbat, the very foundations of which set the stage for the development of all subsequent Jewish moral-ethical conduct and much of the evolution of the liturgy itself. Indeed, Passover may be characterized as the archetypal redemptive experience of the Jewish people, so central is it to historic and contemporary Jewish existence.

At the heart of the celebration is the home-based Passover *Seder* (Hebrew, "order") meal, with its fixed liturgy contained within its own prayer book, the *Haggadah* (Hebrew, "The Story"), retelling the *Shemot*/Exodus tale of slavery in Egypt and liberation into the desert on the way to a return to the Promised Land. The name of the festival itself—Pesach—is derived from the angel of death "passing over"—*pasach*—the houses of the Israelites on the way to slaying the firstborn of Egypt's sons (one the ten plagues visited on a recalcitrant Pharaoh and his people because of his stubborn reluctance to let the Israelite slaves go forth in freedom to worship their God).[5]

The food most associated with the observance of this *major* festival is the flat, unleavened cake known as *matzah*, eaten for either seven or eight days (liberal or traditional observance), replacing all manner of leavened products and a constant reminder of the haste with which the Israelites left their Egyptian prison-home of four hundred years without sufficient time to let their breads rise. Such leavened products are called *chametz*, and are understood to be those made with one or more of five grains (wheat, rye, barley, oats, and spelt). Ashkenazic/Germanic Orthodox (and some other) Jews will also not eat rice, corn, peanuts, and legumes (beans). Because of these restrictions, for many religious Jews, prior to Passover is the occasion on which to conduct a thorough spring cleaning of one's home, most especially one's kitchen, and either sells symbolically or donates those prohibited food items.

Traditionally observant Jews observe the Passover/Pesach in the home both the first and second nights of the festival. Liberally observant Jews tend to observe the first night, with synagogues and communities gathering to celebrate on the second night.

The prescribed outline of the Passover Seder with the meal embedded within is as follows:

1. **Kadesh**: sanctification over festival wine. (First of four cups based on the four places in the Torah/Hebrew Bible where God's redemption of the people Israel is mentioned using four different Hebrew words. A fifth cup has been added to many Passover celebrations to remind Jews that not all are free to celebrate.)

2. **Urchatz**: symbolic washing of the hands (without blessing).

3. **Karpas**: eating a green leafy vegetable (symbolic of both Israel's lowly and agricultural beginnings) into salt water (symbolic of the tears of the enslaved).

4. **Yachatz**: breaking the middle of three *matzot* (pl. of *matzah*). (These symbolize the three distinctions of ancient Israelite society: *kohanim*, high priests; *Levi'im*,

Fig. 6.7
The Passover seder plate
On this plate are shown the traditional foods associated with the celebration of the festival of Passover.
Photo courtesy Creative Commons: http://commons.wikimedia.org/wiki/File:Seder_Plate.jpg

"ordinary" priests; *Yisraelim,* "ordinary" Israelites. One piece will be hidden for the *afikoman* [see below]. (Some Christian communities have transmuted the three to stand for God, Jesus, and the Holy Spirit, though, to be sure, this would be an interpretation outside of Jesus' own celebration.)

5. **Maggid**: telling the story of the Passover. (Traditionally beginning with the youngest child present asking the "four questions" of the meaning of the celebratory event,[6] the *Hagaddah* itself details the story of enslavement and liberation according to the Book of *Shemot*/Exodus together with appropriate rabbinic [and modern] commentaries. It concludes with a second cup of festival wine.)

6. **Rachtzah**: rewashing the hands (with blessing).

7. **Motzi**: blessing the food. (Generic blessing: "Praised are you, O Lord our God, ruler of the universe, who brings forth food [literally "bread/grains"] from the earth.")

8. **Matzah**: blessing the *matzah.* (Blessing specific to the eating of the unleavened cake, "Praised are you, O Lord our God, ruler of the universe, who has sanctified us by your commandments, and commanded us concerning the eating of the matzah.")

9. **Maror**: eating the *Maror.* (Usually this bitter herb is a horseradish root or mixture symbolic of the bitteness of slavery. It is "softened" somewhat by adding *charoset,* a mixture of apples, wine, nuts, and cinnamon, symbolic of the mortar used in the brick-building of the Egyptian pyramids.)[7]

10. **Korech**: eating the "Hillel sandwich" of *maror* and *charoset* (named in honor of the

first-century rabbi who first suggested the two be eaten together).

11. **Shulchan Orech**: eating the festival meal. (Meal traditions are many, depending on region, geography, and ethnic customs. Chicken, beef, turkey, or fish are not uncommon, as is by now the world-famous "matzah ball soup," made with matzah meal.)

12. **Tzafun**: finding the *afikoman*. (Believed to have possibly derived from a Greek word for "dessert," the evening's celebration cannot continue until the hidden matzah has been found. Young children are invited to search for it, and a prize or prizes are given as reward.)

13. **Barech**: blessings after the meal. (After a third cup of wine is enjoyed, appropriate blessings of grace are offered by the participants. A fourth cup is poured and set aside for Elijah, the prophet of the Torah/Hebrew Bible, who, as forerunner and announcer of the much-sought-for *mashiach*/messiah, will visit Jewish homes during the Festival of Passover. At a later point in the celebration, an outside door is opened to let him in.)

14. **Hallel**: offering psalms of praise to God.

15. **Nirtzah**: closing prayers. (Relatively short and concluding with *L'shanah ha-bah-ah b'Yirushalayim*, "Next year, [may we be free to celebrate this Passover] in Jerusalem! The celebration now continues with many songs.

At the end of the Passover holiday celebration, there is an additional service of *Yizkor*/Memorial in the synagogue akin to that at Yom Kippur (as well as at the end of Sukkot and Shavuot).

Sefirat Haomer: Counting the Omer and Lag B'Omer

For the next seven weeks, traditionally observant Jews will count the days between the end of the Passover and the beginning of the Omer, or barley harvest, as referenced in both *Vayyikra*/Leviticus 23:15-16 and *Devarim*/Deuteronomy 16:9-10, with both blessings and announcement. ("Today is the twelfth, thirteenth, fourteenth [and so on] day of the counting of the Omer.")

This period is one of seriousness among traditional Jews. Parties, weddings, and celerations with dancing are not scheduled (nor is haircutting among the most scrupulously observant, as well as refraining from sexual relations), with one exception.

On the thirty-third day of the counting of the Omer (33 in Hebrew equals the numeric expression "lag," the Hebrew letter *lamed*, or *l*, equalling 30, and the Hebrew letter *gimmel*, or *g*, equalling 3). According to historical tradition, a devasting plague killed many Israelites during the time of Rabbi Akiva (50–135 c.e.), but the plague ended on this day. Thus, it is not uncommon in the more observant communities to find many celebratory events, weddings included, scheduled on this day.

Shavuot: Festival of Weeks

This third (technically the second) of the three *Sh'losh Regalim* (Hebrew, "pilgrimage festivals," to Jerusalem, the other two being Passover and Sukkot), celebrated seven weeks after the conclusion of the Passover, it is a reminder to the Jewish people of its agricultural beginnings (since it is also known as *Hag Habikkurim*, "Festival of the First Fruits"), as well as *Hag Matan Torahteinu*, the "Festival of the Giving of the Torah" (when, according to religious tradition, Moses returned to the children of Israel from his mountaintop experience at *Har Sinai*/Mount Sinai and shared with them God's holy words). As a *major* festival, along with others who trace their origins from the First Five Books of the Torah/Hebrew Bible, it is a no-work day (observed for two days by traditional Jews). There is also *Tikkun Layl Shavuot*, when Jews will stay up all night, if possible, to study and to eat dairy foods during the days of the observance, themselves a reminder of the Land of Israel (Hebrew, *eretz z'vat chalav*, "a land flowing with milk and honey").

A modern accretion to the celebration of the festival among Reform, Conservative, and Reconstuctionist Jews is the celebration of "Confrmation," making the end of the formal religious education ("Sunday School") of tenth, eleventh, and twelfth graders, depending on congregational and rabbinical predilection. It is usually a yearlong study with the rabbi(s) of the congregation and culminates in a more creative group worship experience than the normative liturgy which has evolved.

Tisha B'Av: The Ninth Day of Av

Only perhaps the most naïve among us would presume that the enemies of the Jewish people would be totally unfamiliar with the texts and traditions of those to whom they wished to do harm. (Two such well-known examples are, first, Nazi Adolf Eichman [1906–1962], who was responsible for the deaths of thousands upon thousands of Jews during the Holocaust/Shoah by his efficient transportation system of Jews from ghettos to concentration and extermination camps—he read Jewish history, visited Palestine, and attempted to learn Hebrew— and, second, the Nazi assault on the Warsaw Ghetto, which began on the first day of Passover in 1943.) So, too, thought the rabbis of the Jewish religious tradition and recorded such in their texts, as well as the Torah/Hebrew Bible itself.

According to a Judaic understanding, the temple of ancient Israel was destroyed by both the Babylonians and the Romans on the ninth of Av, and with both, the fall of Jerusalem; the exile of the Jews from Spain, according to the Hebrew calendar, which

occurred in 1492, was on the ninth of Av; Cossack nobleman and revolutionary Bogdan Chmielnitski slaughtered Jews in Poland in the mid-1600s on the ninth of Av; and the mass killings at Treblinka death camp in 1942 began on the ninth of Av. Thus, a day set aside to mourn the collective tragedies that have overtaken the house of Israel during its journey makes perfect religious sense. Tisha B'Av is that day, preceded by a three-week period of somber introspection when no weddings or parties take place, Jews refrain, again, from haircutting, sexual relations, and the like. The biblical text read/chanted in the synagogue is that of *Eicha*/Lamentations with a most funereal- or dirge-like melody. Some observant Jews will light their sanctuaries with candles during the worship period and rend their garments (including placing ashes on their foreheads) to commemorate the observance.

Yom Hashoah (Holocaust Memorial Day) and Yom Ha'atzmaut (Israel Independence Day)

The mid-twentieth-century tragedy of the Holocaust/Shoah and the celebratory birth of the Third Jewish Commonwealth in its aftermath has resulted in the two newest days of the religious calendar, whose forms of observance have yet to be fully worked out.

Yom Hashoah, now observed on the twenty-seventh day of the Hebrew month of *Nisan*, occurs in April and associates itself, again, with the Warsaw Ghetto Uprising of 1943. In many if not most communities, there is a communal gathering at either a particular synagogue (rotated among the denominational movements annually) or a Jewish community center, featuring a speaker (either a survivor or scholar) or program, an honoring of those survivors still living, and a closing with the traditional prayer of Jews associated with death, the *Qaddish* ("sanctification of the holy name of God"). In Israel itself, home to *Yad Vashem*, the official Holocaust memorial authority, the nation-state itself stops for a brief two-minute period of memorial at 10:00 A.M. while air-raid sirens are sounded. While some in the most traditional of Jewish communities do not participate in the collective observances (seeing no need for an additional day to Tisha B'Av for such memorialization), their numbers continue to diminish.

Shortly thereafter, on the fifth of Iyar, Jews throughout the world celebrate *Yom Ha'atzmaut*, Israel Independence Day (May 14, 1948). In Israel itself, it is marked by a military parade of troops and armaments,[8] among other celebrations, while in Jewish communities outside of Israel, such events as Jewish cultural fairs, Israeli speakers and programs such as theater and dance, and "Yom Ha'atzmaut Seders" (following the model of the Passover Seder) are held. In its own way, it is a counterweight to the tragedy of the Holocaust/Shoah.

Conclusion

Thus, even with these relatively brief descriptions, the reader can plainly see that for religiously observant Jews, of whatever denominational movement, the Jewish calendar of holidays, holy days, festivals and fast days is a rich, full, and complete one. It, however, tell only one-half of a story, for Jews live their lives by two calendars, the other being the celebration of life-cycle events (from birth to death) which, like the festivals, have themselves evolved over the centuries, and to which we now turn in chapter 7.

IN REVIEW

We have now been introduced to *all* of the Jewish holidays, holy days, festivals, and fast days that comprise the Jewish calendar, one-half of which constitute the reality of Jewish doing and Jewish celebrating. Together with the Jewish life-cycle events we will encounter in the next chapter, we will come to fully appreciate that "the Jews" and "Judaism" are not abstract concepts but the warp and woof of a living reality.

KEY TERMS

Hanukkah	Simchat Torah
Pesach	Sukkot
Purim	Tisha B'Av
Rosh Hashanah	Tu B'Shevat
Sefirat Haomer	Yom Ha'atzmaut
Shabbat	Yom Hashoah
Shavuot	Yom Kippur
Shemini Atzeret	

Questions for Review, Study, and Discussion

1. Imagine yourself an anthropologist of religion/Judaism about to embark on an ethnographic fieldwork study in your community. Contact the local Jewish congregation and secure permission to attend a "regular" Sabbath worship service (either Friday evening or Saturday morning) and a festival worship service (either evening or morning). What additional research do you need to do before attending (for example, if you happen to know a Jewish person, consider the possibility of an interview)? If there is more than one Jewish congregation in your community, so much the better! Ideally, commit yourself to attending each of these different Jewish congregations. After attending, record your impressions of what you have experienced: What are your immediate impressions of these worship experiences? In what ways are they the same? Different? How do they compare with your own experiences of other worship services you have attended? In what ways are they the same? Different?

Suggested Readings

Greenberg, Irving. *The Jewish Way: Living the Holidays*. Northvale, N.J.: Jason Aronson, 1998.

Kozodoy, Ruth. *Book of Jewish Holidays*. Chappaqua, N.J.: Behrman House, 1997.

Olitzky, Kerry M., and Daniel Judson. *Jewish Holidays: A Brief Introduction for Christians*. Woodstock, Vt.: Jewish Lights, 2006.

Schauss, Hayyim. *The Jewish Festivals: A Guide to Their History and Observance*. New York: Schoken Books, 1996.

Strassfeld, Michael. *The Jewish Holidays: A Guide and Commentary*. New York: Harper & Row, 1993.

CHAPTER 7

Cycles *of* LIFE

The Life-Cycle Journey

OVERVIEW

In this chapter, we now introduce ourselves to the other "half" of the Jewish equation, the unique ways in which Jews, both historically and contemporarily, have "marked the moments" that compose the life-cycle: birth, growth, maturation, decay, and death. All religious communities mark these moments; here is one community whose own celebrations are unique in themselves. As before, have fun!

Introduction

The parallel way in which one can study Judaism and the Jewish people—and attempt to answer the questions "What is Judaism?" and "Who are the Jews?"—starts with a further bit of anthropological ethnography: attending the various life-cycle celebrations by which Jews "mark the moments" of the human journey from birth to death. Like the holy days themselves, some of the moments are of biblical and thus quite early origin; others are of recent vintage, brought about by the dramatic changes of historical circumstance and, of course, modernity. And, like the holidays themselves, two caveats frame this chapter:

First, respectful attendance at events that dramatically and centrally mean much to the participants themselves requires of the attendee a good bit of background reading, not only to ask appropriately sensitive questions (and, later, to return back to "home base" and think about what one has experienced), but also to have a frame of reference to experience the events.

Second, the various denominational movements within the Judaic religious tradition—Orthodox Hasidic, Orthodox non-Hasidic, Conservative, Reform, Reconstructionist[1]—all tend to follow the same general plan with regard to their overall celebrations that make the participation of the Jews in their Judaism meaningful. However, in the creation and evolution of their own movements and traditions, diversity and variation have arisen due to their differing interpretations of how the events are to be celebrated. Therefore, as we travel the Judaic life-cycle, from birth to death, we will do so, as before, in the broadest of outlines, aware at all times that movement differences and variations apply every step of the way. We begin, of course, with birth.

Brit Milah:
The Covenant of Circumcision

Unique among all the life-cycle rituals of the Jewish people is that of circumcision (the surgical removal of the vestigial flap of skin covering the head of the penis, and thought by historical biologists to possibly have been there as a protective covering). It is the *only* physical ritual in the whole of the Judaic religious tradition, and traces its origin to the Torah/Hebrew Bible. In *Bereshith*/Genesis 17:9-14, we find the following instructions to the patriarch *Avraham*/Abraham:

Then God said to Abraham, "As for you, you must keep my covenant, you and your descendants after you for the generations to come. This is my covenant with

you and your descendants after you, the covenant you are to keep: Every male among you shall be circumcised. You are to undergo circumcision, and it will be the sign of the covenant between me and you. For the generations to come every male among you who is eight days old must be circumcised, including those born in your household or bought with money from a foreigner—those who are not your offspring. Whether born in your household or bought with your money, they must be circumcised. My covenant in your flesh is to be an everlasting covenant. Any uncircumcised male, who has not been circumcised in the flesh, will be cut off from his people; he has broken my covenant."

Thus, circumcision is done at God's command. Every male, Israelite (and, at least early on, those within Israel's orbit) *must* be circumcised. It *must* be done to all male newborns after eight days. And finally, it is *the sign* of all Israelite males bound eternally to covenant with their God. No other event, no other celebration in the whole of the Judaic religious tradition carries with it the dramatic evidence of this beginning point of the journey.[2] As it has evolved, certain changes, however, have become apparent:

If, for example, the infant male is in some kind of physical stress (up to and including the possible cessation of life), circumcision is, of course, delayed until he is able to safely undergo the procedure. And what of adopted males, either infants soon after birth or young boys prior to the age of *bar mitzah* (which Judaism regards as the age of beginning religious maturity for males, and thus capable of making personal decisions)?

Then, too, what of the postbiblical non-Jew (most likely an adult) who wishes to join the Jews? He may be circumcised or not, necessitating different physical procedural responses. And in the modern period, what of the one who wishes to become Jewish who refuses (for reasons of conscience) to undergo such a physical procedure (or Jewish or mixed parents who reject the rite of Brit Milah)? Can they still be considered members "in good standing" of the Jewish people—or not?

All things being "normal," however, the following would take place: Eight days after the birth a son, the brit milah ("covenant of circumcision") would take place. The actual surgery and attendant rituals are usually performed by a *mohel* (a specially trained Jewish ritual circumciser), often also an Orthodox or Conservative rabbi or cantor. Jewish religious tradition, however, provides other options where such a person is unavailable: A Jewish doctor such as a surgeon, obstetrician, and/or pediatrician (even one unfamiliar with the ritual traditions) may perform the surgery on the eighth day provided there is also someone present who can perform the rituals. If neither a *mohel* nor Jewish doctor is available, one is permitted to use the services of a non-Jewish doctor, again, provided someone knowledgeable in matters of Jewish rituals offers the appropriate prayers.

Fig. 7.1 Issac's circumcision This illustration, from the Regensburg Pentateuch (German, c. 1300 c.e.), depicts the circumcision of Issac (Gen. 21:4). Photo courtesy Creative Commons: http://commons.wikimedia.org/wiki/File:Isaac%27s_circumcision,_Regensburg_c1300.jpg

The Reform/Liberal/Progressive movement in Judaism also addressed a further circumstance of modernity: Cases where either the mother or father is herself or himself not Jewish, but their agreed-on wish is to raise their son within the orbit of the organized Jewish community—what then? If the father is not Jewish, he may (or may not) have a role in the rituals, depending on the rabbi and the congregation. Because the status of the child in postbiblical Judaism follows that of the mother, the child is Jewish, no matter what. Reform rabbis, in the main, are not trained in the surgical procedures, and thus have long relied on medical professionals. In recent years, the movement itself has created educational opportunities for those professionals to learn the attendant Judaic rituals and textual sources (such as Torah/Hebrew Bible, Talmud, Codes, Midrash) to enable them, after certification, to officiate where no rabbi or cantor is present. Both male and female physicians have participated in this educational endeavor, a cause of some consternation among the more traditional adherents of religious Judaism. Equally, as a liberal religious movement, it will welcome both children and their families into their congregations as full participants, even where no such circumcisions have taken place.

Because this ritual is mandated to be held on the eighth day—the first day of life is counted as day one—thus the circumcision will take place one week later. Rabbinic midrashic tradition says that no matter what day of the week the boy is born, he will have celebrated his first Shabbat by the time of his Brit Milah in preparation for his entry into covenant with the God of Israel. Thus, it overrides *all* other Jewish events, including that of Yom Kippur. First things first—literally!

At the ceremony itself, the boy, presented by his father and honored by his grandfather or perhaps a close family friend (the *sandek* or "godfather," that is, God's representative), is usually given his first taste of sacramental wine after the required blessing ("Praised are you, O Lord our God, ruler of the universe, creator of the fruit of the vine"),

and his Hebrew name ("So and so, the son of his father [and mother]") is publicly announced. There does tend to be a party/reception, *not* in honor of the surgery itself, but rather, in celebration of the welcoming of this new life into the Jewish people.

As regards the adopted boy, infant, or young boy, the surgical procedure is the same as is the party/reception.

With regard to one who is already circumcised, there is a symbolic circumcision (usually the appearance of a single drop of blood taken from the shaft of the penis), which thus meets even the most stringent of Judaic interpretations, and applies in the cases of both underage males and those adults who would wish to convert.[3]

Naming a Daughter

Far different is the case of a daughter, for there is no Torah/Hebrew Bible passage anywhere on which one could create a comparable ritual with the power of the Brit Milah. Postbiblically, rabbinically, toward the latter Middle Ages, there arose the tradition of inviting the father of a newly born daughter on the Shabbat (Sabbath) after her birth to offer the incumbent blessings surrounding the reading/chanting of the Torah at worship, a practice that continues in many, many communities even today.

With the rise of modernity, and the ordaining of women to the rabbinate beginning in the last quarter of the twentieth century (the first women rabbi, Sally Priesand of Cleveland, Ohio, was ordained by the Reform Hebrew Union College-Jewish Institute of Religion in 1972), new doors have opened with regard to the birth of daughters. Some have created neutral "naming ceremonies" for both boys and girls, to be held on the eighth day after birth, but with rituals devoid of the specific focus on the circumcision itself. Others have created specific ceremonies focusing directly on the birth of daughters, also to be held on the eighth day, drawing on biblical stories of women and traditionally associated rituals such as the lighting of candles. Both of these are equally attentive to the reception-celebration and welcoming into the Jewish people the new life. Today, Reform, Reconstructionist, Conservative, and Humanistic Judaisms all have specific ritual ceremonies for welcoming daughters into their communities. Even within some Orthodox communities, rabbis and/or cantors will come and offer blessings to celebrate the birth of daughters. (There is, however, no standardization whatsoever of any rituals within any interpretation of Orthodox Judaism, Hasidic or non-Hasidic.)

One of the most creative suggestions to have been put on the table was that presented by Reconstructionist woman rabbi Sandy Eisenberg-Sasso of Temple Beth El Tzedec of Indianapolis, Indiana, who suggested, already in the mid-1970s, that the *power* of the physical ritual of Brit Milah mandated a comparable experience: her suggestion was that, on the eighth day, regardless of the other rituals and benedictions, newly born daughters would have their ears pierced and a small gold ball earring would be affixed to both ears. While she herself may conduct such within her own congregation (of which the author has no specific knowledge), and her suggestion makes intellectual sense, it has *not* become the norm of any Judaic religious movement whatsoever.

Pidyon Haben:
The Redemption
of the Firstborn Son

A most interesting biblically based ritual is that of the *pidyon haben*, the redeeming of the nonpriestly Israelite firstborn son from service to the ancient temple.

In *Bemidbar*/Numbers 8, we read the following text:

After the Levites lay their hands on the heads of the bulls, use the one for a sin offering to the LORD and the other for a burnt offering, to make atonement for the Levites. Have the Levites stand in front of Aaron and his sons and then present them as a wave offering to the LORD. In this way you are to set the Levites apart from the other Israelites, and the Levites will be mine.

After you have purified the Levites and presented them as a wave offering, they are to come to do their work at the Tent of Meeting. They are the Israelites who are to be given wholly to me. I have taken them as my own in place of the firstborn, the first male offspring from every Israelite woman. Every firstborn male in Israel, whether man or animal, is mine. When I struck down all the firstborn in Egypt, I set them apart for myself. And I have taken the Levites in place of all the firstborn sons in Israel. Of all the Israelites, I have given the Levites as gifts to Aaron and his sons to do the work at the Tent of Meeting on behalf of the Israelites and to make atonement for them so that no plague will strike the Israelites when they go near the sanctuary.

Though directed specifically toward the Levites, firstborn males in ancient Israel were still regarded as possessing a level of sanctity necessitating their "redemption" from a fuller life of religious obligation.

Today, as the ritual is practiced among the more traditionally observant (far less so if at all among the modernist movements of Reform and Reconstructionist Judaisms, both of which reject any dividing of the Jewish people as somehow discriminatory), it is celebrated on the thirty-first day of life of the newborn male. One who is known communally as a *kohen* (that is, one whose family tradition is that of descent from the ancient high priests of Israel and of Aaron's, Moses' brother's, family) symbolically receives from the observing family five *shekels* (ancient Israelite coinage, though recreated in the modern State of Israel as a monetary unit), which he returns to the family for the boy's future (an early male dowry, perhaps). The gold coins used are themselves symbolic, though some have used actual gold or silver dollars or other such currencies. In addition, there are attendant rituals of redemption, blessings, and reception-celebrations.

Consecration

A modernist innovation of the Reform movement within the last two hundred years, and now adopted and adapted by both Conservative and Reconstructionist Judaism (and, most interestingly, even within some, though far from all, non-Hasidic Orthodox congregations) is Consecration, celebrated on or around Simchat Torah in the fall.

As both boys and girls begin their formal Judaic religious education in either preschool, kindergarten, or first grade in their congregations, they are the ones to lead the first parade around their sanctuaries in honor of the completion of yet another year's Torah readings. In many congregations, prior to doing so, however, they are collectively invited onto the *bima*/pulpit and given the opportunity to recite *Devarim*/Deuteronomy 6:4 ("Hear O Israel: Adonai is our God, Adonai is one"). For those who, for whatever reason, have not yet had publicly announced their Hebrew names, this too may become part of the pulpit experience. Some congregations have even created special "sweet treats" (such as cookies with icing) for those who celebrate this new beginning.

The ceremony of Consecration, like the welcoming of the newborns, is a concrete and dramatic reminder to Jews that Jewish life, despite the tragedies of the past, continues, the future is not yet fixed, and thanksgiving to God is its most appropriate expression.

Bar and Bat Mitzvah

Perhaps the best known celebration in the larger world is that of bar mitzvah, the coming-of-age celebration of Jewish boys on the road to maturity at age thirteen, the actual celebration of which would occur closest to the actual birthday itself. The phrase itself, *bar mitzvah*, is a mix of the Aramaic *bar* ("son of") with that of the Hebrew word *mitzvah* ("command" or "obligation"), and signifies one who has reached the age of religious respon-

Fig. 7.2 Bar Mitzvah Bar mitzvah is the coming-of-age ceremony for Jewish young men at age thirteen; its equivalent for young women is bat mitzvah at age twelve years plus one day. The ceremony itself centers around reading and chanting from the Torah and a speech, usually a commentary on the scriptural selection. Photo: © Philippe Lissac/Godong/Corbis

Fig. 7.3
Bat Mitzvah
A teen-age girl is celebrating her bat mitzvah in her temple, as her parents look on during the ceremony.
Photo: © Comstock/Corbis

sibility by now being included in the *minyan* (the quorum of ten males necessary for the conduct of a full worship service). It is a noun phrase of affirmation, not a verb—that is, one *is* a bar mitzvah; one is *not* "barmitzvahed."

The communal/congregational expectation is that, after appropriate prior education in either a supplemental religious educational program or Jewish parochial school, the young man is able to lead his congregation in a smaller or larger part of a worship service, recite/chant the blessings before and after both the Torah portion (selection from the *Chumash*, Five Books of Moses) and *Haftarah* (additional scriptural reading, usually from the *Nevi'im*/Prophets, but possibly from the *Ketuvim*/Writings), and deliver a brief *drasha*/discourse/speech on the Torah selection read and studied. Depending on the young man's intellectual capabilities, rabbis and congregations have sensitively modified these expectations and requirements and tailored them somewhat to the celebrant. Jewish newspapers are

regularly filled with stories of young men with various learning disabilities who have "climbed the mountain" to celebrate their *barei mitzvah* (Hebrew plural) and their family's, friends', and congregation's joy and celebration with them.

Though not as well known, nor as practiced, the ceremony itself can take place any time there is a worship occasion with Torah reading. Traditionally, the Torah is read Monday, Thursday, and Saturday mornings, and the mornings of all holy days and festivals. (Because there is a tradition, however, that one does not mix two occasions of celebration—for example, bar mitzvah and a holiday other than the Shabbat—such celebrations do not usually take place on holidays and festivals.) Thus, Mondays, Thursday, and Shabbatot (plural of Shabbat) are all appropriate occasions, though, to be sure, Shabbat is when the overwhelming majority take place, with *Kiddush* luncheon celebrations and late, after Shabbat, parties.[4] (Though, at times, the butt of humor at the oversized lavishness of some attendant celebrations—the "classic" examples being that of American-Jewish author Phillip Roth [b. 1933] in his books *Goodbye Columbus* [1959] and *Portnoy's Complaint* [1969][5]—this is certainly not the norm for the overwhelming majority of Jewish families, where family and friends gather and modestly enjoy this milestone event.)

Approaching the one hundredth anniversary of the first bat mitzvah—that of the founder of Reconstructionist Judaism's Rabbi Mordecai Kaplan's (1881–1983) own daughter Judith (1905–1995) in 1922—this coming-of-age ceremony for young women is now the norm in Reform and Reconstructionist Judaisms, and is fast becoming the norm in Conservative Judaism. Young women become such at age twelve plus one day (so no birth-dating error occurs), perhaps a symbolic recognition that girls *do* mature fast than boys. Because the heart of the celebration is both the Torah reading and the conduct of worship (and within traditionally observant circles, women do not normatively do either), both Conservative and Orthodox Judaisms continue to wrestle with how best to do so in a Western world where gender equality itself is more and more becoming the norm. Unlike its male counterpart, the two-word phrase is fully Hebrew (*bat* = daughter of; *mitzvah* = "commandment" or "obligation"); its affirmation of the young woman's coming-of-age to religious maturity is the same, however (though traditional Orthodox Jews do not yet count them as part of the *minyan*).

Both Reform and Reconstructionist congregations and training programs draw no differentiations whatsoever: their classes are mixed, and young men and women take the same training. While it is usually the case within Conservative Judaism, the more and most traditional congregations still tend to have different tracks for boys and girls, but this too is fast becoming a thing of the past. Orthodox communities may have some kind of female group celebrations, but they do not celebrate *batei* (plural of *bat*) *mitzvah* as described here.

Confirmation

In early nineteenth-century Germany, the burgeoning Reform movement came to the conclusion that the bar mitzvah celebration of young males was religiously discriminatory and incompatible with their own desire for gender equality—without innovatively creating a parallel ceremony for young women. Their solution was the creation of "Confirmation," a group coming-of-age ceremony for both boys and girls, age approximately thirteen but celebrated together. This term and idea was already in place in the Protestant Christianities to which these "modernist" Jews were exposed, and may, in truth, have been the source of their inspiration.

It has evolved, however, not in the way its creators could have imagined: Reform Judaism in its seeming return to more traditional forms of Judaic religious practice—having reintroduced bar mitzvah and added bat mitzvah—(Reconstructionist and Conservative Judaisms doing the same) has upped the celebration of Confirmation to tenth grade (primarily), but also in some congregations to either eleventh or twelfth grade, and marked it as the moment of "graduation" from the congregation's formal school process, and as noted in the previous chapter, associated it with the celebration of the holy day of Shavuot ("Weeks," seven weeks after the Pesach/Passover), when traditionally, Jews affirm Moses' return from *Har Sinai*/Mount Sinai with the *Aseret Hadibrot*/Ten Commandments, symbolic of the whole of the Judaic religious tradition.

The yearlong program of study is usually one conducted by the rabbis of the congregation, involving text study, practical activities ("doing mitzvot," in this case understood in its more popular form as "good deeds," and some social service project, either within or outside of the Jewish community—for example, helping with a food kitchen for the less fortunate or raising money for charitable purposes), and culminating in a creatively crafted worship service drawing on contemporary sources, additional readings, youth-oriented music, but one that still follows the basic outline of classical Judaic worship, no matter how innovative. Its purpose is to allow these further maturing Jewish young people to affirm their faith as Jews as they go on to higher education (the communal and familial expectation) and make their way in the world.

There is, interestingly enough, no ceremony in any of the streams of religious Judaism when the last child leaves home and the parents find themselves alone together for the first time in more than two decades, though there is "marriage dance" when the last child marries. These "religiously quiet" years are filled with expectation and promise as both parents and community—and the child—plan for the future.

Marriage
(and Engagement)

Those who are familiar with the character of the *shadchan*, or marriage broker, in the play and film "Fiddler on the Roof" (though, in part, created for comic relief) know that so-called arranged marriages were already prevalent in the biblical period even as the Torah/Hebrew Bible addressed marriage resulting from "falling in love" (the cases of *Yitzchak*/Isaac and *Ya'akov*/Jacob in the Book of *Bereshith*/Genesis 21 and 24, in the case of the former, and 28 and 29, in the case of the latter, are mixtures of both). Marriage, either to one "favored

Fig. 7.4 Jewish wedding under the chuppah (marriage canopy) Wedding of Barry and Hilit Edelstein at the History Edridge Street Synagogue, New York City, November 9, 2003. Photo: Mario Tama/Getty News Images/Getty Images

wife" among many or to only one wife (as has been the Ashkenazic custom for more than one thousand years and the Sephardic custom fully even since the creation of the modern State of Israel in 1948) has remained the foundational societal concept of communal stability and the rock on which all else has been built.

And, like their non-Jewish counterparts, Jews have also understood the journey to marriage to have two parts: a period of engagement (Hebrew, *erusin*), where personal commitment is in evidence, whether arranged or by personal choice, and the marriage itself (Hebrew, *nissu'in*, "holy separation," for the wedding, and marriage itself or *qiddushin*, "sanctification"; for some, these terms are interchangeable), both of which are understood to have legal implications and ramifications, and thus require the signing of formal and witnessed documents. Ideally, the former was to last approximately one year, and the latter a lifetime (although divorce is a religious reality and is consequently discussed in the next section). In essence, marriage, family, and children are and have been the three building blocks upon which Jews continue to base their lives, and on which they center both their communities and their religious lives. (Note that in all interpretations of the Jewish religious tradition, *all* members of the family are to be treated with honor and respect: husbands to their wives, wives to their husbands, children to their parents, and parents to their children.)

Jewish wedding ceremonies are relatively short, approximately thirty minutes; indeed, all Jewish life-cycle ceremonies are relatively short, understood as "gateways" to the actual events themselves (Brit Milah [circumcision] to life; weddings to marriage; funerals to eternal life). The actual length of the ceremony varies with its various accoutrements: numbers of those in attendance for the *hatan* (Hebrew, groom) and *kalah* (Hebrew, bride); length of the wedding *derasha*/sermonette by the officiant, rabbi, or cantor; length of processional and reces-

sional; and so on. What follows is an outline of its component parts as they have evolved in postbiblical or rabbinic Judaism. (The Torah/Hebrew BIble is remarkably silent about such ceremonies.)

1. **Welcoming Blessings**, welcoming not only the bride and groom and blessing them, but all those in attendance.

2. **Declaration of Intention**, by which the bride and groom publicly announce the reason for the gathering.

3. **First *Kiddush***, sanctification of wine because of the joy of the occasion, and, for some, reminder that the couple had completed their *erusin*, their period of engagement.

4. **Seven Wedding Blessings** (Hebrew, *Sheva Berachot*), all of which begin "Praised are you, O Lord our God, ruler of the universe . . ." and include (a) "who has created all things for your glory," (b) "who has created man/humanity," (c) "who has created man/humanity in Your image," (d) "who gladdens Zion though her children," (e) "who gladdens bride and groom," (f) "who creates joy and gladness," and (g) "who has created the fruit of the vine" (Second *Kiddush*). Traditionally and historically, the bride has paraded herself at this point in the ceremony around her groom seven times in honor of these benedictions. Some modernists have understood this to be an example of gender inequity, and have either dispensed with it entirely or have both bride and groom parade around each other. (In traditional circles, however, the bride may circle her groom upon arrival at the chuppah, rather than at this point in the service itself.)

Fig. 7.5 The chuppah The chuppah is the canopy under which a Jewish wedding is performed. This chuppah was used at a synagogue in Washington, D.C. Photo courtesy Creative Commons: http://commons.wikimedia.org/wiki/File:Chupah_closeup.JPG

5. **Giving of the Bride's Ring**, by the groom with the traditional formula, "Behold you are consecrated unto me with this ring [as my wife] in accordance with the laws of Moses and Israel." (Historically, males' wearing of wedding rings was seen as a non-Jewish custom, and thus there was no equivalent exchange. In the modern period, however, as more and more Jewish men outside of Orthodox circles continue to do so, there has been an exchange of such with the bride saying to her groom the same affirmation.)

6. **Reading of the Wedding Contract** (Hebrew, *ketubah*), and spelling out the groom's obligations to his bride. Contemporary innovative *ketubot* (Hebrew plural), resulting from the movement toward gender equality, have resulted in texts where both spell out their obligations to each other. Although stark in their original writing, they continue to be created by both *soferim*/scribes and calligraphers and have become, ever since the Middle Ages, a form of Judaic art. (The *ketubah* is signed prior to the start of the ceremony; in traditional circles with the bride and groom separated from one another; in more liberal circles together. Also, depending on tradition, the bride appears to her groom before the ceremony with her veil lifted, which he will then place over her face as the biblical *Ya'akov* did to *Rivka*/Rebecca, a moment called *bedekin*, or "veiling.")

7. **Declaration of the Authority of the Officiant**, usually a rabbi or cantor or both together, with the rabbi conducting the service and delivering the *derashah*/sermonette, and the cantor singing/chanting various parts of the liturgy.

8. **Blessing of the Couple**, for their future, their home, and their family.

9. **Groom Stepping and Breaking the Glass**, interrupting momentarily the joyous occasion with a startling reminder of past sadnesses, including the destructions of the temples, the incompleteness of a world in need of the couple's own unique contributory gifts and energies. Upon its breaking, those gathered will shout *Mazal tov!* ("Congratulations!") to the new family just created.

Before the new husband and wife join their guests for their reception, they will momentarily go to a room and enjoy a piece of cake and drink (Hebrew, *cheder yichud*, "room for privacy"), for some traditional Jews the very first time they have been alone together; for others honoring a tradition; but for both symbolic of the privacy central to family life.

There is no one primary location for Jewish weddings: synagogues, homes, outdoors, hotels, restaurants, all can be appropriately sanctified by and for such occasions. However, Jews, no matter where, tend to be married under a chuppah, or canopy, symbolic of their future home (and/or the marriage bed itself where they become truly one as husband and wife).

As mentioned before, there is a tradition practiced among all streams of Judaism that, when the last child on either side is married, the parents are seated and all the married children dance around them, celebrating the gift of life they have been given, their debt to their parents, and their commitment to continuing in their own parents' ways, creating a Jewish present and future.

A word here about what is perhaps the most vexing problem of modern Jewish life for those who live outside of structured Jewish communities, whose interactions with the larger societies of non-Jews bring them into contact—in the workplace, in the colleges and/universities where their children study—more and more with people whose moral-ethical value systems are compatible with their own, and whose "only" differences are those associated with religion: the topic of inter- (religious) marriage or "mixed" (religious) marriage.

Many years ago, the author chanced to read *Jews and Non-Jews Falling in Love* by Reform Rabbi Sanford Seltzer.[6] Sensitively written and addressing this complex reality, only the title seemed to be wrong: Jews do not fall in love with non-Jews: People fall in love with people (exactly how we do not know, and the scientific community has been of little help in this area); sometimes they happen to be Jews and sometimes not. Prior to that, one of

his now late professors, Rabbi Dr. Eugene Mihaily, *alav hashalom* ("May he rest in peace," the traditional appellation for one fondly remembered), at the Hebrew Union College-Jewish Institute of Religion, Cincinnati, Ohio, made the rather astute observation that "intermarriage is the price we Jews pay for life in an open society. The alternative is to return to our Pre-Modern ghettoes. The question is how best to address it."

Indeed, that is the question: How best to address this new reality of modern Jewish life, made all the more difficult where Jews are both accepted and warmly welcomed, where access to residence, profession of choice, and even marital partners no longer present themselves as obstacles to either present or future. It is made still more complicated wherever Jews live by the simple fact that no one has yet been able to determine with any degree of accuracy the *critical mass number* needed for Jewish communal viability. (Is it 1,000,000 or more? 500,000? 250,000?) And because the overwhelming majority of Jews have no plans whatsoever to return to a ghettoized form of communal life, and their children less so, how to meet what many continue to regard as a "crisis of concern" remains on the public agendas of Jewish communal and religious organizations.

One "solution," if that is indeed the correct term in this instance, has been to try to inculcate in the younger generations of Jews so strong a Zionist orientation that, when able to do so, they will move to the State of Israel and become part of the "Jewish State," and thereby increase their chances of marrying Jewish partners. Another "solution" has been that of the more traditional religious streams of Judaism, essentially shunning those who would marry non-Jews and/or making the process of conversion (see below) so difficult as to prohibitively discourage such interactions on the part of their children and thus keeping them within their own structured communities. A third "solution" has been to welcome into Jewish religious life (and Jewish communal life) such families while at the same time strongly and creatively encouraging conversion of the non-Jewish partners and offspring. Here, both the Reform and Reconstructionist movements have pioneered various approaches, the Conservative movement less so but still concerned and struggling to articulate a consistent position. The various streams of Orthodoxy are less welcoming and more reluctant to address the issue in a noncondemnatory way. Ideally, perhaps, some combination of all these possibilities makes the best sense, as the Jewish people collectively continues to struggle with these concerns, but no such collective solution appears in the present or on the horizon. Crystal balls are notorious for their inability to predict the future, as are those in positions of Jewish leadership. What will prove to be the best solution to the dilemma of intermarriage/mixed marriage has yet to be decided.

Divorce

Unlike some aspects of Christianity and some interpretations of the New Testament (in which one finds the sentence, "That which God has put together, let no man put asunder" [Mark 10:9], understood to prohibit divorce), Judaism accepts divorce as among life's tragedies, but one at times necessary if families and communities are to survive and endure. Indeed, the Torah/Hebrew Bible makes reference to a *Sefer Kri'tut* in *Devarim*/Deuteronomy 24:1 ("a document of cutting"), which scholars understand to mean a document of marital divorce, but no archaeologist has yet to unearth one. The Talmud, in *Tractate Sanhedrin* 22a, weighs in on the topic, acknowledging that "Even God sheds tears when a man divorces his wife."

As Judaism has evolved from its biblical beginnings into its rabbinic period and now its modern period, divorce has become somewhat standardized, first among the Orthodox Jews, second among Conservantive and Reconstructionist Jews, and last among Reform Jews, who heretofore accepted as fully valid only the legal documents offered by the state before officiating at remarriage but which are more and more issuing and using their own documents of divorce.

The Jewish document of divorce is called a *get* (Hebrew), and is traditionally twelve lines of text (Hebrew letter *gimmel* = 3; Hebrew letter *tet* = 9), written by a *sofer*/scribe, and given by the husband to his wife. Among the reasons that have been given historically are a woman's inability to bear male children, or children at all (no acknowledgment here of either male sterility or low sperm count), inability to maintain the home and perform those duties associated with its upkeep, falling out of love, and into love with another, and of course (though rarely), sexual improprieties. The problem, however, is gender inequity for those who wish to follow halakha (Jewish law) strictly: the process is that of husband to wife; the wife has no option other than appealing to the *bet din* (a rabbinic court consisting of three rabbis) to pressure her husband to do so. If he, for whatever reason, refuses to do so, he *cannot* be compelled to grant a divorce. His wife then becomes known as an *agunah*, or "chained woman," living in limbo, where she remains married to someone with whom she does not live; whom she does not love and does not love her; is unable to remarry; and is simply and tragically bound to a system with no apparent resolution. Attempts to find a resolution in the United States, in Israel, and in other locations where sizable Orthodox Jewish communities exist have yet to meet with success.

As to the actual presentation of the document, which occurs in the presence of the rabbi of one's congregation or a rabbinic court, neither party need be present but may send representative agents instead (Hebrew, *shelichim*, emissaries). Prior to its acceptance by the woman or her representative, the document itself is cut with a knife (acknowledging the Torah/Hebrew Bible's understanding of its own document as one which was somehow "cut," even if only symbolically). Once divorced, and after a sufficient waiting period, each party is free to remarry, with the exception of the tradition that those who are *kohanim* (Hebrew, descendants of the Aaronide priestly tradition) and who cannot marry those who have been divorced.

There is no religious ceremony as such associated with the presentation of the *get*; it is a legal proceeding within the parameters of the Jewish religious tradition. Its very starkness drives home its sadness. While some more liberal rabbis have suggested the need for such a ritual ceremony, taking place perhaps within a synagogue sanctuary context with both parties involved, and especially where there are children, no one has thus far created such a liturgy acceptable to any of the Jewish denominational religious movements.

Conversion

Conversion, that is, the welcoming into a religious community one not born into the group, is a post-biblical or rabbinic creation. In the biblical period, non-Israelites became Israelites by surrendering their former identities, taking upon themselves their new identities, and after the birth of their children, their former identities became irrelevant as they and their progeny were fully Israelite in every sense of the term.

In the post-Roman, postbiblical period, the rabbis essentially established the outline of practices that remain consistent within the major denominational streams of religious Judaism.

First, all candidates for conversion within any of the movements undergo an intensive educational journey, lasting anywhere from one to three years, and reinforcing the Talmudic dictum, *Lo am-haaretz hasid*, to wit, "An ignorant Jew will never be a pious Jew."

Second, all candidates involve themselves in the religious lives of Jewish communities by regular attendance at Shabbat and holiday observances,

often hosted by mentoring families who take them under their wing and share with them Jewish customs in a more relaxed and informal educational setting.

Third, all candidates involve themselves in the "civic life" of Jewish communities by their participation in events not related to either classroom or sanctuary (for example, Jewish community lectures or theatrical or other programs), all part of the rich cultural life of organized Jewish communities.

Fourth, both men and women undergo ritual immersion in the *mikveh* (Hebrew, Jewish ritual pool), and thus are symbolically reborn into new

Fig. 7.6 A medieval mikveh This mikveh (or mikvah) (Hebrew: מ ק ו ה; Tiberian *Miqwāh*, Standard Hebrew *Miqva*; plural, *mikvaot*) is located in Speyer, Germany, first mentioned in the year 1128. The bath was forgotten and built over until being rediscovered and made accessible to the public. This is one of the best preserved medieval mikvaot. Photo courtesy Creative Commons: http://commons.wikimedia. org/wiki/File:Judenbad_Speyer_3_First_Room_view.jpg

Jewish selves. While, unlike the other Jewish religious movements, Reform Judaism historically shied away from this ritual (as well as the next), it has reembraced ritual immersion more and more in its ceremonies of conversion.

Fifth, all men are expected to undergo either Brit Milah (circumcision) or ritual recircumcision as evidence of their becoming part of the covenanted community of *Avraham*/Abraham and his descendants.

Once the process has been fully completed, all streams of Judaism have ritual-ceremonial traditions, which allow candidates to affirm their new religious identity and affords them the opportunity for the public announcement of their Hebrew name. (Because the candidate has no Jewish parents, the patriarch *Avraham*/Abraham and his wife *Tzarah*/Sarah are the "new Jew's" spiritual parents, and one's name becomes "So-and-so, the son/daughter of Abraham and Sarah.")

So seriously did the rabbis of old (and Jews today) take conversion (Hebrew, *gerut*) that, upon completion, the candidate, now a Jew, was considered 100 percent Jewish, so much so that those who are Jews are forbidden to acknowledge previous religious identity, though the "new Jew" may choose to share such information. In effect, these "Jews by choice" as the now-popular translation has it, are understood to be the equal of all other Jews (though human realities being what they are, one still on occasion hears sad stories of less than full acceptance by either new families or existing communities, practices frowned on and actively discouraged by rabbis in all movements)

One problem that continues to remain unresolved, however, is that of crossdenominational acceptance of other movements' conversionary practices. Creative resolutions have been attempted in both Israel and the United States, but without sustained success. The problem, as it has survived, is that two of the Jewish religious movements—Orthodox and Conservative—are halakhic (legally interpretive understandings), and two—Reform and Reconstructionist—are not halakhic in their interpretive understandings. While the nonhalakhic movements have no difficulties in accepting halakhic conversions, the reverse has not been the case (that is, not meeting the legal requirements has led to continued questioning of the validity of those conversions as well as those who officiate at them, both in Israel and throughout the rest of the world where Jews reside). The problem is most acute in Israel itself, where Jewish life-cycle affirmations (birth, marriage, and death) are under the control of a centrist to rightist Orthodoxy, which continues not to acknowledge the religious validity of other movements, to the point of so far unsuccessfully attempting to amend Israel's Law of the Right of Return for Jews to become automatic citizens for those who have converted in all non-Orthodox movements. Like the *agunah*/divorce problem addressed above, Jews the world over eagerly await creative solutions from their leadership.

Death, Burial, and Mourning

The Jewish religious tradition may best be described as a "fast burying tradition," stemming as it does from a desert world of intense heat and no refrigeration, but one which is guided by two governing principles and framed by respect for the body itself (understood already in *Bereshith*/Genesis as the vessel of the "holy soul," which connects humanity to God—what is perhaps meant by "being created in the divine image"). Those two principles are, first, simplicity of behavior as it has evolved its patterns of response to death, burial, and mourning, and, second, recognition of the *reality* that a death has taken place (that the deceased did not "pass away" or "pass on" or some other euphemistic phrase; he or she *died*). This orientation is most seen (literally) not only in the brevity of its funeral services themselves, about fifteen minutes, but the lack of flowers and/or other forms of beautification surrounding the funeral. (The only exception to the latter is cemeteries throughout the world where highly decorative crypts, above ground, are in evidence for those wealthy enough to afford them. Many Jews, however, tend to be buried in "plain pine boxes" or simple coffins, and their gravesites marked by either ground-level stone markers or simple above-ground headstones or footstones.) What follows, then, as always, in broad brushstrokes and in recognition of the degree of variance within the Judaic religious movements is the outline of Jewish mourning practices as they have come to be observed by the Jews the world over.[7]

Aninut

Once the actual death has occurred, prior to the funeral, the mourner, along with close family and friends is involved with initial preparations. (The responsibility of friends is to provide for food needs, both during this period and afterward.) Visitation by those less close is actively discouraged, as the surviving family members must now confront the enormity of their loss (even if supposedly

Fig. 7.7 Burial ceremony This burial ceremony of Jewish religious leader Hacham Yedidia Shofet took place in Mission Hills, California, 25 June 2005. Photo courtesy Creative Commons: http://commons.wikimedia.org/wiki/File:Burial_Ceremony.JPG

pre-prepared because of illness). In Orthodox and Conservative congregations, less so in Reform and Reconstructionist congregations but increasingly so, there are *chevrei kaddisha* (Hebrew, "holy societies") that will claim the bodies and prepare them for burial by washing them, paring fingernails and toenails, and dressing them in white linen shrouds. Because Jewish funerals *must* be close-coffined, physical disfigurement the result of war or disease is not particularly relevant. Prior to the actual funeral in the funeral home, there is the traditional practice of having someone, or a rotation of people, stay up all night with the body to read from the Book of Psalms.

The funeral, itself short, is usually conducted by rabbis or cantors (or other knowledgeable persons) and consists of passages from the Book of Psalms, other readings, a *hespaid* or eulogy (which Jewish tradition suggests one is obliged to tell only half a person's goodness at that occasion), and the actual physical burial of the deceased in Jewishly consecrated ground (either a cemetery wholly owned by a congregation or community, or a section, usually cordoned off, of a larger cemetery). Traditionally observant Jews will fully lower the body into the ground and be responsible for its burial. (Funeral homes and non-Jewish cemetery workers are a modern accretion.) Less traditional Jews will have others lower the coffin, usually after the service has been completed, and shovel three symbolic mounds of dirt onto the coffin, and allow those in attendance, family and friends, to also participate. Both upon entering and upon leaving the cemetery, some Jews will symbolically wash their hands, as they will also do upon entering and leaving a house of mourning.

Shivah

For the next seven days (*shivah* is Hebrew for "seven"), those in mourning will now deal with the pain of their loss. In many homes, mirrors are covered, mourners sit on low benches (evidence that they have "been brought low"), neither shave nor wear cosmetic makeup, refrain from going to work or school, do not participate in celebratory events (though they may attend regular worship) including sexual relations with spouses, and begin the process of learning to deal with the new reality of their loss. There is usually a daily worship service in the home, attended by family and friends, though not on the Shabbat, when the family goes to the synagogue to hear the name of the deceased called out during the memorial part of the service.

Sheloshim

Sheloshim is Hebrew for "thirty." This period marks the gradual reintegration of the mourners back into communal life: returning to work and worship (though again refraining from celebrations while attending religiously connected events), the resumption of normal family activities as, gradually and increasingly, family and friends go about their business without the benefit of the physical presence of the one who has died.

This entire journey of mourning is extended into an eleven-month period from the initial moment of the death of the deceased. Religiously observant Jews will say the daily *Kaddish* (memorial prayer which is a litany of praise to the God of Israel while making no mention of mourning and death whatsoever), attending daily or weekly worship services, and slowly and ideally successfully rejoining the society of which they are a part. Psychologists and other healing professionals tell us that healthy reintegration after the death of a loved one *should* take approximately one year. After that, the continuing inability to reconnect may be a sign of unhealthy psychological reactions and the need for therapeutic intervention.

Approximately one year later—the *Yahrtzeit* (German, "year-time") anniversary of the death—it is common to dedicate or consecrate the stone marker with a brief ceremony, not understood to be a second funeral but a brief reflection on the life of the one now gone. Such markers have traditionally been inscribed with, in addition to the person's name in both Hebrew and local language and dates of birth and death, the phrase at the top, "Here lies . . . " along with, "May his/her soul be bound up in the bond of eternal life." Additionally, the name will be announced at the Shabbat worship after the actual date of death. From now on, it will become an annual occurrence, as well as inclusion in the four *yizkor*/memorial services during the holy day calendar: Yom Kippur, Sukkot, Pesach, and Shavuot.

Last, rabbinic tradition is extremely vague about the concept of the "soul," that is, the non-physical part of the human person, though there is in the literature the idea that, prior to birth, all such entities reside with the God of Israel, and after death, such entities return to the God of Israel, where they dwell forever. (The dualistic distinction of the soul's purity and the body's impurity, which is largely uncorrectable in Christianity, does not find its resonance within Judaic religious tradition.) As regards the *olam haba* (Hebrew, "the world to come"), the rabbis are purposely vague, preferring to leave such thinking to others, though we do know that, historically, the Pharisees themselves—rabbinic precursors—were committed to the literal physical resurrection of the dead and that this concept is very much alive among some in the most traditional expressions of Judaic religion today. Also, this future world was not limited only to Jews or even righteous Jews, to wit, the Talmud (*Tosefta* to *Sanhedrin* 13) includes the often-quoted phrase "the righteous of all nations have a share in the world to come." Further, for Jews, "heaven" and "hell," as understood by Christianity, are also understood vaguely, though heaven, as the abode of the God of Israel does exist and must be akin to the ancient Garden of Eden. Hell, on the other hand (though in the Torah/Hebrew Bible there are references to the "netherworld"), must be like *Gehinnom* or *Gehenna*, the foul-smelling garbage dump outside of ancient Jerusalem. The bottom line of Judaic faith on these matters is to leave all in the hands of

God: one's earthly job is to live life in accord with the highest moral-ethical principles as defined by the Jewish religious tradition and to practice religious observance as scrupulously as humanly possible, and when the earthly journey is at its end and one is in God's presence, deeds will be weighed and determinations made.

Addendum: Jewish Synagogal and Communal Life

Not strictly speaking part of the life-cycle as such, but appropriate as an addendum in this context, Jewish life, both synagogal and communal, is organized and regulated. Though we do not know the true origins of the synagogue, many scholars think its beginnings can be traced back to the period of the Babylonian Captivity (post-586 B.C.E.), when the Israelites were forced to restructure their religious regimen, without benefit of the temple and priestly sacrificial cult, and turned to Scripture-story retelling, direct prayerful communication with God, and a renewed emphasis on moral-ethical behavior (which the prophets had unsuccessfully tried to renew in their critiques of their fellow Israelites, and which, they argued, led to the downfall of both the northern and southern kingdoms).

As the synagogue had been created as the portable home of Jews in their wanderings for the last 2,000 years, its raison d'être is threefold: as a *beit hatefila* (Hebrew, "house of prayer or worship"), a *beit hamidrash* (Hebrew, "house of study or learning"), and a *beit haknesset* (Hebrew, "house of assembly or gathering"). It is, truly, the Jew's home away from home, the only institution ever created by Jews to concern itself with the life of the Jew as individual and Jew as communal member from first breath until last. Today, not unlike all professionalizations, it is staffed by one or more rabbis (senior, associate, and/or assistant), who are charged with overall responsibility for the religious life of the congregation; a cantor, tasked with specific responsibility for the liturgical life of the congregation; a director of education of either its supplemental or parochial school; a business administrator responsible for the practical realities of running an institution (bill paying and collection, building maintenance); support staff (secretarial and janitorial); and governed by an elected board of trustees headed by a president, one or more vice-presidents, elected corresponding and recording secretaries, treasurer, and board members in varying numbers depending on the size of the congregation. Constituent organizations include a sisterhood or ladies guild, a men's club or brotherhood, and a high school youth group, and possibly a junior high youth group as well. Institutionally, synagogues (sometimes called "temples" in non-Orthodox movements) tend to be parts of larger regional, national, and international organizations and affiliated with their own denominational movements. Support monies are raised through the payment of dues, both in individual synagogues as well as movement affiliations. Those with more give more; those with less give less; everyone contributes; and, ideally, no one is turned away for an

Fig. 7.8 Beth Sholom synagogue, Elkins Park, Pennsylvania Here is a truly unique example of American synagogue architecture by the famous American architect Frank Lloyd Wright (1867–1959). Photo courtesy Creative Commons: http://commons.wikimedia.org/wiki/File:Frank_Lloyd_Wright_-_Beth_Sholom_Synagogue_3.JPG

inability to contribute. Programmatically, synagogues are themselves centers of Jewish life: in addition to full worship and educational calendars, they sponsor social events, speakers, cultural programs and the like, and their rabbis in their *drashot* (Hebrew plural of *derasha*, or sermon) address not only the texts and interpretations of Torah/Hebrew Bible, Talmud, Midrash, but issues of concerns to Jews (for example, Israel and the Middle East crises, antisemitism, and intermarriage/mixed marriage).

Communally, already in the post-Roman world in Babylonia, and the movements west and east, Jews organized themselves, clustering themselves together for safety, security, and survival. In periods of instability, communal leaders arose who spoke for their communities directly to the seats of power and attempted to mediate between them and their people. In periods of stability, they turned their focus inward and involved themselves in the present and future direction of their communities, and their economic and social well-being. Rabbis served their people as both religious and communal leaders, attempting to mediate disputes among their own, and on occasion serving as representatives outside the ghetto walls.

Today, Jewish life throughout the world is made up of a plethora of organizations of which the synagogue or synagogues are only a part. There are Jewish community centers that focus primarily on social communal programming, defense and educational organizations, religious organizations, interest organizations, fraternal organizations, and cultural organizations. Indeed, no matter where one wants to invest one's Jewish energies, there are, in all likelihood, one or more organizations compatible with one's desires. In the United States, there is even an organization of organizations, that is, the Conference of Presidents of Major American Jewish Organizations, composed of fifty-one such groups (and based on the size of their memberships). Such a "surfeit of blessings" is indicative of a healthy Jewish people, not immune from the problems, stresses, and strains of its own existence, but a people facing its future wherever it leads.

IN REVIEW

We have now completed our journey of "Jewish life on the ground," as it were. With the celebration of the Jewish holidays, holy days, festivals, and fast days and the human journey from birth through maturation, decay, and death, what has emerged is a clearer picture of who the Jews are in real life and how they practice their Judaism in real life. We next turn to a somewhat "darker side" of that reality, which takes us all the way back into history and explores present-day Jewish concerns.

KEY TERMS

Aninut	*Beit hatefila*
bar mitzvah	*Chevra kaddisha*
bat mitzvah	confirmation
Bedekin	consecration
Beit haknesset	*Erusin*
Beit hamidrash	*Get*

continues on following page

interreligious marriage	Nissu'in
Kaddish	Pidyon Haben
Ketubah	Sefer Kri'tut
Kiddush	Shabbat
Kiddushin	Shelichim
Kohanim	Sheloshim
Mazal tov	Shivah
mixed marriage	sofer
mohel	Yahrtzeit

Questions for Review, Study, and Discussion

1. Again, imagine yourself as an anthropologist of religion/Judaism about to embark on an ethnographic fieldwork study in your community. Again, contact the local Jewish congregation and secure permission to attend a bar and bat mitzvah, consecration, and confirmation worship service. (While a Brit Milah, wedding, and funeral would also certainly be appropriate, they tend to be somewhat private events, usually by personal invitation only.) What additional research do you need to do before attending (for example, if you happen to know a Jewish person, consider the possibility of an interview)? If there is more than one Jewish congregation in your community, so much the better! Ideally, commit yourself to attending each of these different Jewish congregations. After attending these life-cycle events, record your impressions of what you have experienced: What are your immediate impressions of these events? In what ways are they the same? Different? How do they compare with your own experiences of other life-cycle events you may have experienced? In what ways are they the same? Different?

Suggested Readings

Goldberg, Harvey E. *Jewish Passages: Cycles of Jewish Life*. Berkeley: University of California Press, 2003.

Gutman, Joseph. *The Jewish Life Cycle*. Leiden: Brill, 1997.

Isaacs, Ronald H. *Sacred Moments: Tales from the Jewish Life Cycle*. Northvale, N.J.: Jason Aronson, 1995.

Marcus, Ivan G. *The Jewish Life Cycle: Rites of Passage from Biblical to Modern Times*. Seattle: University of Washington Press, 2004.

Milgram, Goldie. *Living the Jewish Life Cycle: How to Create Meaningful Jewish Rites of Passage at Every Stage of Life*. Woodstock, Vt.: Jewish Lights, 2009.

CHAPTER 8

Cycles *of the* HERE AND NOW

The Twenty-first-Century Moment and Beyond

OVERVIEW

In this chapter, we will address those concerns that continue to occupy not only Jewish thinkers and writers but Jewish communities and their leaderships as well: concerns such as the safety, security, and survival not only of the Israeli Jewish community but the American Jewish community and Jews worldwide; the ever-present specter of antisemitism ("the longest hatred and the biggest lie") not only in the West but the Middle East; and the still-irresolvable Israeli–Arab/Palestinian conflict. In so doing, we are preparing ourselves for our final chapter on the future of Judaism and the Jewish people.

Introduction

Given the extraordinary historical journey of the Jews—the goods with the bads; the ups with the downs—and the evolving creativity of its religious expressions throughout its journey, at the beginning of this twenty-first century, only the most naïve reader would suggest a present and future free of difficulties (but certainly ones also filled with promises and successes). In their excellent edited compendium *Modern Judaism*,[1] Nicholas de Lange (University of Cambridge) and Miri Freud-Kandel (University of Oxford) brought together thirty-one academic colleagues to address a variety of "issues" under ten rubrics: (1) historical, (2) religion and modernity, (3) local, (4) societal, (5) religious,

(6) theological, (7) philosophical, (8) halakhic, (9) gender, and (10) the other. To address all of them would require, equally, a text of comparable length (459 pages!). Instead, this chapter will focus on three of those issues, ones that loom largest in Jewish thinking and consciousness and that, in the process, bring forth more publications and presentations, both within and outside of Jewish circles than others. The three issues are under the three following headings: (1) "American, Israeli, and Worldwide Jewish Survival," (2) "Antisemitism: The Hatred Old and New," and (3) "The Middle East: Israel and Her Neighbors." (Readers are urged, however, to examine de Lange and Freud-Kandel's text on these specific issues and those not addressed here.)

American, Israeli, and Worldwide Jewish Survival

As addressed in chapter 2 ("Cycles of History: The Judaic Journey"), Adolf Hitler, *yemach sh'mo* ("May his name be blotted out!" the ultimate Hebraic and Judaic curse), and his minions were perhaps more successful in their attempt to *globally* exterminate and annihilate the Jewish people than has been heretofore realized. The true *meaning* of this mid-twentieth-century destruction of Jewish lives is a present and future population diminished by half: that is, if the demographers are correct, had these horrific events not occurred (and one certainly wishes they would not have, but history is not reversible), it is both likely and probable that the current worldwide Jewish population, taking into consideration post–World War II realities, could presently be approaching 28 to 32 million persons, rather than the current 14 to 16 million persons. With the American Jewish communities approximately 6 million persons, the Israeli Jewish communities approximately 6 million, and 2 to 4 million Jews scattered elsewhere (predominantly Canada and South America, Western Europe, the former Soviet Union, and Australia/Oceania), Jews throughout the world share a common concern with their collective survival. And it is no wonder!

For among the worldwide Jewish people are those for whom their Judaic identity, religious as well as nonreligious, is central to their existence, those for whom it is central most of the time and peripheral at other times, and those for whom it is peripheral all the time. Coupled with this is the sociological reality that the longer one's period of education (a primary Judaic value), the later one marries and the fewer children in one's family, which adds yet another level of anxiety. Third, in environments where Jews are increasing welcomed and accepted (the United States being the prime example), diminished Jewish commitments resulting from intermarriage/mixed marriage increase the angst.

For those in the first category, issues and concerns with Jewish survival (that is, the literal *physical* survival of those who identify with and positively wear the label "Jew") is paramount. For those in the second category, they too are somewhat concerned if perhaps less committed, but are more willing to be on the receiving end of innovative programs to ensure such survival, rather than on the so-called frontlines of addressing the question. For those in the third category, the "accident" of their birth is just that, neither a fortuitous nor disadvantageous event, but a simple fact, one of questionable meaning in the working out of their lives and, following the normal human progression of plodding the path of least resistance, they are as likely as not to remain within the structures of the organized Jewish communities where they reside, but do not communicate to their own offspring the positivity of Jewish involvement. That is, they *may* join Jewish religious congregations in diminishing numbers, they *may* educate their children Jewishly, they *may* contribute financially to Jewish causes, and they *may* remain current in their knowledge of issues of Judaic concern.

Thus, in surveying the worldwide communities of Jews, two opposite approaches appear to present themselves: organizations and communities that invest their energies and resources in programs and opportunities directed toward those who are already committed to Jewish life and Jewish survival, regardless of denominational affiliation, and others who direct their energies and resources in "outreach" (the currently preferred term) toward those who are only marginally identified and marginally concerned. As regards the latter, however, while their publications and presentations are always framed by "successes" in reclaiming and returning their fellow Jews to the fullness of Jewish life, objective investigation concludes that the juries and evidence are still out—for example, how many intermarriages *have* resulted in the conversion of the non-Jewish spouse out of the overall population of the mixed married? How many of their children *are* enrolled in Jewish educational programs out of the total of those children? How many Jews worldwide see themselves as Zionists, committed to Israel's survival, and have visited the Jewish state at least once? What are the *real* figures for worldwide Jewish *aliyah* (Hebrew, "immigration to Israel"), and which countries predominate, and why? How many Jews *are* affiliated with and active participants in Jewish religious life in each of the movements and overall, in both their personal and their communal lives, out of the total number of Jews? And similar questions.

American Jewish Communities

Turning first to the American Jewish communities, the presently prevailing myth is that of unity—the American Jewish *community*—when the reality is that there is a plethora of organizations and voices, and divisiveness is the norm rather than the exception, even on issues of agreed-on concern (for example, Israel and antisemitism). And yet, there is also a strong feeling and sense of "privilege" at the opportunities to be Jews in a country still evolving its own relationships to its subpopulations, where overt discrimination is addressed legally, where

Fig. 8.1 An American Hanukkah This example of a Jewish *objet d'art* by Mae Rockland Tupa, entitled "Miss Liberty," for the holiday of Hanukkah is but one contemporary example of Jewish artistic creativity. Photo: Art Resource and Mae Rockland Tupa

governments are neither controlled by nor answerable to religious institutions, and where the very diversity of populations is its strength. For Jews, the United States continues to be—in the old Yiddish phrase *der goldiner medina* ("this golden land")—a land of seemingly limitless opportunity, where access to residence, profession, economic success, and life-partners are more or less obstacle free.

What such freedom, however, portends for America's Jews remains the question. One could survey the Jewish past and conclude that Jewish survival was successful at least in part because the enemies of the Jews limited Jews' access outside of organized Jewish life: Jews could *not* live outside their ghettos or own land; Jews could *not* enter most professions; Jews could *not* marry whomever they chose; nonforced conversion was an option for very, very few; economic success (and the benefits it carries) also for the very, very few. Thus, the external pressures of outside forces played a decisive role, larger at times and smaller at others, in keeping Jews together and enabling them to develop their communal structures, their religious and intellectual traditions, and the like.

In twenty-first-century America, where Jews are freer, not only to accomplish much but less afraid

of antisemitism (to which we shall turn in the next section), safer and more secure than anywhere else in the world, including present-day Israel, Jews now confront what it means to be "free Jews," with all

Fig. 8.2 Emma Lazarus (1849–1887) Lazarus, an American Jewish writer, wrote the words used in the inscription on the base of the Statue of Liberty in New York Harbor.
Photo: Art Resource, N.Y.

BOX 8.1

Inscription at the Base of the Statue of Liberty, New York

The New Colossus

Not like the brazen giant of Greek fame,
With conquering limbs astride from land to land;
Here at our sea-washed, sunset gates shall stand
A mighty woman with a torch, whose flame
Is the imprisoned lightning, and her name
Mother of Exiles. From her beacon-hand
Glows world-wide welcome; her mild eyes
    command
The air-bridged harbor that twin cities frame.

"Keep, ancient lands, your storied pomp!"
    cries she
With silent lips. "Give me your tired, your poor,
Your huddled masses yearning to breathe free,
The wretched refuse of your teeming shore.
Send these, the homeless, tempest-tossed
    to me,
I lift my lamp beside the golden door!"

Emma Lazarus (1849–1887)
Jewish-American Poet

of the strengths and weaknesses, complexities and simplicities, that freedom carries with it. How such communities of Jews will ultimately work out their personal and collective identities is a chapter in a text yet to be written.

State of Israel

Turning next to the State of Israel, the freedom to be Jews and to "do Jewish" is a hallmark of a nation-state arising like a phoenix from the ashes in the aftermath of the Holocaust/Shoah of the mid-twentieth century, and welcoming all those Jews who would come to participate in its creation, but one facing two problems radically different and potentially disastrous for its Jews: first, an entrenched right-wing, politically militant religious Orthodoxy, which actively discourages any and all attempts to allow non-Orthodox religious alternatives for its Jewish populations (forcing the Israeli Reform and Conservative movements to carry their concerns into the courts), and which, in the process, furthers the secularization of much of Israeli life (for example, less than 20 percent of Israelis define themselves as "religious" [Hebrew, *dati*], understanding such identification as Orthodox, with which they prefer *not* to identify). And, second, a perpetually tense, hostile residence in a militarily at-the-ready part of the world that has seen armed conflicts beginning in 1948 and continuing in 1956, 1967, 1973, 1981, and most recently in 2006. While political and military scholars *do* acknowledge that the likelihood of the Israeli state "being wiped off the map"[2] is extremely unlikely—given its highly developed military system and armaments, including nuclear capabilities—more than fifty years of ongoing tension has resulted in the creation of a kind of "new Jew" (Hebrew *sabra*, the term for the Israeli cactus): fluent in Hebrew, knowledgeable in the Judaic sources of Torah/ Hebrew Bible, Talmud, Midrash, and so on, but increasingly estranged from a Judaic religious life.

Fig. 8.3 The Old City, Jerusalem This photo shows the citadel and David's tower within Jerusalem's old city. Photo: © DeA Picture Library/ Art Resource, N.Y.

Whether such estrangement will result in a schism of incalculable proportions for future Jewish survival remains an open-ended question.

Jews Worldwide

For the remaining Jews worldwide, however, these questions and concerns play directly into their own. They are, however, coupled with their own real and evident concerns about their abilities to nourish and sustain their own populations, concerns about economic, institutional, and leadership resources, birthrates versus death rates, intermarriage/mixed marriage, and other issues. Examples include the following: The Jewish population of Great Britain is not growing to any appreciable degree. The Jewish people of France is remaining stable in a country where its increasing Muslim population (large portions of which are antisemitic as well as anti-Israel) is fast approaching 10 percent. The Jewish populations of other European countries remain small (Poland, Romania, Bosnia, the Scandinavian countries; all evidence of Hitler's tragic *success*), with long-range prognoses for their survival more negative than positive.

An ironic "bright spot," however, may very well be that of the former Soviet Union, which appears to be experiencing a "religious revival" of sorts among its approximately three million Jews (actual numbers are still difficult to determine, a legacy of Communism)—despite a resurgent antisemitism—as its Jewish populations are publicly identifying themselves with the various streams of religious Judaism (Reform Conservative, Orthodox, Hasidic-Chabad Orthodox) and are making their presence felt.

For a people who have journeyed so far, concern with its physical survival and the ability to sustain and grow its numbers remains. But worldwide, Jews continue to be optimistic; and the overwhelming majority of them appear to be working hard to sustain themselves in the present and prepare for the always-unknown future.

Fig. 8.4 Ethiopian Jews in Israel
Here, an Ethiopian Jew is following behind a Kes or Ethiopian Jewish priest.
Photo: Marco Longari/ AFP/Getty Images

Antisemitism:
Hatred Old and New

At the end of the nineteenth century, the "father of modern political Zionism," Theodor Herzl (1860–1904), published his tract *Der Judenstaat* (German, "The Jewish State"), arguing for the creation of a Jewish state that would, in effect, "level the playing field," making the Jewish people a nation-state among equals, and consequently, leading to a lessening of worldwide antisemitism. Sadly and tragically, such has *not* proven the case; indeed, some have even argued that, as a result of the reality of the modern State of Israel and its ongoing confrontations in the Middle East, antisemitism has not lessened but increased. Whether or not that is true, antisemitism (again, simply defined as "hatred of the Jews and Judaism")—this oldest hatred and biggest lie—continues to rear its ugly head and has experienced something of a resurgence in the latter part of the twentieth century and on into this twenty-first century, primarily in Europe, and certainly in the Middle East itself. Some have argued, however, that while Jews and Muslims/Arabs had long had their differences and at times manifested these differences in far less than honorable disagreements, up to and including violence, this antisemitism is understood to be essentially transportable to and from Europe.

Why so and why now? Certainly and to be sure, the September 11, 2001, American tragedy has pointed toward a difference in worldviews between Western and European and American, and Middle Eastern perspectives. (Whether or not one wishes to elevate these differences to Harvard University professor Samuel P. Huntingdon's [1927–2008] "clash of civilizations" remains highly contestable.[3]) Yet those who have opposed the integration of Jews into fuller participation in the civic life of the various countries of the world have done so for many, many years, and have based their hatred on social and cultural distinctions ("We do not like these people; their ways are not our ways; and we do not wish

to associate with them."); religious and theological convictions ("They are primarily responsible for the death of our Lord [Christ], and their descendants must be made to pay continuously for the iniquities of their predecessors."); political biases ("Their collective agendas are to maneuver themselves into power to the disadvantage of everyone else and must be stopped."); to the most perverse of all its manifestations, the racial-biological construct of the Nazis, evidences of which remain today ("Jews are a different order of physical creatures, seemingly looking like the rest of us, but genetically different, and if we allow them to breed with us, we weaken the whole of the human race. Their blood is different from our blood and their *unnatural* perverted talents [money-making and sexual preoccupations] will further lead to a destroying of the rest of us and create a world where they reign over us. They must be stopped before they put into place a Jewish world government!")

As a minority population in every country in the world with the exception of Israel itself, Jews *do* remain somewhat at risk where those who oppose them feel free to take matters into their own hands, violate the laws of the nation-state (or do so with either the sanction of the government or its blind eye), and see the only way to oppose Jews is by acts of violence.

In the post–World War II era, Western countries continue to show a remarkable *intolerance* for those who practice antisemitism, and often prosecute its perpetrators to the fullest extent of the law. Even the United Nations, with its remarkable record of consistent biases and denigrations of the State of Israel, in 2007, condemned antisemitism by reaffirming its passage of a 2005 resolution condemning any denial of the Holocaust/Shoah as an anathema to its own global vision of the world community, and declaring January 27 as the Annual International Day of Commemoration in Memory of the Victims of the Holocaust.

Yet, antisemitism continues, and Jews continue to worry—their own history has taught them the

Fig. 8.5 Antisemitism then (above)
The Nazi Secret Service (SS) set fire to the Synagogue of Baden-Baden in Germany on November 10, 1938, which is known as *Kristallnacht* ("Night of Broken Glass").
Photo: Bildarchiv Preussischer Kulturbesitz/ Art Resource, N.Y.

Fig. 8.6 Antisemitism now (left)
These Jewish graves were vandalized in 2008 in a cemetery in Berlin, Germany.
Photo: Sean Gallup/Getty News Images/Getty Images

truth of the cliché "forewarned is forearmed." Jews, especially in the West, have learned what they perceive as *the* lesson of the Holocaust/Shoah: that silence in the face of such overt hatred of Jews and Judaism cannot be met with silence, indifference, or tolerance, but must be met instead with legal, political, religious, social, and educational responses, not only on the part of agencies created specifically for this task (for example, in the United States, the Anti-Defamation League), but in the workplace, college and university settings, the courtrooms, and in everyday life.[4] While its total eradication may be something of a pipe dream (given the human reality that there will always be people and groups who do not like others, for whatever reason, and base their own failing on the supposed "power" of those same others without the courage to confront their own failings), lessening the power of antisemitism to do evil to Jews and Judaism remains high on the agendas of organized Jewish communities worldwide. Significantly, already in the last century, networks of concern confronting antisemitism exist not only among Jews but now include non-Jews in support of Jews, governmental agencies—the United States State Department, for example, has begun monitoring global antisemitism and publishing its reports[5]—Christian religious communions, and ordinary citizens. In this arena, too, there is hope, as Jews continue to join among themselves and with others to fight what must be understood and has been understood as a frontal assault on their very right to exist and continue to be a part of the human community.

The Middle East:
Israel and Her Neighbors

Throughout the world, more newspaper column inches and live media coverage continue to be devoted to events in the Middle East than any other

topic, long before the events associated with America's 9/11 tragedy, and perhaps a reflection of the intimate bond between Jews and Christians in the rise of Western civilization, the intimacy of religious connections between Judaism and Christianity, and the simple fact that the central personage of Christianity—the Christ—was born into this Jewish people in that place. Like *every* topic addressed in this text, the ins and outs of this ongoing Middle East conflict between Israel and her neighbors is complex, long-standing, and worthy of the many, many volumes that have been published, are being published, and will be published, both analyzing the historical story of the conflicts themselves, their temporary resolutions, and suggestions for their long-term solutions. Consistent with our overall intensions, however, as we move toward a conclusion, we offer the following observations and comments.

Fundamental to *any* discussion of the Middle East and its conflicts *must* be a discussion of the religious and theological understandings that both unite and divide Jews and Muslims, and the place of historical Christianity in the conversation. The "Zionist theology" of the Torah/Hebrew Bible is the place to start, and *Bereshith*/Genesis 12 (though there are many, many others texts from which to choose) is as good a place as any. In verse 1, the God to whom *Avram*/Abram (his initial name) has submitted himself tells him to "Leave your country, your people, and your father's household and *go to the land I will show you.*" Later on, in verse 7, He again appears to him, and says, "To your offspring *I will give this land.*" There *in that place* the Hebrews/Israelites/Jews will develop into the people they will become, never fully leaving it, believing wholeheartedly that their God (the *only* God!) loved them enough not only to enter into *berith*/covenant with them but gifted them—and no other people—with that land (including those who already lived there). There they lived both prior to and after their enslavement in Egypt and ever since, losing political control several times (721 B.C.E., 586 B.C.E., 70 C.E.), but reclaiming, at long last, political hegemony in 1948, and fully determined "never again" (a catchphrase most closely identified among Jews as a post-Holocaust/Shoah response to all further attempts at extermination/annihilation) to allow others to take it from them. That they have behaved, collectively, marvelously well toward others in that place can historically be documented; that they have behaved far less than their best, both in the distant past and in the recent present, can likewise be historically documented and verified. But for Jews—and not only those who live there or who have lived there, those who live outside the land and who fully support the right of Jews to live in their land—it is their land, and the decisions that flow from that ownership—by divine fiat—must *always* take that fact into consideration, the present moment notwithstanding.

For the last two thousand years, with the birth and development of the various adumbrations of Christianity (first Roman Catholicism and Eastern Orthodoxy, and later the various Protestantisms), their relationships with Jews and their relationships with the land itself have been uneven and ambivalent. Some have a longstanding support of the right of Jews to return and own the Land of Israel, out of a theological matrix in which Jewish return is the first step to their Christ's eventual return. Others, out of their own biases and prejudices against Jews, seem unable to integrate present Jewish hegemony into their own theological worldview, for how can Jewish "success" in returning to the land of their birth be squared with a people who continues to deny the reality of the Christ on whom all success is built and from whom all goodness flows? Still oth-

Fig. 8.7 Suicide bombing attack on Israeli bus A Palestinian suicide bomber exploded this Israeli bus in Haifa, Israel, in 2003.
Photo: David Silverman/Getty News Images/Getty Images

BOX 8.2

The Hamas Covenant

This charter, issued in 1988, seeks the establishment of an Islamic state in Palestine in place of where Israel and the Palestinian territories exist currently.

Introduction

And if they who have believed the scriptures [that is, the Jews] had believed, it had surely been the better for them: there are believers among them, but the greater part of them are transgressors. . . . They are smitten with vileness wheresoever they are found . . . unless they obtain security by entering into a treaty with Allah, and a treaty with men; and they draw on themselves indignation from Allah, and they are afflicted with poverty. This they suffer, because they disbelieved the signs of Allah, and slew the prophets unjustly; this because they were rebellious, and transgressed.

Article 7

The Day of Judgment will not come until Muslims fight the Jews, when the Jew will hide behind stones and trees. The stones and trees will say, "O Muslims, O Abdullah, there is a Jew behind me, come and kill him." Only the Gharkad tree would not do that because it is one of the trees of the Jews.

Article 11

The Islamic Resistance Movement believes the Land of Palestine is an Islamic Waqf consecrated for future Muslim generations until Judgment Day.

Article 15

The day that enemies usurp part of Muslim land, Jihad becomes the individual duty of every Muslim. In the face of the Jews' usurpation of Palestine, it is compulsory that the banner of Jihad be raised.

Article 20

In their Nazi treatment, the Jews made no exception for women and children. . . . They deal with people as if they were the worst of war criminals.

Article 28

The Zionist invasion is a vicious invasion. . . . It relies greatly in its infiltration and espionage operations . . . [and arms] undermining societies, destroying values, corrupting consciences, deteriorating character and annihilating Islam. It is behind the drug trade and alcoholism in all its kinds so as to facilitate its control and expansion.

Conclusion

The Arab Palestinian people, expressing themselves by the armed Palestinian revolution, reject all solutions which are substitutes for the total liberation of Palestine and reject all proposals aiming at the liquidation of the Palestinian problem or its internalization.

---

ers, out of a far more negative theological interpretation of Jews and Judaism (and perhaps a strong desire to link to the Arabs and Muslim there for religious as well as political agendas) see no legitimacy whatsoever for present-day Jewish ownership of the land and still view the last two thousand years of exile as concrete evidence of divine punishment and Jewish perfidy, the present moment only a temporary reprieve before a return to exile.

Six hundred years after the birth of Christianity comes a new voice to the table, that of Muhammed (570–632 C.E.), experiencing anew God's revelations, coupled with a strong political desire to unite this entire geography under one sovereignty, *Dar al-Islam* (Arabic, "house of submission") versus the world of the others, *Dar al-Harb* (Arabic, "house of war"). That all of the lands under this extended banner would be regarded as sacred and holy to Muslims makes sense: a "spot" under the political and religious control of Jews (originally regarded and respected as the "People of the Book [Torah]") would thus prove and has proven to be an anathema, and thus must be conquered and their leadership and followership subjugated and worse. That they have thus far been unable to do so "ups the ante," and makes the ongoing crises from an Arab and Muslim perspective, coupled with successive military defeats, that much worse.

Thus, two religious traditions understand the same pieces of land as sacred to both, given by God first to one and then to the other, and for whom each represents a continuing threat. That the Christianities in their own religio-theological assessments overwhelmingly continue to support the Israeli/Jewish side only exacerbates the problem. And while some Protestants—for example, Presbyterianism with its own long history of residence and support of the Arab and Palestinian peoples—have sided with Muslims and Arabs and against Jews and Israel has not significantly diminished their perception of one-sidedness.

Into this heady brew of conflict comes a previous vision of realpolitik that saw and sees Israel as the one true democracy in the Middle East, and for years the *only* true "window" in the affairs of the now-former Soviet Union. During the heyday of the Cold War between the two superpowers of Russia and the United States, Israel (already perhaps perceived by some as a vassal state rather than ally of the United States) sided consistently with the United States, and proved a physical base from which to launch an attack should the need have arisen. But now, in the realignment of the world's nation-states, can such a past history of friendship and service sustain a relationship presently and on into the future? Also, given the West's all-consuming need for oil resources, can Israel continue to count on the United States and her allies as it has in the past, or will other, Arab voices and nation-states, including those of the Palestinians, displace Israel in coming generations? Israelis worry and Jews outside Israel worry (See box 8.2 on page 179).

Conclusion

At the beginning of this twenty-first century, America and the West are engaged in what has been labeled a "war against terrorism," which their enemies have seemingly linked directly to the continuing instability in the Middle East and Israel's treatment of its Palestinian population. Whether this is wholly or partially accurate can be seriously questioned and debated. What is true, however, is that within the current geopolitical boundaries of the sovereign State of Israel exist a people who do not wish to be governed by Israel and Jewish Israelis. Increasingly many, Jews and non-Jews alike both within Israel and throughout the world, have come to the conclusion that a two-state solution is the *only* viable solution to end this crisis of now more than half a century: a Jewish state governed by Jews and those who wish to live under its flag, and a Palestinian state, contiguous to Israel, composed predominantly of Arabs and Muslims and those who wish to live under its flag. Only time and goodwill on both sides, coupled with an overriding commitment to end the bloodshed that has gone on for far too long, will determine if the Jewish dream of *shalom*/peace and the Muslim dream of *salaam*/peace can become a reality before it is too late for both sides. Whether this solution in this volatile part of the world will bring about an end to terror remains to be seen.

IN REVIEW

We have now explored, albeit ever so briefly, contemporary Jewish realities from a Judaic perspective, both the positives and the negatives. What both portend for the future of Judaism and the Jewish people remains an ongoing guessing game. In our next and final chapter, your author will attempt his own assessments as to that future.

KEY TERMS

Aliyah	Holocaust/Shoah
antisemitism	intermarriage
Dar al-Harb	mixed marriage
Dar al-Islam	orthodoxy
Dati	*Sabra*
Der goldiner medina	Zionism
Der Judenstaat	

Questions for Review, Study, and Discussion

1. *Before* securing a copy of de Lange and Freud-Kandel's book *Modern Judaism*, attempt your own assessment of the ten issues they themselves address. Now compare your list with theirs. Where do you agree? Differ?

2. What is your prognosis for the future survival of the American Jewish communities (based on and including your own reading, observations, and experiences)?

3. Given the present state of the Israeli–Arab/Palestinian crises, how would you resolve such hotly contested issues? What, then, becomes your prognosis for the future of Israel in the context of the Middle East?

4. Overall, how would you assess the future of both Judaism and the Jewish people? Why so?

Suggested Readings

American Judaism

Glazer, Nathan. *American Judaism*. Chicago: University of Chicago Press, 1988. A classic!

Kaplan, Dana Evan. *The Cambridge Companion to American Judaism*. Cambridge and New York: Cambridge University Press, 2005.

Kaplan, Dana Evan. *Contemporary American Judaism: Transformation and Renewal*. New York: Columbia University Press, 2009.

Kaplan, Mordecai M. *Judaism as a Civilization: Toward a Reconstruction of American-Jewish Life*. Philadelphia: Jewish Publication Society of America, 1994.

Raphael, Marc Lee. *Judaism in America*. New York: Columbia University Press, 2005.

Sarna, Jonathan. *American Judaism: A History*. New Haven, Conn.: Yale University Press, 2005.

Antisemitism

Berenbaum, Michael, ed. *Not Your Father's Antisemitism: Hatred of the Jews in the 21st Century*. St. Paul: Paragon, 2008.

Laqueur, Walter. *The Changing Face of Anti-Semitism: From Ancient Times to the Present Day*. New York: Oxford University Press, 2008.

Perry, Marvin, and Frederick M. Schweitzer. *Anti-Semitism: Myth and Hate from Antiquity to the Present*. New York: Palgrave Macmillan, 2005.

Prager, Dennis, and Joseph Telushkin. *Why the Jews? The Reason for Antisemitism*. New York: Touchstone, 2003.

Israel and the Middle East

Cleveland, William L. *A History of the Modern Middle East*. Boulder, Co.: Westview, 2004.

Hertzberg, Arthur. *The Zionist Idea: A Historical Analysis and Reader*. Philadelphia: Jewish Publication Society of America, 1997.

Laqueur, Walter, and Barry Rubin, eds. *The Israel–Arab Reader: A Documentary History of the Middle East Conflict*. New York: Penguin, 2008.

Lewis, Bernard. *The Middle East*. New York: Charles Scribner's Sons, 1997.

Oren, Michael B. *Power, Faith, and Fantasy: America in the Middle East: 1776 to the Present*. New York: W. W. Norton, 2008.

Sachar, Howard M. *A History of Israel: From the Rise of Zionism to Our Time*. New York: Knopf, 2007.

World Jewry

Kurlansky, Mark. *A Chosen Few: The Resurrection of European Jewry*. New York: Ballantine, 2002.

Mendes-Flohr, Paul, and Jehuda Reinharz, eds. *The Jew in the Modern World: A Documentary History*. New York: Oxford University Press, 1995.

CHAPTER 9

Conclusion

The Future of Judaism and the Jewish People

OVERVIEW

In his office at The University of Alabama, this author keeps three crystal balls—to remind him that none of them work! Predicting the future for any group of persons or religious traditions is the work of fortune-tellers and other prognosticators and charlatans, some of whom occasionally get it right. Making no claims to accuracy, these final thoughts serve to open doors to further study and conversation regarding not only the future of Judaism and the Jewish people but of the past and present as well. The journey of the Jews from their earliest beginnings and with it the creation of what we now call Judaism has been a long, complex, and at times tortuous one. Ideally, the journey will continue far into an unknown future, but one filled with promise and success.

Final Thoughts

At the conclusion of the celebration of Pesach (Passover), after the fourth cup of sacramental wine is drunk (and after its appropriate blessing), we find the following words, poetically expressed in the Reform or Liberal *Hagaddah* (Passover prayer book), beginning with the Hebrew *Chasal Siddur Pesach k'hilchato*:

The Seder service now concludes:
Its rites observed in full.
Its purposes revealed.
This privilege we share will ever be renewed.
Until God's plan is known in full,
His highest blessing sealed:
Peace!
Peace for us! For everyone!
For all people, this, our hope:
New year in Jerusalem!

Next year, may all be free

L'shanah haba-ah b'Yirusalayim! ("Next year in Jerusalem!")[1]

So, too, might we say of this text—on a far less grandiose level to be sure! We have told the briefest of stories of both Judaism as the religious expression of the Jewish people over the course of their journey of several thousand years, and the stories of their lives lived in various places as well. We have also addressed both their philosophical and theological conceptualizations, as well as the texts that have provided the foundations for those conceptualizations. And we have outlined both the religious calendar to which religious Jews commit themselves—regardless of their denominational/ movement affiliation—and the celebrations of their lives from birth to death. In these chapters, despite their brevity, we have painted (or perhaps sketched) a modern group of people who trace themselves lineally to the ancient biblical period and who understand themselves as inheritors of a rich legacy. They are committed to this legacy not only in the present generation but for future generations as well, and not only in their largest settings (Israel, the United States, the former Soviet Union), but wherever Jews reside—no matter the size of their communities, their birthrates, or the threats to their lives.

For religious Jews, their faith in their future is not one augured in crystal balls or other tools of the magician or soothsayer: for them, the *berith*/covenant with the God of Israel—the one, true God of *all* humankind—is an *eternal* one. And while at times abused by the disobedient (and punished in response), it is ultimately indestructible, shatter-proof, even by those (both Christians and Muslims) who would claim its limitations as a result of their newer readings of past, present, and future. For these Jews, as long as this planet endures, there *will* be Jews, perhaps in different locations than those where they presently dwell, perhaps in different numbers than those we can presently count; perhaps in different religious configurations than those

Fig. 9.1 Looking toward the future An Israeli girl in the capital of Tel Aviv celebrates the sixtieth anniversary of the founding of the State of Israel.
Photo: Jack Guez/AFP/Getty Images

we presently see, though this latter point remains open to continuous internal debate: the Orthodox convinced that *only* their approach will guarantee Jewish survival, and non-Orthodox interpretations arguing that the diversity of approaches is the surest guarantor of that survival.

From an historical perspective, there is truth indeed in this *weltanschauung* (German, "world-perspective"). The great German-Jewish historian Heinrich Graetz (1817–1891), whose monumental eleven-volume *Geschichte der Juden* (*History of the Jews*), published between 1853 and 1875, perceived the journey as one of "peaks and valleys." That is to say, one could graph the journey using such a framework: as one Jewish community begins its descendancy, another begins its ascendancy, from the very beginnings, still shrouded in mystery, in the Middle East, through this present moment and on into the future. Though Gratez and others who have followed him (for example, Salo Wittmayer Baron [1895–1989], whose twenty-seven-volume *A Social and Religious History of the Jews* was published between 1952 and 1983) have applied the very best scientific methods of their discipline, they, perhaps like their Jewish religious counterparts, despite all the evidence at times to the contrary, were reluctant to say the *Kaddish* memorial prayer for the Jewish people.[2] (One is almost inclined to agree with the American humorist Mark Twain [1835–1910], who upon reading his own obituary written by another, remarked that the "report of my death was an exaggeration.")

Perhaps, indeed, as a group, Jews *are* somewhat unique. All attempts at easy definitions have come up short. Mordecai Kaplan (1881–1983), the founder of Reconstructionist religious Judaism, for example, used the term "civilization" to describe both the people and their extended systems of beliefs, values, cultures, and so on, and possessing all of the component parts of any civilization; regardless of whether or not they lived in their own land and were governed by those who were like them. Others, including the founders of early Reform Judaism, sought to confine Jews and Judaism to religious categories only, divorcing ideas of peoplehood and/or nationhood from their vocabulary, only to be "shocked back" in the aftermath of the Holocaust/Shoah of the Second World War.[3] Even the definition supplied by the author of this text in chapter 1 is *only* a point of departure, attempting to address a whole host of topics rather than a complete description of the people and the things to which they commit themselves. Perhaps, then, this continuing inability to define either the group or its systems of thought and behavior is indicative of its amazing ability to surmount all obstacles and impediments to its ongoing survival.

Based on all the available evidence and given the sweep of Jewish history, the people known as the Jews and the religious traditions known as Judaism should not be here. As stated previously in chapter 2, the story should have come to its end, or been greatly diminished, following the destruction of the northern kingdom of Israel in 721 B.C.E. after the Assyrian invasion. It should have come to its end following the destruction of the southern kingdom of Judah in 586 B.C.E. after the Babylonian invasion. It should have come to its end following the destruction of Palestine in 70 C.E. after the Roman debacle. It should have come to its end, or been greatly diminished, after the expulsion from Spain in 1492 by King Ferdinand and Queen Isabella. It should have come to its end in the largest Jewish community (Poland) in the seventeenth century after the Khmelnitsky massacres. It should have begun its unrecoverable descendancy after the Holocaust/Shoah of World War II. All of these "shoulds," however, do not accord with what has taken place: in the aftermath of every destructive tragedy, the Jews have refused to succumb; though initially reduced in numbers, they have survived, married and remarried, given birth, recreated devastated communities—sometimes in the exact same locations, sometimes in other locations—and continued to celebrate their religious traditions, both as they have known them in the past and modified them to meet new realties. The threefold mandate of preservation, adaptation, and innovation continues to serve as a cornerstone of their religious survival.

Twenty-first-century reality? The American Jewish communities are seemingly growing in number even as they are beset by concerns of intermarriage/mixed marriage in a welcoming environment where antisemitism continues its own downward spiral. The Jewish communities in the former Soviet Union, in the aftermath of the fall of Communism in the late 1990s, are beginning the long, slow road back to vibrancy both culturally and religiously, even as rightist antisemitism, never fully out of the picture, continues to rear its ugly head. The Jewish communities in a now-reunited Germany (of all places!), surprisingly, reveals a healthy and diverse population religiously and culturally, slowly growing in numbers, and protected, in large measure, by both a government and a population determined to confront their past, and less tolerant of neo-Nazism than in the past. The Jewish communities of Great Britain and France and Australia, while not growing numerically to any appreciable degree, are stable, their institutions stable, and are committed to addressing problems such as antisemitism and anti-Israelism and determined not to be overwhelmed by them. The Jewish communities of Israel are growing in numbers and continuing to build a viable culture and nation-state, despite the internal worrisome agendas of rightist religious Orthodoxy and the as-yet-unresolved external threat of enemies intent on her destruction, but continuously unable to do so. Jewish communities in Latin America, South Africa, and a whole host of other places where Jews live continue to maintain their Jewish populations and celebrate their Jewish lives as Jews have done, continue to do, and will continue to do.

Conclusion

Thus, the story of Judaism and the Jewish people continuously appears to be one of a people who live their lives at the very precipice of their own collective existence, but who continue to take steps away from that edge only to be met by obstacles and barriers that not only prevent them from doing so but propel them back to that edge as well. Only time will ultimately tell which direction will meet with success. Until then, Jews will leave their fate—and their faith—as they have always done, in the hands of their God. More than that, one cannot say—or write.

Fig. 9.2 Only in America! As evidence of religious pluralism in the United States, a cross and a Star of David are displayed in front of the same building in Ann Arbor, Michigan, which serves as both St. Clare of Assisi Episcopal Church and Temple Beth Emeth.
Photo: AFP/Getty Images

IN REVIEW

We hope you have enjoyed this text and learned much about Judaism and the Jewish people in the process. Do consult the various readings supplied at the end of each chapter as well as at the end of the book itself to learn even more. The story is told of a Gentile who requested of the great sage Rabbi Hillel that he teach him everything he needed to know while standing on one foot. Rabbi Hillel responded, "That which is hateful to you do not do to your neighbor. All the rest is commentary." *Zil g'mar*: Go and Study! Enough said!

KEY TERMS

berith/covenant

Hagaddah

kaddish

Pesach

weltanschauung

Questions for Review, Study, and Discussion

1. The question remains, "How would you explain the continuing existence not only of the Jewish people but of Judaism as well?"

2. What conclusions do you now come to as to the present and future of Judaism and the Jewish people?

Suggested Readings

Hartman, David. *Israelis and the Jewish Tradition: An Ancient People Debating Its Future*. New Haven, Conn.: Yale University Press, 2000.

Van Diggele, Els. *A People Who Live Apart: Jewish Identity and the Future of Israel*. Amherst: Prometheus, 2003.

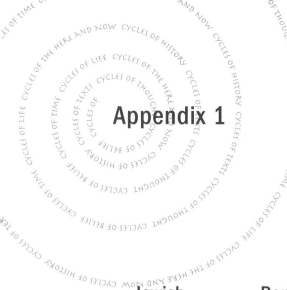

Appendix 1

Torah/Hebrew Bible, Roman Catholic Bible, and the Protestant Bible

Jewish (Torah/Hebrew Bible)	Roman Catholic (Old Testament)	Protestant (Old Testament)
FIVE BOOKS OF MOSES	**PENTATEUCH**	
Genesis	Genesis	Genesis
Exodus	Exodus	Exodus
Leviticus	Leviticus	Leviticus
Numbers	Numbers	Numbers
Deuteronomy	Deuteronomy	Deuteronomy
PROPHETS	**HISTORICAL BOOKS**	Joshua
		Judges
Preliterary prophets	Joshua	Ruth
	Judges	Samuel 1 and 2
Joshua	Ruth	Kings 1 and 2
Judges	Samuel 1 and 2	Chronicles 1 and 2
Samuel 1 and 2	Kings 1 and 2	Ezra
Kings 1 and 2	Chronicles 1 and 2	Nehemiah
	Ezra	Esther
Major prophets	Nehemiah	Job
	Esther	Psalms
Isaiah		Proverbs
Jeremiah	**WISDOM BOOKS**	Ecclesiastes
Ezekiel		Song of Songs
	Job	Isaiah
Minor prophets	Psalms	Jeremiah
	Proverbs	Lamentations
Hosea	Ecclesiastes	Ezekiel

continues on following page

Appendix 1 (cont.)

Jewish (Torah/Hebrew Bible)	Roman Catholic (Old Testament)	Protestant (Old Testament)
Joel	Song of Songs	Daniel
Amos		Hosea
Obadiah	**PROPHETS**	Joel
Jonah		Amos
Micah	**Major Prophets**	
Nahum		
Zephaniah	Isaiah	Obadiah
Habakkuk	Jeremiah	Jonah
Haggai	Lamentations	Micah
Zechariah	Ezekiel	Nahum
Malachi	Daniel	Habakkuk
		Zephaniah
THE WRITINGS	**Minor Prophets**	Haggai
		Zechariah
Wisdom	Hosea	Malachi
	Joel	
Psalms	Amos	
Proverbs	Obadiah	
Job	Jonah	
Song of Songs	Micah	
Ruth	Nahum	
Lamentations	Habakkuk	
Ecclesiastes	Zephaniah	
Esther	Haggai	
	Zechariah	
Nonwisdom	Malachi	
Daniel	**APOCRYPHA**	
Ezra		
Nehemiah	Tobit	
Chronicles 1 and 2	Judith	
	Maccabees 1 and 2	
	Ben Sirach	
	Ecclesiasticus	
	Baruch	

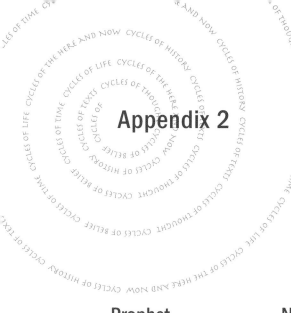

Appendix 2

Rank-Ordering of Prophetic Books included in Jewish Sabbath and Festival Worship Services

Prophet	Number of Readings	Number of Readings
	Sabbath	Festival
Isaiah	15	6
Kings 1 and 2	11	5
Ezekiel	6	5
Jeremiah	8	2
Samuel 1 and 2	3	4
Hosea	3	2
Joshua	2	2
Micah	1	3
Judges	3	0
Zechariah	1	2
Amos	2	0
Malachi	1	1
Joel	0	1
Obadiah	1	0
Jonah	0	1
Nahum	0	0
Habakkuk	0	0
Zephaniah	0	0
Haggai	0	0

Notes

1. Unpacking a Definition

1. The course was "Introduction to Jewish Philosophy," at the graduate level, taught by the late Professor Alvin Reines at the Hebrew Union College-Jewish Institute of Religion, Cincinnati, Ohio, Spring Semester, 1972.

2. Indeed, though we will be "formally" introduced to the Jewish process of conversion later on in the book, at this juncture, suffice it to say that there was no religious (or any other) vehicle in the biblical period for what we know today as "conversion." A non-Israelite who lived among the community, either voluntarily or as the result of capture in battle, and who later chose to identify with the host community, simply surrendered whatever his/her previous identity and status were, married into the community, had children, and within one or at most two generations, such a prior history was all but forgotten. Conversion, as we understand it today—as a religious ceremony marking one's change of religious status and identification—is a postbiblical or rabbinic construct.

3. After a lengthy introduction, the operative statement is the following:

Therefore: The Central Conference of American Rabbis declares that the child of one Jewish parent is under the presumption of Jewish descent. This presumption of the Jewish status of the offspring of any mixed marriage is to be established through appropriate and timely public and formal acts of identification with the Jewish faith and people. The performance of these *mitzvot* serves to commit those who participate in them, both parent and child, to Jewish life.

Depending on circumstances [according to the age or setting, parents should consult a rabbi to determine specific *mitzvot* that are necessary], *mitzvot* leading to a positive and exclusive Jewish identity will include entry into the covenant, acquisition of a Hebrew name, Torah study, bar/bat mitzvah, and *Kabbalat Torah* (Confirmation). [A full description of these and other *mitzvot* can be found in *Sharrei Mitzvah*.]

Resolution Adopted by the CCAR (Central Conference of American Rabbis), "The Status of Children of

Mixed Marriages," Report of the Committee on Patrilineal Descent, Adopted March 15, 1983.

4. For an interesting contemporary Judaic view of the seeming "conflict" between two different mythic visions of the Jewish past and present, see Jacob Neusner, "Stories Jews Tell to Explain Themselves and How They Conflict," *National Jewish Post and Opinion,* November 23, 2005, 13, 16.

5. Among the more well-known American Jewish gangsters are the following: Isadore "Kid Cann" Blumenfeld (1900–1981); Louis "Lepke" Buchalter (1897–1944); Meyer "Mickey" Cohen (1913–1976); Moe Dalitz (1899–1989); Arthur "Dutch Schultz" Flegenheimer (1902–1935); Gus Greenbaum (1894–1958); Max "Boo Boo" Hoff (1892–1941); Edward Osterman ("Monk Eastman," 1873–1920); Arnold Rothstein (1882–1928); Moe Sedway (1894–1952); Jacob "Gurrah" Shapiro (1899–1947); Benjamin "Bugsy" Siegel (1906–1947); Charlie "King" Solomon (1884–1933); Irving Wexler ("Waxey Gordon," 1886?/1889?–1952); Jack Zelig (1888–1912); and Abner "Longy" Zwillman (1899?/1904?–1959). A delightful but rather "dark side" of the American Jewish story is Robert A. Rockaway's book *But He Was Good to His Mother: The Lives and Crimes of Jewish Gangsters* (New York: Gefen, 2000).

6. David Biale, *Cultures of the Jews: A New History* (New York: Schocken Books, 2002).

7. This translation, which the author truly believes to be a more accurate rendering of the Hebrew text, suggests, by implication, that the genius of God was not *creatio ex nihilo* (Latin, "creation out of nothing"), but, rather, taking already-existing materials ("stuff") and organizing the formless chaos of the universe. The question of whether or not God did, in fact, create this original matter thus becomes secondarily relevant, if at all.

8. While the historical outline used primarily follows that of the 1972 *Encyclopedia Judaica,* it has been further refined by dividing the period known as the "Middle Ages" into (1) the eighth to the fourteenth centuries, and (2) the fourteenth to the seventeenth centuries; the period "Modern Times"—to 1880—into (1) the sixteenth to seventeenth centuries and (2) the eighteenth to nineteenth centuries.

9. Such continuous interactivity puts to bed the false understanding perpetuated by the great British historian Arnold J. Toynbee (1889–1975), author of the monumental twelve-volume *A Study of History* (1934–1961), who is said to have labeled the Jews a "fossilized people" for both its seeming lack of internal intellectual development and its seemingly nonexistent influence on and participation in the development of Western civilizational ideas.

2. Cycles of History

1. Jakob J. Petuchowski (1925–1992), late Professor at the Hebrew Union College-Jewish Institution of Religion, Cincinnati, Ohio, used to tell his students that "Jews read Torah with a twinkle in their eyes while Christians read Torah as a pretext to and for their reading of the New Testament." I trust this double entendre needs no further clarification.

2. Even this difference in perspective is not without its controversies, at least in the United States. In June of 2006, for example, the Kentucky State Board of Education, in approving its seven-hundred-page Program of Study, reaffirmed it use of B.C. and A.D. without the *additional* use of B.C.E. and C.E. Representatives of conservative Christian groups, misreading the Board's intentions, wrongly accused it of undermining the very foundations of United States history. ("Kentucky school board decides to keep B.C., A.D. in curriculum," *Huntsville Times,* June 15, 2006; Jennifer Siegel, "Religious Groups Push Kentucky To Use 'Before Christ,' " *Forward,* June 9, 2006.)

3. Attempts to somehow connect the "Hebrews" (or Israelites) with a variety of disparate groups subsumed under the more global designation *HaPiru, HaBiru* or *'Apiru* has thus far proved unconvincing.

4. In the Jewish religious tradition, opposition to the act of self-destruction (suicide) unites all streams of religious Judaism. Suicide is understood to be the desecration of a holy vessel of one "created in the image of God," according to the Book of *Bereshith*/Genesis. How then do the rabbis of later Jewish tradition explain what must have been viewed by Saul's own contemporaries as a noble act? By concluding that there are some stories in the Hebrew Bible or Torah from which Jews may draw no positive conclusions. (Another example would be the marriage of Esther the Jew to the non-Jewish monarch Ahashuerus [Hebrew, *Ahashwerosh*], the Persian king in the biblical book of her name, which, while resulting ultimately in Jewish success over attempted genocide, gives no religious sanction to interreligious marriage between Jews and non-Jews.)

5. A medical reading of this text would seem to indicate the story of the dead child may be the *first* recorded instance in literature of a death resulting from Sudden Infant Death Syndrome (SIDS), about which we continue to know very, very little (i.e., how a seemingly healthy child may go to sleep and fail to wake up). In numerous conversations with medical practitioners, the author has had it repeatedly confirmed that no mother, unless she is in either an alcohol- or drug-induced stupor, can simply roll over and smother her child during sleep; some genetic or other reflex would prevent her from doing so.

6. An excellent text addressing this myth in all its configurations is Tudor Parfitt's *The Lost Tribes of Israel: The History of a Myth* (London: Weidenfield & Nicolson, 2002).

7. The dual religious and theological interpretations of these events by the normative Jewish community and the still minority dissident group who will later evolve into Christians will have enormous consequences for the next two thousand years of Judaic history: for the former, at least Talmudically and reflective of dominant thinking, the destruction was the result of internal Jewish dissension, the Romans acting, consistent with biblical thinking, as "agents of God." For the latter, it was a confirmation of the failure of the Jewish community to accept the *truth* of Jesus Christ as the long-sought-for Jewish messiah, and God's punishment of them for their failure to do so, again the Romans functioning as agents of God. Even with the "parting of the ways" several centuries later, the so-called crime of deicide (i.e., killing the god), reflected not only in New Testament texts but in generation after generation of Christian interpretation and implementation (i.e., ghettoization, expulsion, forced conversion, even extermination) remains current. It was only with the 1965 Roman Catholic enactment of *Nostra Aetate* ("In Our Age") at the Second Vatican Council, initiated under the inspired leadership of the late Pope John XXIII (1881–1963 C.E.), exonerating all Jews, then and now, for participation in the death of the Christ, and condemning antisemitism in the process, that the winds of change for Jews in the West began to blow, and continues to this day.

8. A rather delightful read with interesting implications by the late famed Viennese Nazi hunter Simon Wiesenthal (1908–2005 C.E.) is a book called *Sails of Hope: The Secret Mission of Christopher Columbus* (New York: Macmillan, 1973).

9. The text to read is that of Joshua Trachtenberg, *The Devil and the Jews: The Medieval Conception of the Jew and Its Relation to Modern Anti-Semitism* (1961; reprint, Philadelphia: Jewish Publication Society of America, 1984).

10. For English-speaking readers, the best-known edition is that translated by Solomon Ganzfried, with additional material by Judah Goldin, *Code of Jewish Law* (New York: Hebrew Publishing Company, 1963).

3. Cycles of Texts

1. Included among these Jewish texts are: 1 and 2 Esdras, Tobit, Judith, Ecclesiasticus or the Wisdom of Ben Sirach, Bel and the Dragon, Susanna, and 1 and 2 Maccabees.

2. In 2001, the Pontifical Biblical Commission of the Roman Catholic Church produced a lengthy document titled "The Jewish People and Their Sacred

Scriptures in the Christian Bible," which strengthened Jewish–Christian relations by recognizing the inherent integrity of the Torah/Hebrew Bible for Jews and its interpretive methodologies, even as it affirmed its own incorporation of those texts together with the New Testament texts in proclaiming the "Good News (Gospel) of Jesus Christ." See also appendix 1, "Torah/Hebrew Bible, Roman Catholic Bible, and Protestant Bible" for a charting out of the three different Bibles according to each of these three traditions.

3. As would be expected, part of the "magic" of the text is lost in translation, most especially with regard to the names of the various biblical personages, a supreme example of which is the following: Jacob, the second-born twin after Esau is named *Ya'akov*, which we may presently translate as "Heel-grabber," the name by which he will be known until his wrestling match with the *Ish* (Hebrew, "man"), after which he will be known as *Yisra'el* or "God-wrestler," the sobriquet by which the Jewish people will forever be known, not only "Israel-ites,"—*Yisra'elim*—but the Children/People of Israel—*Benai Yisra'el* or *Am Yisra'el*—as well. Such naming conventions were obviously a source of descriptive pleasure and punning amusement to the ancients.

4. Barry W. Holz, ed., *Back to the Sources: Reading the Classic Jewish Texts* (New York: Simon and Schuster, 1986).

5. Far and away, the First Five Books of Moses—the *Chumash*—have produced outstanding volumes in English that are not only valued in Jewish denominational communities, but across the board: These volumes include the Reform commentary edited by W. Gunther Plaut, *The Torah: A Modern Commentary* (New York: Union of American Hebrew Congregations, 1974); the Conservative commentary edited by David L. Lieber, *Etz Hayim: Torah and Commentary* (Philadelphia: Jewish Publication Society of America, 2002); the now-classic 1937 Orthodox commentary of the late Chief Rabbi of the British Empire Joseph H. Hertz, *The Pentateuch and Haftorahs with Hebrew Text, English Translation and Commentary* (New York: Soncino Press, 1958); and the cross-denominational *JPS Torah Commentary* in five individual volumes and edited by the late Nahum M.

Sarna and Chaim Potok (Philadelphia: Jewish Publication Society of America, 1996).

6. For comparison purposes, here is the Deuteronomic version:

> I am the Lord your God, who brought you out of Egypt, out of the land of slavery.
>
> You shall have no other gods before me.
>
> You shall not make for yourself an idol in the form of anything in heaven above or on the earth beneath or in the waters below. You shall not bow down to them or worship them; for I, the Lord your God, am a jealous God, punishing the children for the sin of the fathers to the third and fourth generation of those who hate me, but showing love to a thousand generations of those who love me and keep my commandments.
>
> You shall not misuse the name of the Lord your God, for the Lord will not hold anyone guiltless who misuses his name.
>
> Observe the Sabbath day by keeping it holy, as the Lord your God has commanded you. Six days you shall labor and do all your work, but the seventh day is a Sabbath to the Lord your God. On it you shall not do any work, neither you, nor your son or daughter, nor your manservant or maidservant, nor your ox, your donkey or any of your animals, nor the alien within your gates, so that your manservant and maidservant may rest, as you do. Remember that you were slaves in Egypt and that the Lord your God brought you out of there with a mighty hand and an outstretched arm. Therefore the Lord your God has commanded you to observe the Sabbath day.
>
> Honor your father and your mother, as the Lord your God has commanded you, so that you may live long and that it may go well with you in the land the Lord your God is giving you.
>
> You shall not murder.
>
> You shall not commit adultery.
>
> You shall not steal.
>
> You shall not give false testimony against your neighbor.

> You shall not covet your neighbor's wife. You shall not set your desire on your neighbor's house or land, his manservant or maidservant, his ox or donkey, or anything that belongs to your neighbor.

7. This notion of the loving critique, no matter how harsh or severe, would later be enshrined by the rabbis of the postbiblical Jewish religious tradition in their notion of *yesurin shel ahava* (Hebrew, "chastisements out of love"). That is, just as one's own parents reprimand and punish out of love with the betterment of their child always before them, so God reprimands and punishes his own children of Israel, always taking them back and allowing them to return to him in love. Then, too, the relationship between God and Israel, symbolized by the *berith*, or covenant, places significantly more responsibility on Israel for proper moral-ethical behavior and ritual-ceremonial observance because they are God's own special and unique people, just as one's parents' expectation of their own children is greater than their expectations of others' children.

8. In Talmudic times, under the prying eyes of the Palestinian Roman censors, the rabbis critiqued historic Edom, which their own audiences understood to mean quite clearly their Roman enemy.

9. Note that the correct understanding of all of these prophetic critiques is not that the prophets were themselves contra ritual or ceremonial behavior. It was that such temple-related activities were only properly performed by those who came into the holy presence of God morally and ethically upright. The word, therefore, that would perhaps best describe the object of both their contempt and their wrath would be *hypocrisy*, i.e., the one who behaves in an immoral/unethical manner but who continues to bring his sacrifices to the temple, who engages in unethical behavior for his own selfish betterment but who brings his tithes to the priest and receives his blessing in return.

10. Originally, scholars were more than convinced that this third and final section consisted of *eleven* rather than thirteen books, both Ezra–Nehemiah being one text and Chronicles 1 and 2 being one text, later divided by an unknown *Christian* editor, evidently early enough for Jews to also adopt this convention.

11. If these Wisdom texts were (and are) understood as the possible curriculum of the ancient settled community, and designed to produce good husbands, good fathers, and good citizens, then at least initially, these were used in some academic setting about which we do not know, taught by teachers about whom we know nothing, and presented to the middle-class and upper-class sons (not daughters!) of ancient Israel in formats about which, again, we know nothing. Whatever insights into their use may be gleaned from Talmudic materials is ex post facto (Latin, "after the fact") their actual reality.

12. This attribution is, however, itself somewhat problematic for the following reasons: Many of the psalms have superscriptions and unknown attributions. Others use the Hebrew phrase *Mizmor leDavid*, which may be translated "A Psalm *of* David," "A Psalm *for* David," "A Psalm *to* David" or "A Psalm *by* David." How to distinguish between them with regard to specific psalms is nearly impossible, which is not to totally dismiss Davidic authorship but rather to suggest that perhaps not all of those attributed to him are indeed his compositions. The Torah/Hebrew Bible does, however, take great pains to paint David as one possessed of both a military genius *and* a religio-spiritual sensitivity for whom psalmic composition would make logical sense.

13. One such system of categorization is the following: enthronement psalms, zion psalms, torah psalms, national lament psalms, personal lament and appeal psalms, confidence psalms, thanksgiving psalms, royal psalms, wisdom psalms, and combination psalms.

14. An alternative translation would be "*Awe* of God is the beginning of wisdom/knowledge," thus suggesting that a certain recognition of one's limited humanity in God's eternal presence carries with it a humility that *should* reflect itself in a positive predisposition to learning.

15. Verses 1:16 and 1:17 have been incorporated into the Liberal (Reform) Ceremony of Conversion through the Jewish Religious Tradition to the Jewish people:

> But Ruth replied, "Don't urge me to leave you or to turn back from you. Where you go I will go,

and where you stay I will stay. Your people will be my people and your God my God. Where you die I will die, and there I will be buried. May the LORD deal with me, be it ever so severely, if anything but death separates you and me."

16. This resolution is not without problems itself. Some scholars have suggested that this text is an appendage to what was originally an unresolved or negative assessment of the meaning of life, i.e., that it is ultimately devoid of meaning, and that whatever comfort is to be derived from living, it is found in the journey itself for however long it endures.

17. The only other place where the antisemitic enemy of the Jewish People—in this case the prime minister of Persia, Haman—is given voice is in this text of the Book of Esther. In 3:8-9, we find him making the following comment:

> Then Haman said to King Ahashverosh, "There is a certain people dispersed and scattered among the peoples in all the provinces of your kingdom whose customs are different from those of all other people and who do not obey the King's laws; it is not in the King's best interest to tolerate them. If it pleases the King, let a decree be issued to destroy them, and I will put ten thousand tal-

ents of silver into the royal treasury for the men who carry out this business."

18. Louis Ginzberg, *Legends of the Jews* (Philadelphia: The Jewish Publication Society of America, 2003).

19. Hayim Nahman Bialik and Yehoshua Hana Ravnitzky, *The Book of Legends*, trans. William G. Braude (New York: Schocken Books, 1992).

20. Ginzberg, *Legends of the Jews*, 286–87.

21. *The Soncino Classic Collection*, CD-ROM (Chicago: Davka Corporation, 1991–1996).

22. torah.org/advanced/shulchan-aruch/classes/orach chayim/chapter5.html.

23. torah.org/advanced/shulchan-aruch/classes/chapter6 .html.

24. Orthodox (Hebrew and English): www.halachabrura .org. Conservative: www.responsafortoday.com. Reform: www.ccarnet.org. All sites accessed January 29, 2010.

25. The whole question of the role/place/function of women in Jewish religious life—like their role/place/ function in the religious life of other communities— remains a contested one. The more historically traditional communities, in this case Jewish Orthodoxy, tend to reaffirm the positions of the past, while the more moderate and liberal denominational communities continue to negotiate between the past and the fluctuating realities of the present.

4. Cycles of Thought

1. http://www.iep.utm.edu/p/philo; accessed January 29, 2010.

2. The Hebrew word *midrash* ("to search out," "to draw out") will give rise to an extensive literature of biblical commentaries "filling in the gaps" where the Torah/ Hebrew Bible is silent, a set of rules for explication, stories, and legal commentaries, a process that continues today.

3. Note here the differentiation as before indicated by the use of a lowercase *t* rather than a capital *T*. Such orthographical distinctions do not exist in Hebraic writing.

4. A concrete example of this difference is found within this author's own personal library: My Palestinian Talmud is four volumes in length; my Babylonian Talmud is twenty volumes!

5. The conservatizing nature of Jewish organizational and communal structures seemingly unable to countenance contrary or perceived heretical views will again come to the fore in the person of Benedict Spinoza in Amsterdam in the seventeenth century.

6. http://www.jewishvirtuallibrary.org/jsource/biogra phy/HermannCohen; accessed January 29, 2010.

7. The "classic" survey of the field is that of Julius Guttman, *Philosophies of Judaism: The History of Jewish Philosophy from Biblical Times to Franz Rosenzweig* (New York: Holt, Rinehardt & Winston, 1964). The latest and even more up-to-date survey is that of Daniel Frank, *History of Jewish Philosophy* (New York: Routledge, 1997).

8. An excellent source of information regarding the controversy is the edited collection of essays by Carol Rittner and John Roth, *Memory Offended: The Auschwitz Convent Controversy* (Westport, Conn.: Praeger, 1991).

9. Whether Fackenheim intended this phrase metaphorically or literally was never fully clarified and thus remains a source of controversy. According to the rabbis of the Jewish religious tradition, embedded with the Torah/Hebrew Bible are 613 *mitzvot*/commandments/obligations, both positive ("You shall . . . ") and negative ("You shall not . . . "). To elevate this response to the Holocaust/Shoah on the part of the Jewish people is to accord it the status of Torah/Hebrew Bible, and with it, the sanctity and power of halakha/Jewish law, the central behavioral model of Judaism.

5. Cycles of Belief

1. The Hebrew term *perushim*, from which we derive our English term "Pharisees," means "separatists," and alludes to their religious commitments more than their political allegiances during the period of Roman oppression. Jesus himself, to the degree to which we may wish to align him with any other group of Jews during his time, would certainly have been comfortable with these "democrats," whose concern for the people he shared. On the other hand, the term *tsadokim*, "Sadducees," or "followers of [the high priest of the Solomonic era] Tzadok," would have been those most interested in preserving the status quo under Roman hegemony and a way of life and religious system that had been in existence for almost six hundred years (586 B.C.E. and onward).

2. On this very point, the great Christian scholar of Judaism George Foote Moore (1851–1931) summarizes well the prevailing scholarly consensus:

> Judaism, in the centuries with which we are concerned, had no body of articulated and systematized doctrine such as we understand by the name theology. Philo, indeed, endeavored to harmonize his hereditary religion with a Hellenistic philosophy, but the resulting theology exerted no discoverable influence on the main current of Jewish thought. As in the case of the Bible itself, any exposition of Jewish teaching on these subjects, by the very necessity of orderly disposition, unavoidably gives an appearance of system and coherence which the teachings themselves do not exhibit, and which were not in the ids of the teachers. This fact the reader must constantly bear in mind. It must further be remarked that the utterances of the rabbis on this subject are not dogmatic, carrying an authority comparable to the juristic definitions and decisions of the Halakah; they are in great part homiletic, often drawing instruction or edification from the words of Scripture by ingenious turns of interpretation, association, and application, which seized upon the attention and fixed themselves in the memory of the hearers of the novelty, not of the lesson, but of the way the homilist got it into the text and out again. Large liberty in such invention has always been accorded to preachers, and every one knows that scholastic precision is not be to looked for in what is said for impression. (George Foote Moore, *Judaism* [Cambridge, Mass.: Harvard University Press], 357).

The best available work in English, with large numbers of quotations and organized by topic, remains that of Claude Montefiore and Herbert Lowe, titled *A Rabbinic Anthology* (London: Macmillan, 1938) and republished both in the United States and England.

3. Orthodox Judaism, as it has seen and understood itself, perceives the "oral tradition" (Hebrew, *Torah she b'al peh,* "Torah which is upon the mouth"), later written down in the Talmuds, as equally given by God to Moses as Sinai, and therefore the job of later generations is to interpret the ethical and ritual "truths" of these divinely given texts. Halakhic or "legal" Judaism thus becomes God-given Judaism as they affirm and present it to their adherents. Others outside of Orthodox Judaism, which is not one strand only but, like other subcultures, reveals much diversity, take a more objectively critical view, understanding this interpretive (and innovative) tradition as one evolving over generations in response to both internal and external pressures and forces. Hence, today the divisions are historical—e.g., between non-Hasidic Orthodox Judaism or *Misnagdic* (Hebrew, "Oppositional") and Hasidic Judaisms—and Halakhic Judaism—primarily both strands of Orthodox Judaism—and non-Halakhic Judaisms—Reform Judaism and Reconstructionist Judaism (a twentieth-century American innovation). Conservative Judaism, attempting to balance itself between its dual commitments to both halakha and modernity, finds its leaders and adherents opting for more traditional Jewish approaches (e.g., chanting the liturgy) and more modern and less historically traditional Jewish approaches (e.g., ordaining women).

4. Israel's birthplace of Medzhybizh was at one time or another under the political governance of each of these four sovereignties.

5. Rabbi Shneur Zalman's own followers today have achieved particular successes during the 1960s in the United States in helping Jewish young people exchange their commitment to the all-pervasive drug culture for that of religious Judaism, as well as sending married couple emissaries into Jewish communities throughout the world to evangelize and proselytize among their fellow Jews for a more traditionally observant Jewish religious way of life. Controversy, however, continues to surround Chabad Hasidism, primarily due to the fact that its last rebbe, Menachem Mendel Schneerson (1902–1994), died childless without a designated heir (either his own son, as has become normative Hasidic tradition, or someone not related), but has been viewed by some among his followers as not having died at all but is in fact the long-sought-for Judaic *mashiach* (Hebrew, "messiah"), who will return, smite the enemies of the Jews, and restore peace and harmony among the world's peoples.

6. Not one to shy away from controversy, his taking over the helm of a failing academic institution— one associated with the Unification Church of Korea minister Rev. Sun Myung Moon (b. 1920)—and reversing its fortunes both fiscally and academically has estranged him somewhat from the organized American Jewish communities, as have his writings, though in later years much of this rancor and enmity have dissipated.

6. Cycles of Time

1. While scholars of the Torah/Hebrew Bible have yet to definitively explain the rationale for the word choice of *Shemot*/Exodus 20:8—*zachor,* "remember"—versus that of *Devarim*/Deuteronomy 5:12—*shamor,* "observe"—rabbinic tradition pragmatizes its understanding that the Shabbat itself is inaugurated with the lighting of *two* holy candles, one in observance of each command. (A Hasidic expansion on this theme of candle lighting, practiced among some not all, is to allow unmarried daughters still living at home to each light one candle in honor of the Shabbat, since the task has historically been associated with the woman of the home, though halakha (legal tradition) insists on the obligation without gender fixity.

2. The Talmud itself already recognized reality with its well-known statement *Pikuach nefesh docheh et hashab-*

bat, "Where the saving of a life is concerned, this overrides even the most stringent of Sabbath proscriptions."

3. *High Holyday Prayer Book: Yom Kippur*, trans. Philip Birnbaum (New York: Hebrew Publishing Company, 1951), 46.

4. These four species, or kinds, have led to a variety of rabbinic interpretations. One such equates the four with body parts (palm branch = spine; myrtle leaf = eye; willow = mouth; lemon = heart), all of which can participate in sinful activity, but should instead be used to fulfill the *mitzvot*, commanded obligations of the religious Jew. A second equates the four with different kinds of Jews (lemon = Jew with both religious knowledge and religious practice; palm branch = Jew with religious knowledge but no observance; myrtle = religious practice but little or no knowledge; willow = Jew who has neither). In bringing them together, the hope is that the ideals of both knowledge and practice will "rub off" on the other three. (See http://www.jewfaq.org; accessed January 29, 2010.)

5. The rabbinic rereading of the biblical text regarding the Pharaoh of Egypt, believed to have been Ramses II (c. 1302–c. 1290 B.C.E.), is a more nuanced portrayal of a tragic figure whom the God of Israel needed to manipulate for divine designs without making moral judgments either way. Thus, his heart-hardening reluctance was understood to have been necessary to advance the story of Israel's liberation, but not the portrait painted by later generations of one paradigmatically evil.

6. All four begin with "Why is this night different than all other nights?" (1) Since on all other nights we are permitted to eat both leavened and unleavened products, but on this night only unleavened? (2) Since we ordinarily eat vegetables, but on this night we add the bitter herb? (3) Since we ordinarily do not dip our food, but on this night we dip food twice? (4) Since we ordinarily eat either sitting up or reclining, but on this night we recline when eating? (This latter practice may have been initiated during Roman times in Palestine, when the Jews saw such reclined eating as an expression of free Roman conduct.)

7. As a child, the author has a memory of being terribly upset at one Passover celebration with family and friends. Having just learned to read, he had gotten quite scared upon learning that one was to eat "the bitter Herb" (the name of one of the adult participants). Thankfully, of course, no such thing transpired.

8. An interesting historical footnote: Early on after the founding of the State of Israel in 1948 and its military celebrations, some in the more traditionally observant Jewish communities in Israel (and, to a lesser extent, abroad) decried what they described as a "glorification of the ways of war," in contradistinction to a religious tradition, which "sanctifies the ways of peace."

7. Cycles of Life

1. Nonreligious Zionists, both in Israel herself (the collective farming communities known as *kibbutzim* and *moshavim* were, historically, composed of socialists, and, to a lesser, degree, communists, who celebrated their lives, but without recourse to the Jewish religion as such) as well as outside of Israel also celebrate life's journey. Also, the newest expression of Judaic religion—"Humanistic Judaism"—finds the use of the term *God* terribly problematic for its adherents, but celebrates Jewish lives nonetheless within its own congregational settings. (It is, by the way, originally an American movement, founded in the latter half of the twentieth century, but has adherents in Israel and other locales as well.) Finally, the Yiddish socialist movements of Jews who came primarily from Soviet Russia prior to the mid-twentieth century and flowered in the larger cities and metropolitan areas in the United States (and elsewhere) established schools and organizations of kindred spirits that, in turn, equally celebrated their lives and their journeys.

2. This author would argue, at least in part, that among the reasons for the very power of Brit Milah are its

explicit association with two of the "life forces" that are crucial to the very survival of the human race: blood and semen.

3. Like all surgical procedures, circumcision itself is not without controversy: some have long argued that the procedure is itself medically sound and healthful (males undergoing it evince less incidents of penile cancers and their partners less incidents of cervical cancers); others arguing that it may increase the potential of later erectile dysfunction. Both positions have their advocates and detractors. Jews, however, regardless of supposed medical benefits or not, do so for *religious* reasons, which they tend to regard as wholly sufficient. Additionally, so powerful is this event on the life of Jews, that even those most estranged from the organized Jewish community and/or religious life will contact rabbis, cantors, or *mohelim* (pl. of *mohel*) to arrange for the Brit Milah (surgery and ritual) of their newborn sons.

4. A midrashic innovative reinterpretation of bar mitzvah is that when a man approaches eighty-three years of age, he becomes eligible for a *second* bar mitzvah: having met the requirement of a "normal" lifespan of "three score years and ten" (3 x 20 + 10), he begins to count again (70 + 13 = 83).

5. A more gently humorous and often-told story is that of the young man who began his speech with such nervousness (and perhaps subconsciously remembering the gifts he had already received) that his first words were "Today, I am a fountain pen!"

6. Sanford Seltzer, *Jews and Non-Jews Falling in Love* (New York: Union of American Hebrew Congregations, 1976).

7. Here, we may use the understanding of mourners being included in two circles: the *inner circle* of those whose loss is most immediate—husbands, wives, brothers, sisters, fathers, mothers, sons, and/or daughters; and the *outer circle*—aunts, uncles, cousins, grandparents, grandchildren—as well as close family friends who, while equally feeling the pain of such a death are not obligated to take upon themselves the various responsibilities associated with mourning rituals, but *may choose* to do so. No judgment whatsoever is made regarding either the pain or grief of such persons. Inner-circle mourners may also rend their garments or affix to them black ribbons that can be torn or cut in response to the benediction "Praised are you, Adonai, judge of truth."

8. Cycles of the Here and Now

1. Nicholas de Lange and Miri Freud-Kandel, eds., *Modern Judaism* (New York: Oxford University Press, 2005).

2. A phrase associated with the public statements of the Iranian president Mahmoud Amadinejad, *yemach sh'mo*, "May his name be blotted out!"

3. His original essay "The Clash of Civilizations?" was first published in the journal *Foreign Affairs* (Summer 1993): 22–49, and later published in book form as *The Clash of Civilizations: Remaking of World Order* (New York: Simon and Schuster, 1996). His thesis continues to generate enormous controversy both in support of and opposed to his position.

4. While a book titled "A Brief History of Antisemitism" could conceivably be a companion volume to this one, and there is already a substantial library of published works addressing this topic from a variety of perspectives (historical, psychological, sociological, theological), two recent works suggest a more pragmatic approach: Kenneth S. Stern, *Anti-Semitism Today: How It Is the Same, How It Is Different, and How to Fight It* (New York: American Jewish Committee, 2006), and *Confronting Anti-Semitism: Myths . . . Facts . . .* (New York: Anti-Defamation League, 2006).

5. Its "Report on Global Anti-Semitism," covering the period July 1, 2003–December 15, 2004, for example, can be accessed online at http://www.state.gov/g/drl/rls/40258.htm; accessed January 29, 2010.

9. Conclusion

1. *A Passover Haggadah*. (New York: Central Conference of American Rabbis, 1975), 93.
2. Even the British historian Arnold Toynbee (1889–1975), in his twelve-volume *A Study of History* (1934–1961), who referred to the Jews as "a fossilized people," could not write them out of existence.
3. Even the perverse Nazi attempt to define Jews as the descendants of one Jewish grandparent in the infamous and notorious Nuremberg Racial Laws of 1935 was a failed enterprise: to attempt to falsely equate biology with belief, physicality with identity, could not and cannot be done. Jews who say they are Jews do so with a variety of interpretive judgments, accepting some definitions (religious, cultural, ethnic) even while rejecting others (Zionist, non-Zionist, secularist, humanist).

Glossary

Ale malei rachamim "O God, full of compassion." Prayer text included in Jewish funerals, asking divine blessing and eternal caring upon the deceased.

Aliyah Immigration to Israel. Literally, a "going *up*" to the Land of Israel. (Its opposite is *yeridah,* literally a "going *down*" from the Land of Israel.)

Al Kuzari **(Arabic, "The Khazar")** Written by Yehuda Ha-Levi (Judah the Levite, 1085/86–1140), it is a philosophical discussion divided into five sections why Judaism is superior to philosophy as well as Christianity and Islam regarding the "true path" to the One God.

antisemitism Hatred of the Jewish people and the Jewish religious faith, heritage, and tradition. Throughout history, the forms antisemitism has taken have included expulsion, ghettoization, forced religious conversion, denial of civil rights, and extermination-annihilation. (The preferred spelling here is without the hyphen; to use a hyphen is to imply its opposite, that there is such a thing as "Semitism," which is nonexistent.)

Aninut The initial period of mourning according to the Jewish religious tradition when the death is first realized and the family gathers prior to the funeral, supported by friends and extended family members.

Apocrypha Additional biblical texts many of which were co-existent with those canonized in the Torah/Hebrew Bible and largely preserved today in Roman Catholic versions of the Holy Bible.

apostasy Rejection of one's birth faith—in this case Judaism—and the embracing of another. Such persons are, more likely than not, viewed by the original communities as "enemies," "traitors," or worse.

Aron Kodesh **(Hebrew, "Holy Ark")** The cabinet or closet on the synagogue sanctuary *bema* or elevated front containing one or more scrolls of the First Five Books of the Hebrew Bible.

Aseret Hadibrot Usually translated as the "Ten Commandments," as found in the Torah in *Shemot* (Exodus) 20 and *Devarim* (Deuteronomy) 5. A more accurate translation would be the "Ten Essential Statements," without which no society could endure.

Ashkenazim Historically understood as those Jews residing in or coming from so-called Germanic lands.

assimilation Sociologically understood as the process by which immigrant individuals or groups surrender their distinctive identities in exchange for blending into the larger cultural, social, and political environment. Such a process is seen by large numbers of Jews as particularly threatening to the ongoing survival of Jews outside the Land/State of Israel, and, consequently, a strong argument in favor of *aliyah.*

Atzai Hayyim (Hebrew, "Trees of Life") The two wooden rollers which enable the Torah/Hebrew Bible scrolls to be manipulated for synagogal use as part of the worship liturgy.

Babylonian Talmud The five-hundred-year encyclopedic compendium of Jewish legislative materials whose core is an extended commentary on the Mishnah*,* and reveals much about Jewish life during the period of its composition (200 c.e.–700 c.e.). It remains today among the primary sources of Jewish religious authority, especially in the more traditionally observant communities, and the central curriculum of study of both students and rabbis.

Bar or Bat Mitzvah Literally, "son" or "daughter of the Commandment." The "coming of age" in the Jewish religious tradition of a boy at age thirteen and a girl at age twelve years plus one day (girls maturing faster than boys). Usually the ceremony involves the conduct of any or all of a worship service, the reading or chanting of selected portions of Scripture, and a speech, possibly a commentary on that Scripture. Usually celebrated with, at times, too elaborate social parties.

Baruch de Spinoza (1632–1677) The Dutch Sephardic Jew whose philosophic views and conclusions ultimately led him to be excommunicated from the Jewish community. Today, he is regarded as one of the major figures foundational to modern philosophy and whose major works were his *Theological-Political Treatise* and *Ethics.*

b.c.e. (**Before Common Era**) The term used by Jews (and others, especially academics in the secular academy) to identify a particular date according to the Western or Gregorian calendar without referencing the Christ and before the year "0."

Bedekin The momentary ceremony prior to a Jewish wedding when the bride is "veiled."

Behirah (Hebrew, "Chosenness") The biblical understanding of the people of Israel "chosen" by God for a special purpose, to be "a light unto the nations and a banner unto the peoples," giving evidence by the lives led of a true commitment to and following in the ways of God. Over the course of the centuries, this concept has led to misunderstandings between Jews and Christians as well as to false claims of arrogance and superiority on the part of Jews, and a desire to supersede them on the part of those who were/are not.

Beit Haknesset One of the three primary functions of the synagogue to serve as a site of assembly or gathering of its members.

Beit Hamidrash Another of the primary synagogue functions—to serve as a place of Jewish study and learning.

Beit Hatefila The third—or perhaps—first primary function of the synagogue the serve as the place of prayer and worship.

Bemidbar/**Numbers** The fourth book of the Torah/Hebrew Bible, and detailing the wilderness experience of the ancient Israelites prior to their arrival in the Holy Land.

Bereshith/**Genesis** The first book of the Torah/Hebrew Bible telling the story of both the creation of the world and the creation of the Israelite people through the stories of their patriarchs Abraham, Isaac, Jacob, and Joseph.

Berith (Hebrew, "Covenant") The "covenant" entered into between God and the people of Israel at Sinai after their escape from Egypt and their wanderings in the desert, prior to their entrance into the Promised Land of Israel. According to *Devarim* (Deuteronomy), entered into both with those at Sinai as well as with the generations yet to come. If Israel honors God and follows in God's ways, then God will protect and save Israel from its enemies.

Bible The commonly accepted term by both Jews and Christians for their sacred Scriptures. For Jews, it comprises the books from Genesis to Second Chronicles. For Protestant Christians Genesis through Revelation, and for Roman Catholics the additional texts known as the Apocrypha.

Borei Olam God as "Creator of the world or universe." The place at which all Jewish theological investigation must begin; the place at which the Torah/Hebrew Bible, the sacred scriptures of the Jewish people, itself begins. (In the aftermath of the Holocaust/Shoah, for me, the only initially logical and honest concept still able to address contemporary reality.)

Brit Milah Literally, the "covenant of circumcision." The religious ceremony marking the entre of an eight-day-old Jewish boy into the "covenant of Abraham" by his parents and welcoming him into the Jewish community. The ceremony consists of two distinct parts: the attendant religious ritual and the actual surgical procedure of the removal of the additional flap of skin covering the head of the penis. (Debate continues as to its medical benefits as well as its religious value.)

C.E. (**Common Era**) The term used by Jews (and others, especially academics in the secular academy) to identify a particular date according to the Western or Gregorian calendar without referencing the Christ and after the year "0"

Chabad Hasidism A form of Hasidic Orthodox Judaism founded by Rabbi Shneur Zalman (1745–1812) of Liadi, Lithuania. "Chabad" is an acronym standing for wisdom, understanding, and knowledge, the three pillars governing their interpretation of Jewish thought and practice.

Cherem The Hebrew term for excommunication.

Chevra Kaddisha The burial society tasked with the responsibility to properly prepare the body for interment in the cemetery by washing the body, combing the hair, cutting the fingernails and toenails, wrapping the body in a linen shroud, and placing it in the plain pine box of Jewish religious tradition. Separate societies exist for males and females.

Christianity The historical movement which began as a dissident sect of Jews (and others) during the period of the Roman oppression of Palestine 2,000 years ago, and flourished to become a worldwide movement today. At its heart is the person of the Christ regarded as the Son of God who was born, died, and was resurrected—the long-sought-for Messiah. The ongoing tension between Judaism and Christianity over accepting or rejecting him as the Jewish messiah remains today.

chosenness See *Behirah*.

Chumash The Hebrew term for the First Five Books of the Hebrew Bible, and taken from the Hebrew word for five, "hamesh."

Chuppah (**Hebrew, "Canopy"**) The canopy under which the bride and groom are married. Can be erected in either the congregational sanctuary, the home or the outdoors. Symbolic of the future home (and, possibly, of the marriage bed) of the new family.

Chutzpah (**Hebrew: "Brazenness"**) That special quality of stubborn determination associated with the Jewish people that has enabled them to survive—despite all previous attempts at their demise.

cities of refuge Allotted to the Levites in the Book of Leviticus, these cities were understood to be places where those who took the lives of others accidentally and without intention could flee (to be later joined by their families) and could reside in safety and security. Their period of residence remained until the death of the high priest after which they could leave and rejoin their tribal communities.

confirmation The group ceremony important to Reform Judaism usually around tenth grade and celebrated in the spring around the holiday of Shavuot and usually after a year-long intensive study period with the rabbi or rabbis of the congregation.

consecration The group ceremony important to Reform Judaism usually around kindergarten and celebrated in the fall around the holiday of Simchat Torah marking the end of Sukkot and marking the beginning of Jewish religious education. For those children not yet receiving their Hebrew names, they are presented with them at that time.

Conservative Judaism Founded in the middle 1800s in Germany, this "middle-of-the-road" Jewish religious movement was originally known as Positive-Historical Judaism and attempted to form a midpoint between the more liberal Reform Judaism and the stricter Orthodox Judaism. It arose, however, as a response to what it perceived to be the religious excesses of early Reform Judaism, especially its dramatic modifications of traditional Jewish liturgical practices.

conversion The religious ceremony by which an individual comes to embrace a religious faith and tradition different from that of his or her birth. For Jews, the process is of postbiblical or rabbinic origin and consists of study, religious practice, ritual immersion, and the acceptance of a Hebrew name. Each of the Jewish denominational religious communities differs in their specific requirements.

cosmology The study of the universe in all of its various manifestations and the place of humanity within it.

covenant See *Berith*.

culture The sum total of a given human community's endeavors, its music, art, literature, religion, etc.

Da'at Elohim A modern Hebrew expression—literally "knowledge of God"—but better understood as "theology."

Dar al-Harb (Arabic, "World of War") Understood by the followers of Islam as those places outside of Islamic hegemony and thus perceived by many as enemies to be vanquished.

Dar al-Islam (Arabic, "World of Islam") Understood by the followers of Islam as those places governed by Islamic hegemony and thus correctly in harmony with Allah.

Dati Hebrew term designating a Jewish religious person usually Orthodox. Literally, the term may best be understood as one who follows the halakha or Jewish legal traditions.

deicide The antisemitic charge against the Jewish people as primarily responsible for the death of the Christ and derived from a particular reading of the New Testament texts, resulting in a bad history for the last 2,000 years.

Der goldiner medina Yiddish phrase for "the golden land" and understood by Eastern European Jews to designate America as the land of opportunity where the streets were paved with gold.

Der Judenstaat The political manifesto of the father of modern political Zionism Theodor Herzl (1860–1904) arguing that the only way to resolve the European scourge of antisemitism was for Jews to have a land of their own and be the equal of all other nation-states.

Deutero-Isaiah Second Isaiah as argued by some scholars that chapters 40–66 of the Book of Isaiah indicate a different author with a different religious agenda from that reflected in the first 39 chapters.

Devarim/Deuteronomy The fifth book of the Torah/Hebrew Bible telling the story of the approach of the ancient Israelites to the Holy Land and the death of Moses.

Die Endlösung The "'Final Solution' to the Jewish problem" as understood by Adolf Hitler, *yemach sh'mo,* "May his name be blotted out!," and his Nazi minions. Put into practice, it ultimately resulted in the deaths of almost 6 million Jewish men, women, and children; one million below the age of twelve and an additional 500,000 between the ages of twelve and eighteen, in ghettos, concentration camps, and environments in ways that continue to stain the conscience of Western civilization, not only Germany and Poland.

Dialoghi d'amore Written by Judah Abravanel (1465–1523), this philosophical text was a series of dialogues between Philo (love or appetite) and Sophia (science or wisdom) on the subject of love.

Edict of Milan Signed by Emperor Constantine I (272–337) and Emperor Licinius (263–325), it proclaimed religious toleration through the Holy Roman Empire.

Enlightenment The eighteenth-century philosophical moment in France, Germany, Great Britain, Italy, The Netherlands, Portugal, and Spain which effectively ushered in the modern era and sundered the marriage between the church and the nation-state.

Eretz-Israel The "Land of Israel." That place promised by God to the people of Israel according to the Torah/Hebrew Bible, and sacred to the religious traditions of Judaism, Christianity, and Islam. Interestingly and significantly enough, the Torah/Hebrew Bible itself posits more than one set of geographic boundaries for the land. The Land of Israel continues to be a source of political and religious dissension in the world today, as yet unresolved.

Erusin The Hebrew term for the engagement ceremony marking the beginning of the marital agreement according to the Jewish religious tradition.

Exemplar Humanae Vitae Written by Uriel da Costa (1585–1640), this autobiographical text, *Example of a Human Life*, relates his own story as a victim of religious intolerance on the part of the Amsterdam Jewish community.

First Isaiah The first thirty-nine chapters of this major prophet of the Torah/Hebrew Bible. Some scholars have argued that the focus of the text and its writing style indicate a significantly different author from the remaining twenty-seven chapters.

First Jewish Commonwealth The term used to designate the period of ancient Israel's hegemony and sovereignty over its own land which ended with the Babylonian Exile in the year 586 B.C.E.

First Temple Built by King Solomon in Jerusalem after the death of his father King David, and thus fulfilling his father's dream. In order to do so, he heavily taxed the Israelites and enslaved them into labor corveys which led to increasing dissatisfaction.

G-d (Also L-rd) So holy do very devout Jews regard the Four-Letter Name of God in Hebrew, that they will also use this English-language convention in their writing, Additionally, outside of Scripture/Torah reading in the synagogue itself, rather than say "Adonai" as it appears in the Hebrew, they will substitute either "Adoshem" or "Ado-kem."

Gemara The extensive commentaries which accompany the Mishnah in both the Babylonian and Palestinian (Jerusalem) Talmuds and reflect the richness of Jewish life in both communities over the several hundred years of their composition.

Get (Hebrew, "Jewish bill of divorcement") Granted by the husband to the wife in Orthodox religious circles and to each other in Conservative religious circles. Historically, Reform Judaism did not make use of this document, accepting, instead, the civil decree of divorce as sufficient. In recent years, however, Reform liturgists and religious thinkers have presented models of such documents, though no "official" one currently exists.

Haftarah The additional scriptural selection associated with the Torah/Hebrew Bible in the worship service on those occasions—Shabbat, festivals, and holy days, as well as Mondays and Thursdays—when Scriptures are read. Usually taken from either prophetic literature or the additional writings found in Scripture, a word, a phrase, a name or an idea contained within it related directly to the primary scriptural selection taken directly from the *Chumash*/First Five Books of Moses.

Hagaddah The special "prayer book" associated with the celebration of Pesach (Passover). Literally, "The Story," its essence, surrounded by both prayers and commentaries, involves the retelling of the liberation by God of the people of Israel from slavery and bondage in Egypt as first recorded in the *Sefer Shemot* (Book of Exodus). (Historically, such an event is not recorded in Egyptian documents, however.)

halakha Literally, "the way." The system of Jewish law as culled by the rabbis from the Torah itself, and elaborated upon in both the Palestinian and Babylonian Talmuds and subsequent and additional Jewish literatures. For the Orthodox Jew, Jewish law governs *all* facets and aspects of daily and religious living, coming as it does directly from God and interpreted authoritatively by rabbinic spokesmen. Conservative Judaism likewise affirms its sanctity, but attempts to give it a more human cast through its Law and Standards Committee of its Rabbinical Assembly. Reform Judaism has long rejected its sovereignty, acknowledging, instead, that "the past shall exercise a vote, not a veto" (attributed to the late Rabbi Dr. Solomon Freehof of Rodef Sholom Temple, Pittsburgh, Pennsylvania).

Hanukkah The *minor* Jewish holiday celebrating the victory of the Maccabees over the Syrio-Greeks in the year 162 B.C.E. and the rededication of the ancient Temple by the rekindling of the Eternal Light of God's Presence, as recorded in the books of the Maccabees. Usually occurs in the November–December time frame accompanied by gift giving.

Hanukkat Habayit The ceremony that marks the "dedication of the [new] home" by the affixing of the *mezzuzah* and other attendant rituals.

Har Sinai (Hebrew, "Mount Sinai") In the Negev Desert, the sight at which, supposedly, God entered into covenant with the people of Israel after first liberating them from Egyptian slavery.

Hasidism/Hasidic Judaism A Jewish religious movement originally founded at the end of the seventeenth century by Israel Ba'al Shem Tov (1698–1760) as a pietistic movement in responses to a perceived Orthodox joyless rigidity. Known for its distinctive clothing, reminiscent of eighteenth-century Polish nobility.

Haskalah The Russian Jewish secular enlightenment movement of the nineteenth century, which saw the production of many literary texts—novels, short stories, novels, plays, poems, newspapers—in the Hebrew language.

Hasmoneans The ruling dynasty of Jews after the successful defeat of the Syrio-Greeks in 162 B.C.E. and continuing for approximately one hundred years until 37 B.C.E.

Hebrew Bible The religiously neutral term for the texts which comprise the Torah of the Jews, and composed of three parts: the First Five Books of the Bible, the Books of the Prophets, and the Books of the Writings.

Hebrews Translation of the Hebrew word—*Ivri'im*—for the ancient Israelites.

Holiness Code The rabbinic term for those chapters from the Book of Leviticus, 17 to 26, which spell out the religious-ceremonial and moral-ethical responsibilities of religious Jews still in force today, together with the benefit of additional commentaries throughout the generations.

Holocaust Up until recently, the universally acknowledged English word used to describe the wanton murder of nearly six million Jews by the Nazis and their collaborators. Said to have first been used by the noted writer and Nobel Prize–winner Elie Wiesel. Its origin is the Anglicization of the Greek translation of the Hebrew word *'olah*, the totally consumable offering by fire to God as depicted in the Torah. In recent years, the term itself has become increasingly problematic for obvious reasons. Current thinking is to use the Hebrew word Shoah instead. (See below.)

Holy Land One term among many for the Land of Israel according to the Hebrew Bible/Torah. The land where the God of Israel entered into the *Berith*/covenant with the people of Israel.

Holy Roman Empire The term for the union of territories in Central Europe during the Middle Ages, primarily Germany, Italy, and Burgundy.

Hope of Israel Written by Rabbi Menasseh ben Israel (1604–1607), addressing his own longings for a Messianic Age of relief for Jews, an English translation found its way to England from where Jews had been expelled in 1290. This text and Israel himself were instrumental in the return of the Jews to England under Oliver Cromwell (1599–1658) in the seventeenth century.

Ich und Du The actual German title of Martin Buber's (1878–1965) book *I and Thou*, a philosophical work which addresses his central idea of relationship, human to inanimate (I-it), human to human (I-thou), and human to God (I-Thou).

immanent The theological idea of God's presence being relatively near and approachable to humans, primarily through prayer.

interreligious marriage A contemporary Jewish communal concern regarding the question of Jewish survival resulting from marriages between Jews and non-Jews.

Israelites An English term to designate the ancient Mediterranean community of Palestine who later became the Jews. The Hebrew term is *Yisraelim*.

Jews The modern term for those people who trace their ancestry to ancient Palestine, were the recipients of Sacred Scripture at Mount Sinai after enslavement in Egypt, and have maintained their commitment to One God for close to six thousand years.

Judaism The religion of the Jewish people as reflected in its commitment to the Torah/Hebrew Bible, to One God, and its distinctive twin calendars of holidays, holy days, festivals, fast days, and life-cycle events.

Kabbalah The mystical tradition of Jewish religious tradition as reflected in a specific set of texts and rabbinic interpreters. Said to have begun already in the second century, most objective scholars have argued for a stronger Middle Ages construction.

Kaddish Aramaicized prayer usually understood to be the "mourner's prayer" recited by the survivors after the funeral of a loved one, either during the worship service or at home. Reform Judaism, on the other hand, has suggested that, after the Shoah, all Jews are mourners and has the entire congregation stand and recite this prayer.

Karaism A Jewish religious movement which arose in opposition to the Pharisees and took a more literal reading of the Torah/Hebrew Bible. It reached its high point during the tenth and eleventh centuries. Remaining Karaites are no longer viewed as members of the Jewish people.

Ketubah (Hebrew, "Jewish marriage contract") Given by the husband to the wife and spelling out the terms and conditions of the marital agreement in both Orthodox and Conservative religious communities. Reform Judaism initially rejected its use as unequal and condescending, but, in recent years, has sought to revive it with a more egalitarian text.

Ketuvim/Writings The third section of the Torah/Hebrew Bible and consisting of such books as Psalms, Proverbs, Ruth, Esther, Song of Songs, Daniel, and Ecclesiastes.

Kiddush Hebrew for "sanctification" and referring specifically to the act of blessings over wine on the Sabbath and all Jewish festivals (except for Yom Kippur/Day of Atonement).

Kiddushin "Holiness" or "sanctification." The term is used to describe Jewish marriage. There is literally no linguistic equivalency in Hebrew for our English word *marriage*.

Kingdom of Israel Biblical reference to the northern kingdom of Ten Tribes ultimately conquered by the Assyrians in the year 721 B.C.E.

Kingdom of Judah Biblical reference to the southern kingdom of the two tribes of Judah and Benjamin ultimately conquered by the Babylonians in the year 586 B.C.E.

Kohanim (Hebrew, "Priests") In ancient Israel, the community was divided into three groups the high priests, the Levitical assistants, and the remainder of the community of Israel. The priests were the first to perform the rituals associated with both the portable Ark and the Temple in Jerusalem, assisted by the Levites, and were understood to be biological descendants (or extended family members) of Aaron, Moses' brother.

Korban The "sacrificial animal" in the ancient cultic system of worship in biblical times, both pre-Temple and Temple; still associated today with the Pesach (Passover) liturgy as the *korban Pesach*, the Passover sacrifice, reminiscent of that system.

L-rd (Also, G-d) See G-d.

Land of Canaan A geographic term for the land known as Palestine and conquered by the ancient Israelites under Joshua.

Land of Israel The term used to describe the Land of Palestine after the conquering of Canaan by the Israelites under Joshua.

Levi'im The "Levitical priests" whose primary function was to assist the *Kohanim*, the high priests, in the performance of their pre-Temple and Temple cultic rituals and to be responsible for and care for the *clai kodesh*, the "holy vessels" associated with these rituals.

Levitical cities According to the biblical Book of Leviticus, specific cities were set aside for the Levites to settle and survive as they were not among the tribes among whom the land was divided.

Machzor The special "prayer book" of the Jewish religious tradition used for the High Holy Days of Rosh Hashanah (New Year) and Yom Kippur (Day of Atonement) only.

Madrega A term from medieval philosophic Hebrew used to describe a plane or spiritual existence and awareness.

Mazal tov The Hebrew term understood to mean "congratulations." Literally, however, it means "good planet," and may in fact have referenced ancient Israel's acceptance of the influence of the planets on human behavior.

Megillah Generically any "scroll," *Megillah* or *Megillat Esther* is that associated with the festival of Purim (Lots) and tells the story found in the Book of Esther in the Torah/Hebrew Bible.

menorah Generally, a candelabrum, the most well-known the eight branched one associated with the festival of Hanukkah (Festival of Dedication). A seven-branched one is reminiscent of that found in the ancient Temple in Jerusalem, echoing the first story in *Bereshih* (Genesis), that of creation and the seven days of the week.

Mercaz ruchani "Spiritual center." A term attributed to Ahad Ha-Am (Asher Ginzburg, 1856–1927), one of the early Zionist intellectual giants of pre–State of Israel, whose vision for the state was that of a place where the cultural and religious essences of Judaism and the Jewish people would continue to flower and develop, spreading to all parts of the world where Jews dwell and enriching the lives of non-Jews as well.

Medinat Yisrael Contemporary Hebrew term used to designate the modern State of Israel, founded on May 14, 1948.

Merkava/chariot mysticism One of the designated terms for the Jewish mystical tradition and based on the description supplied in the first chapter of the book of the prophet Ezekiel where he spells out his vision of the divine involving a chariot.

Messiah The Jewish (and later Christian) belief in a religiously devout Jew who could trace his ancestry to the Davidic household and who would restore Israel to its former glory. Later Christian tradition saw him in the person of the Christ and regarded him as both fully human and fully divine where as Jewish religious tradition maintained its position that he would be fully and totally human.

mezzuzah The cylindrical container housing two sections of Torah/Hebrew Bible *Devarim* (Deuteronomy) 6:4-9 and 11:13-21, in response to the biblical injunction, also in *Devarim*, "You shall write them upon the doorposts of thy house and upon thy gates, that ye may remember and do all My commandments and be holy unto your God."

Middle East That part of the eastern Mediterranean where the State of Israel finds itself surrounded by hostile neighboring nation-states. Also the birthplace of the world's three great monotheistic religious traditions, Judaism, Christianity, and Islam.

midrash Jewish interpretive literature of a nonlegal nature. Commentary on the Torah/Hebrew Bible as well as additional sermonic and story literature "filling in the gaps," so to speak, in the literary record. Some of it is quite fanciful, allowing the rabbis, the creators of midrashic literature, to give free rein to their imaginations. Others of it are quite insightful, morally, ethically, spiritually, psychologically, as well as intellectually.

midrashic method A way of actually interpreting scriptural materials in a more fanciful manner by "filling in the gaps" in biblical stories and/or imagining events involving the characters which are not part of the actual stories.

Midrash Rabba (Hebrew, "the Great Midrash") A multivolume set of fanciful rabbinic commentaries in sermonic form addressing biblical texts primarily from the First Five Books of Moses.

Mishnah (Hebrew, "Second Teaching") A six-chaptered text comprised of the Jewish laws governing the Jewish community of Palestine in the aftermath of the Roman destruction in the year 70 C.E. The laws themselves were codified by Rabbi Judah the Prince at the end of the second century.

Mishneh Torah The recodification of the laws of the Mishnah and abstracted from the extensive Babylonian Talmud by Moses Maimonides (1135–1204) who, in addition, supplied his own explanations and commentaries.

Misnagdim **(Hebrew, "opponents")** A term used for those Orthodox Jews who opposed the rise and development of Hasidic Judaism in the eighteenth century and continuing today.

Mitzvot Literally, "commanded acts" by God to the Jewish people. The continuum as Judaically understood is that of *Mitzaveh-mitzvot-mitzuvim*, Commander-commandments-commanded. According to the rabbis, 613 "commandments" are found throughout the Torah/Hebrew Bible of both a moral-ethical and ritual-ceremonial nature, of equal sanctity. The commandments of a Torah/Hebrew Bible, given by God, ultimately become, in the eyes of the rabbis, the legal system, halakha (see above), of the Jewish religious tradition. The word has also taken on a popular form in describing any "good deed."

mixed marriage Like the term intermarriage, the term used to designate marriage between Jews and non-Jews and reflective of the ongoing concern of Jews for continuing survival.

mohel Jewish "ritual circumcisor," usually a rabbi or cantor, well versed in both the ritual traditions and the surgical procedures.

Moreh Nevuchim Hebrew term for Moses Maimonides's (1135–1204) philosophic text *The Guide for the Perplexed* in which he attempted to reconcile neo-Aristotelianism and biblical Judaism.

Moses ben Maimon (Maimonides) (1135–1204) Perhaps the greatest figure in Jewish intellectual history. Born in Spain, Maimonides and his family ultimately settled in Egypt where his medical training enabled him to become both rabbi of the Jewish community and physician to the Sultan as well as continue to own philosophic writings.

neo-Orthodoxy A modern descriptive term for Orthodox Jews comfortable in the larger society while maintaining their commitment to a strict interpretation and practice of the Jewish religious tradition.

Nevi'im/**Prophets** The second part of the Torah/Hebrew Bible and comprised of the major prophets Isaiah, Jeremiah, and Ezekiel, and the twelve minor prophets.

Nissu'in The Hebrew term for the Jewish wedding ceremony.

Old Testament The Christian term for the books of the Torah/Hebrew Bible. Both Protestant Christianity and Roman Catholic Christianity differ on the order of the books after the First Five Books from that of the Jews.

oral tradition Hebrew, "Torah sheb'al peh," (literally, "Torah which is upon the mouth"). The Jewish religious tradition, attributed to the biblical Moses, whereby he returned from Mount Sinai, with the fullness not only of the commentary tradition but the interpretative tools as well.

Orthodox Judaism The denominational branch of the Jewish religious tradition which sees itself as lineally descended from ancient Israelites and who interpret Torah/Hebrew Bible in a literal way and whose practices adhere to more of past practices than other denominational communities.

Pale of Settlement The eighteenth- and nineteenth-century term used to describe the proscribed and ghettoized area of restricted residence for the Jews of Russia under the Czars.

Palestinian Talmud The joining of the commentaries (Hebrew, Gemara) to that of the Mishnah organized by Rabbi Judah the Prince at the end of the second century. Upon its completion, due to the exigencies of history, the Palestinian or Jerusalem Talmud is a far smaller text addressing fewer of the laws of the Mishnah by perhaps as much as 75 percent. Also called the Jerusalem Talmud.

pantheism Literally, "God is all," and the theological understanding that everything which exists is part of God, and that the universe, nature, and God are one and the same.

patriarchs Term for the major and larger-than-life figures of the Torah/Hebrew Bible: Abraham, Isaac, Jacob, Joseph, and Moses.

Pesach Hebrew term for the Jewish holiday of Passover.

Pharisees The radical and revolutionary class of Jews who, after the destruction of the Second Temple in the year 70 C.E. by the Romans, saved both Judaism and the Jewish people by reinterpreting the "system of Judaism," calling for study of sacred texts, divine worship, and high ethical behavior. Contemporary religious expressions of Judaism are the descendants of their innovations. Misunderstood by the New Testament writers, especially those who wrote the Gospels, in all likelihood, they would have had more in common with Jesus than their competitors, the Sadducees, who wished to affirm the status quo and return to the priestly system.

Pidyon Haben The symbolic birth ceremony of "redeeming" the one-month-old Israelite boy from priestly service. Still practiced by both Orthodox and Conservative Jews, it was abandoned by Reform Jews as not representative of the equality of males and females.

Positive-Historical Judaism The original term for the Jewish denominational movement which has evolved into Conservative Judaism and originally founded in the Germany in the mid-nineteenth century as a response to the perceived excesses of Reform Judaism founded approximately one-half century earlier.

postbiblical or Rabbinic Period Interchangeable terms for the period subsequent to the canonization of the Torah/Hebrew Bible (70 C.E.) until the beginnings of the modern period in Jewish history.

prebiblical or Biblical Period Term used to designate the beginnings of the ancient Israelites through the period of biblical history and ending with the canonization of the Torah/Hebrew Bible (70 C.E.).

Promised Land Religious term of reference for the Land of Israel according to both Jewish and Christian religious traditions.

Protestant Reformation The term used to describe the rise of Protestant Christianity said to begin with Martin Luther's (1483–1546) critique of the Roman Catholic Church and ending with the Treaty of Westphalia in 1648.

Purim The minor Jewish festival celebrating the successful vanquishing of the attempted genocide of the Jews of Persia according to the Book of Esther in the Torah/Hebrew Bible. Doubts remain as to the actual historicity of the events described.

Pythagoreans Followers of a particular branch of Greek philosophy with a particular focus on the scientific and mathematical.

qiddusha/holiness A core concept of the Jewish religious tradition growing out of the Torah/Hebrew Bible and subsequent Jewish literatures and focusing on human behavior desiring to emulate divine perfection.

Rabbinism or Talmudism Terms used to describe the postbiblical period in Jewish history after the canonization of the Hebrew Bible (70 c.e.) and before the rise of modern period in Jewish history.

rabbi (Hebrew, "my teacher") The postbiblical term for Jewish clergy meaning teachers and following no priestly tradition. Said to be the next stage in Jewish leadership after the Pharisees.

Reconquista Spanish, "Reconquest," and referring to the Catholic retaking of Spain from the Muslims beginning in the 700s and concluding successfully in the 1200s. Two centuries later, it would result in the expulsion of the Jews from Spanish territories (1492).

Reconstructionist Judaism The modern American Jewish religious denominational movement founded by Rabbi Mordecai M. Kaplan (1881–1983) as a more liberal form of Conservative Judaism but less liberal than Reform Judaism, and centered on Kaplan's understanding of Judaism as a civilization. It is the smallest of the Jewish religious movements.

Reform Judaism Founded in Germany in the early part of the nineteenth century, this liberal Jewish movement was originally a movement for liturgical reform and a progressive desire to enter into larger society through university education.

religion The generic term used to describe communities primarily concerned with moral-ethical behaviors and ritual-ceremonial behaviors and seeing themselves connected to their God or gods.

Responsa The tradition of rabbinic literature which is a series of questions addressed to leading rabbis and their answers citing various sources from the Talmuds and works by other rabbis. The questions asked tend to be of a more practical rather than theoretical nature.

Rosh Hashanah The Jewish holy day which marks the beginning of the new Jewish calendar year in the fall and inaugurates a ten-day period of introspection leading to Yom Kippur/Day of Atonement.

Sefirat Haomer Hebrew, the "Counting of the Omer," or barley sheaves harking back to the agricultural history of ancient Israel and marking the seven-week period between Passover and Shavuot.

Sabra Hebrew for "cactus" and used to describe modern-day Israelis, prickly on the outside and sweet on the inside.

Sadducees The oppositional party in power to the Pharisees during the Roman period of oppression in Palestine. Said to be strict readers of the Torah/Hebrew Bible and rejecting the innovations of the Pharisees while upholding the priestly class.

Sanhedrin The governing supreme court of ancient Israel consisting of seventy-one members and tasked with legal responsibilities during the Second Temple/Roman period when the chair of the council was in fact the high priest.

Second Generation The term now used to describe the children of Holocaust/Shoah survivors, children of severely diminished families, who are now adults themselves. Many continue to struggle with the Holocaust/Shoah, some psychologically and others religiously.

Second Jewish Commonwealth The period during which the Temple stood again after its rebuilding following the Babylonian Captivity five hundred years before. It ended in the year 70 c.e. with the destruction of the Temple by the Romans.

Second Temple See Second Jewish Commonwealth.

Sefer Kri'tut Reference in the Torah/Hebrew Bible to a "document of cutting" by which the understanding is that of a divorcing document rending a marriage null and void.

Shabbat Hebrew term for Sabbath, the Saturday event of rest from work in emulation of God's "resting" according to the Book of Genesis. Perhaps the primary contribution of Jews to civilization.

Shavuot Hebrew for "weeks" or "oaths." The Jewish spring holiday seven weeks after the Passover celebrating the harvesting of crops and, according the the religious traditon, the day when Moses returned from Sinai with the Ten Commandments.

She'elot u-T'shu'vot **(Hebrew, "Questions and Answers")** A more technical terms for the *Responsa* literature of questions directed to leading rabbis and their written answers citing various sources in Judaic literature and the writings of other rabbis.

Shelichim **(Hebrew, "agents" or "representatives")** According to the Jewish legal tradition, halakha, persons sometimes do not need to be physically present in order to conduct their business but may use designated persons instead.

Shelosh regalim The three "pilgrimage festivals" according to the Torah/Hebrew Bible when the ancient Israelites would journey to Jerusalem and present their gift offerings at the Temple, Pesach (Passover), *Shavuot* (Festival of Weeks), and *Sukkot* (Festival of Booths).

Shelosha-Asar Ikarim Hebrew, "Thirteen Principles of Faith" summarizing Jewish religious beliefs and enumerated by Moses Maimonides (1135–1204).

Sheloshim The thirty-day mourning period in Jewish religious tradition beginning with the moment of death and continuing for one month.

Shemini Atzeret The eighth day of solemn assembly and the festival of observance taking place at the end of the festival of Sukkot.

Shemot/Exodus The second book of the Torah/Hebrew Bible detailing the story of Israel's imprisonment/enslavement in Egypt and subsequent liberation by Moses and Aaron and forty years of wandering in the deserts on the way to the Promised Land.

Shirat Hayam Reference to the "Song at the Sea" (of Reeds) or "Song of Moses" (Shirar Moshe) Exodus 15, and sung by the Israelites after their successful escape form their Egyptian pursuers.

Shirat Moshe See Shirat Hayam.

Shivah The seven-day mourning period in Jewish religious tradition commencing upon one's return from the funeral.

Shoah The Hebrew, biblical term now preferred more and more to describe the wanton murder and callous slaughter of almost six million Jewish men, women, and children during the years 1939–1945 by the Nazis and their assistants. Best translated as "Destruction" or "Devastation." A singularly unique event in the history of the Jewish people as well as all humankind.

shofar "Ram's horn," a reminder of the *Bereshith* (Genesis) story wherein *Avraham*/Abraham sacrificed a ram rather than his son *Yitzchak*/Isaac. Used in ancient Israel as both a military instrument and a call to gather the community. Associated today with the High Holy Days of Rosh Hashanah (New Year) and Yom Kippur (Day of Atonement).

Shofetim/Judges The religious, political, civil, and military leaders referenced in the Book of Judges, most well known are Deborah and Samson.

Shulchan Aruch The compilation of Jewish law composed by Rabbi Joseph Karo (1488–1575) together with his commentaries and reflective of Jewish life in Spanish and other Mediterranean communities.

siddur The special Jewish "prayer book" for use at Shabbat (Sabbath) and Haggim (festival) services, as distinct from the *Machzor* used for the High Holy Days only.

Simchat Torah The Jewish festival marking the end of the holiday of Sukkot and celebrating the completion of the annual Torah reading cycle (*Devarim*/Deuteronomy) and the beginning of the next cycle (*Bereshith*/Genesis).

Simeon bar Kokhba Palestinian Jewish rebel leader who revolted unsuccessfully against the Roman oppressors in the year 132 C.E. Initially successful, he established an independent Jewish state which survived only three years.

Sofer(im) (Hebrew, "scribes") Those Jewish scholars whose specialty is calligraphic work including Torah scrolls, *mezzuzot*, *getot*, and other documents important to the Jewish religious tradition.

State of Israel The modern State of Israel—the Third Jewish Commonwealth—declared its independence on May 14, 1948, in the aftermath of the tragedy of the Holocaust/Shoah.

Stoics A Greek philosophy which explored the relationship between cosmic determinism and human behaviors as well as the freedom to choose one's path of such behaviors as the fulfillment of one's philosophy.

Sukkot The Jewish festival which begins five days after Yom Kippur/Day of Atonement and commemorates ancient Israel's agricultral heritage by the construction of a temporary outdoor dwelling.

synagogue The religious institution of the Jewish people and fulfilling a threefold purpose a house of prayer and worship, a house of study and learning, and a house of gathering and assembly.

Talmud The encyclopedia commentary of Jewish religious life based on the legal texts of the Mishnah and constructed in both Palestine and Babylonia.

Temple of Solomon The First Temple constructed at King Solomon's instigation after the death of his father David and destroyed during the Babylonian invasion in 586 B.C.E.

Ten Commandments Occurring in two places in the Torah/Hebrew Bible (*Shemot*/Exodus and *Devarim*/Deuteronomy), these ten statements ("You shall" and "You shall not") comprise the core of Jewish moral-ethical and ritual-ceremonial responsibilities.

Ten Lost Tribes The enduring myth that after the ten tribes of Northern Israel were conquered by the Assyrians in 721 B.C.E. they somewhat survived and their descendants are alive today in such places as the Native Americans of North America or the Eskimos of Alaska among other possibilities.

Tetragrammaton The unpronounceable four-lettered name of God—Y-H-V-H—as found in the Torah/Hebrew Bible.

Theodor Herzl (1860–1904) Viennese journalist who became the father of modern political Zionism resulting from his coverage of the antisemitic trial of the falsely accused French Army captain Alfred Dreyfus (1859–1935) and his publishing of *Der Judenstaat* as his solution to the problem of antisemitism.

Theologico-Political Treatise One of the two major philosophic works of Dutch Jewish thinker Baruch de Spinoza (1634–1677) and addressing his critique of Judaism and Christianity as well as their understandings of the Torah/Hebrew Bible.

theology Classically understood as the human attempt to gain knowledge of God through an intensive exploration of Sacred Scriptures (Torah/Hebrew Bible and/or New Testament). For Jews, however, the emphasis is on the *relationship* between humanity and God rather than on direct knowledge of God, regarded as an impossibility.

Theophany at Sinai The event at Mount Sinai in which the people of Israel, both present and future generations according to *Sefer Devarim*/Book of Deuteronomy, entered into a covenantal relationship for all time with the God of Israel.

Third Jewish Commonwealth A synonymous term for the reborn modern State of Israel founded May 14, 1948.

Thirteen Principles A summary statement of the basic principles of Jewish faith and belief and written by Moses Maimonides (1135–1204) and included today in many Jewish prayer books.

Tikkun Olam A principle of the Jewish religious tradition whereby Jews have a moral-ethical responsibility to partner with God in repairing a broken world by addressing its moral and social inequities.

Tisha B'Av (Hebrew, 9th of Av) The summer Jewish holy day marking collectively the various tragedies which have overtaken the people of Israel down through the centuries (e.g. First and Second Temple, Egyptian enslavement, etc.).

Torah (Hebrew, "Way," "Path," "Teaching") The Hebrew term for the Sacred Scriptures of the Jewish people consisting of three parts: First Five Books of Moses, the Prophets, and the Writings.

Torah sheb'al peh Literally, "Torah that is upon the mouth." The Oral Tradition of Rabbinic interpretation later set down in such primary texts as the Mishnah and Talmuds. The so-called "oral tradition" continues to remain authoritative today for Orthodox Jews, less so for Conservative, Reform, and Reconstructionist Jews.

Torah shebichtav Literally, "Torah that is written down." The written text that begins with *Bereshith* (Genesis) and ends with *Divrei Hayamim Bet* (Second Chronicles).

transcendent The religious and theological notion common among both Jews and Christians that the God whom they both affirm is in the heavens beyond human visitation except after death.

Trito-Isaiah A view among some biblical scholars that the final chapters of the prophetic Book of Isaiah are from a third writer after the authors of chapter 1 to 39 and 40 to 59.

Tu B'Shevat (Hebrew, 15th of Shevat) The Jewish festival known as the "New Year of the Trees" and a reminder of the importance of forestation in the history of ancient Israel and the contemporary State of Israel.

usury Literally the charging of interest for loans. While Roman Catholic religious tradition condemned the practice, it has remained as a cornerstone of antisemitic thinking as indicative of a supposed Jewish preoccupation with monetary matters.

V'shamru Popular Shabbat (Sabbath) hymn emphasizing both the covenant and the creation story.

Vayyikra/Leviticus The third book of the Torah/Hebrew Bible and encompassing much of the Jewish legal tradition as well as the sacrificial system of the ancient Temple.

Vidui The "confessional prayer" text to be said by the religious Jew prior to death asking God's forgiveness for any sins committed and not yet atoned. There are such prayers in all Jewish denominations.

Vindiciae judaeorum Text by Rabbi Menasseh ben Israel (1604–1657) articulating his rationale for a return to England by a formerly exiled population.

Wisdom literature A subsection of the third section of the Writings in the Torah/Hebrew Bible and including such books as Psalms, Proverbs, Song of Songs, Ecclesiastes, Ruth, Esther, and Job.

Wissenschaft des Judentums (German: *"Scientific Study of Judaism"*) The nineteenth-century German Jewish intellectual tradition whereby Judaism itself became the object of university study employing the methods pioneered in other fields of academic inquiry.

Y'tziat Mitzrayim (Hebrew, *"Going forth out of Egypt"*) The Hebrew term used to describe the exodus from Egypt and first recorded in Sefer Shemot/Book of Exodus. A cornerstone of Jewish religious memory today and leading to the development of the Jewish ethical tradition.

Yahrtzeit Literally, "year time." The term acknowledging the anniversary of the death of a loved one. On such anniversaries, the names of the deceased are called out at the conclusion of the worship service and *Kaddish* is said by the mourners.

Yavneh The city in ancient Israel where, according to Jewish religious tradition and written in the Talmud, Rabbi Jochanan ben Zakkai and his colleagues canonized the Torah/Hebrew Bible.

Yeridah Emigration from Israel. Literally, a "going *down*" from the Land of Israel. (See its opposite, *aliyah*, a "going *up*" to the Land of Israel.)

Yesurin shel ahavah Literally, "chastisements out of love." The rabbinic tradition of examining critically those aspects of Jews life out of a sense of deep commitment and caring. The objective of such critical analysis is to improve, never to destroy, governed as it must be by love of one's fellow Jews and one's Jewish tradition, however interpreted.

Yism 'chu Popular Shabbat (Sabbath) hymn emphasizing creation rather than creation and covenant.

Yochanah ben Zakkai First-century head of the rabbinical academy in Yavneh and primarily responsible for the canonization of the Torah/Hebrew Bible.

Yom Ha'atzmaut One of the two newest Jewish holidays—Israel Independence Day—and celebrated both in the State of Israel and abroad commemorating May 14, 1948.

Yom Hashoah The other new Jewish holiday—Holocaust Commemoration Day—first commemorated in Israel in the early 1950s and now memorialized by Jewish communities all over the world.

Yom Kippur (Hebrew, **"Day of Atonement"**) Regarded by many Jews as the holiest day of the Jewish religious calendar, occurring ten days after Rosh Hashanah, the New Year, and concluding the Ten Days of Awe.

Zeman matan Torahteinu Literally, "the time of the giving of the Torah." The summary description of the festival of Simchat Torah of the Torah/Hebrew Bible, coming at the end of the festival of Sukkot (Booths).

Zionism The modern political and religious movement of the Jewish people advocating a return of the people to its ancestral homeland. With the founding of the State of Israel on May 14, 1948, Zionism today remains a worldwide movement of support by Jews and non-Jews for the State.

Zohar (Hebrew, *"Book of Splendor"*) The primary text of the Jewish kabbalistic or mystical tradition said to have been authored by Moses de Leon (1250–1305) and remains primarily a highly spiritualized commentary on the Torah/Hebrew Bible.

For Further Reading

Ariel, David S. *What Do Jews Believe? The Spiritual Foundations of Judaism.* New York: Schocken Books, 1995.

Ben-Sasson, H. H., ed. *A History of the Jewish People.* Cambridge, Mass.: Harvard University Press, 1976.

Biale, David, ed. *Cultures of the Jews: A New History.* New York: Schocken Books, 2000.

Boteach, Shmuley. *An Intelligent Person's Guide to Judaism.* London: Duckworth Overlook, 2005.

Breslauer, S. Daniel. *Understanding Judaism through History.* Belmont, Calif.: Thomson/Wadsworth, 2003.

Cherry, Shai. *Introduction to Judaism.* Chantilly: The Teaching Company, 2004.

Chill, Abraham. *The Minhagim: The Customs and Ceremonies of Judaism, Their Origins and Rationale.* New York: Sepher-Hermon, 1979.

Cohen, Henry. *What's Special about Judaism?* Xlibris, 2002.

Cohn-Sherbok, Dan. *Judaism: History, Belief, and Practice.* London: Routledge, 2003.

Cohn-Sherbok, Dan. *The Blackwell Dictionary of Judaica.* Oxford: Blackwell, 1992.

de Lange, Nicholas. *An Introduction to Judaism.* Cambridge: Cambridge University Press, 2000.

———. *Judaism.* Oxford: Oxford University Press, 2003.

de Lange, Nicholas, and Miri Freud-Kandel, eds., *Modern Judaism: An Oxford Guide.* Oxford: Oxford University Press, 2005.

Ehrlich, Carl S. *Understanding Judaism: Origins, Beliefs, Practices, Holy Texts, Sacred Places.* London: Duncan Baird Publishers, 2004.

Eisenstadt, S. N. *Jewish Civilization: The Jewish Historical Experience in a Comparative Perspective.* Albany: State University of New York Press, 1992.

Fackenheim, Emil L. *What is Judaism? An Interpretation for the Present Age.* New York: Summit Books, 1987.

Fine, Lawrence, ed. *Judaism in Practice: From the Middle Ages through the Early Modern Period.* Princeton: Princeton University Press, 2001.

Firestone, Reuven. *Children of Abraham: An Introduction to Judaism for Muslims.* New York and Hoboken, N.J.: The American Jewish Committee and Ktav Publishing House, 2001.

Gilbert, Martin. *Letters to Auntie Fori: The 5,000-Year History of the Jewish People and Their Faith.* New York: Schocken Books, 2002.

Goldberg, David J., and Rayner, D. *The Jewish People: Their History and Their Religion.* New York: Penguin, 1987.

Holtz, Barry E., ed. *Back to the Sources: Reading the Classic Jewish Texts.* New York: Summit Books, 1984.

"Judaism 101," www.jewfaq.org, accessed January 29, 2010.

Kirsch, Jonathan. *The Woman Who Laughed at God: The Untold History of the Jewish People.* New York: Penguin Putnam, 2001.

Konner, Melvin. *Unsettled: An Anthropology of the Jews.* New York: Penguin, 2003.

Kugel, James. *On Being a Jew.* Baltimore: Johns Hopkins University Press, 1990.

Küng, Hans. *Judaism: Between Yesterday and Tomorrow.* New York: Continuum, 1991.

Limburg, James. *Judaism: An Introduction for Christians.* Minneapolis: Augsburg Publishing House, 1987.

MacArdle, Meredith. *The Timechart History of Jewish Civilization.* Edison, N.J.: Chartwell Books, 2004.

Mansoor, Menahem. *Jewish History and Thought: An Introduction.* Hoboken, N.J.: Ktav Publishing House, 1991.

Margolis, Max, and Alexander Marx. *A History of the Jewish People.* New York and Philadelphia: Meridian Books and The Jewish Publication Society of America, 1927.

Neusner, Jacob. *Between Time and Eternity: The Essentials of Judaism.* Belmont, Calif.: Wadsworth, 1975.

———. *An Introduction to Judaism: A Textbook and Reader.* Louisville: Westminster John Knox, 1991.

———. *Judaism: An Introduction.* London and New York: Penguin Books, 2002.

———. *Signposts on the Way of Torah.* Belmont, Calif.: Thomson/Wadsworth, 1998.

———. *The Way of Torah: An Introduction to Judaism.* Belmont, Calif.: Thomson/Wadsworth, 2004.

Neusner, Jacob, and Alan Avery-Peck, eds. *The Blackwell Companion to Judaism.* Oxford: Blackwell, 2000.

———. *The Blackwell Reader in Judaism.* Oxford: Blackwell, 2001.

Neusner, Jacob, Alan Avery-Peck, and William Scott Green, eds. *The Encyclopedia of Judaism.* Leiden: Brill, 2001.

Robinson, George. *Essential Judaism: A Complete Guide to Beliefs, Customs, and Rituals.* New York: Pocket Books, 2000.

Roth, Cecil, ed. *Encyclopedia Judaica.* Jerusalem: Keter Publishing House, 1972.

Scheindlin, Raymond. *A Short History of the Jewish People: From Legendary Times to Modern Statehood.* New York: Macmillan, 1998.

Seltzer, Robert M. *Jewish People, Jewish Thought: The Jewish Experience in History.* Upper Saddle River, N.J.: Prentice-Hall, 1980.

———, ed. *Judaism: A People and Its History.* New York: Macmillan, 1989.

Wylen, Stephen. *Settings of Silver: An Introduction to Judaism.* Mahwah, N.J.: Paulist, 1989.

Yerushalmi, Yosef Hayim. *Zakhor: Jewish History and Jewish Memory.* Seattle: University of Washington Press, 1982.

Index

Aaron, 17

Abraham, 4, 16, 54–55

Abravanel, Judah, 92–93

Absalom, 18

Abulafia, Meir, 91

A.D./C.E., 15

Adonijah, 18

Age of the False Messiahs, 34

Age of Jewish Denominationalism, 113v

Age of the Prophets, 22, 25, 62

agunah, 159

Akiba (Akiva), Rabbi, 29, 142

Aleichem, Sholom (Sholem Rabinowitz), 37

Aleppo Codex, 8

Alexander the Great, 26

Alexandria, 30

Al Kuzari, 88–89

Altizer, Thomas J. J., 121

American Jewish Historical Society, 8

American Sephardi Federation, 8

Amnon, 18

Amos (Amos), 65, 67

Antioch, 30

Antiochus IV, 27, 135

antisemitism, 10, 38, 39, 40, 103, 104, 175–77

    higher antisemitism, 52

Apocrypha, 54

Aquinas, Thomas, 90

Arabs, 31, 177

Arendt, Hannah, 102–3

Arguing with God, 121

Aristobulus I, 27

Aristotle, 85

Ark of the Covenant, 20, 25

Aron Kodesh, 53

Assembly of Jewish Notables, France, 35

Assyrians, 20, 24, 62

Atzai Hayyim, 53

Augustine, Bishop of Hippo, 30

Avimelch, 4

Babylonia, 8, 29, 30

Babylonians, 20, 25, 26

Baeck, Leo, 118

Bamidbar/Numbers, Book of, 29

Banu Qurayza, 31

Bar-Ilan University, Israel, 80

Bar Kokhba (Bar Kosiba), Simeon, 29